# Myths of the North American Indians

# MYTHS OF THE NORTH AMERICAN INDIANS

BY

LEWIS SPENCE

ILLUSTRATED

GRAMERCY BOOKS
NEW YORK • AVENEL

Originally published under the title
*The Myths of the North American Indians.*

*Publisher's Note:* The text has been slightly altered for this edition,
but has not been abridged.

Foreword copyright © 1994 Random House Value Publishing, Inc.
All rights reserved.

This edition is published by Gramercy Books,
distributed by Random House Value Publishing, Inc.
40 Engelhard Avenue, Avenel, New Jersey 07001

Printed and bound in the United States of America

**Library of Congress Cataloging-in-Publication Data**
Spence, Lewis, 1874–1955.
Myths of the North American Indians / Lewis Spence.
p.    cm.
Includes bibliographical references and index.
ISBN 0–517–10158–0
1. Indians of North America—Religion and mythology.
2. Indians of North America—Legends.   I. Title.
[E98.R3S7 1994]
299'.7–dc20
93-40680
CIP

8 7 6 5 4 3 2 1

# CONTENTS

LIST OF COLOR ILLUSTRATIONS      vii

FOREWORD      ix

PREFACE TO THE FIRST EDITION      xiii

I.   DIVISIONS, CUSTOMS, AND HISTORY OF THE RACE      1

II.   THE MYTHOLOGIES OF THE NORTH AMERICAN INDIANS      80

III.   ALGONQUIAN MYTHS AND LEGENDS      141

IV.   IROQUOIS MYTHS AND LEGENDS      217

V.   SIOUX MYTHS AND LEGENDS      266

VI.   MYTHS AND LEGENDS OF THE PAWNEES      304

VII.   MYTHS AND LEGENDS OF THE NORTHERN AND NORTH-
WESTERN INDIANS      312

BIBLIOGRAPHY      363

GLOSSARY AND INDEX      375

# LIST OF COLOR ILLUSTRATIONS

*Section following page 110*

Clasping her in his arms, he bore her to his village.
(Algonquian)

The hunter poised his spear and struck.
(Algonquian)

He suddenly assumed the shape of a gigantic porcupine.
(Iroquois)

She smiled at him and sang a strange, sweet song.
(Iroquois)

He leaned his shoulder against the rock.
(Sioux)

They arrived at the abode of the Water-god.
(Sioux)

He emerged in his own country.
(Sioux)

He seized hold of the hair.
(Haida of the Northwest)

# FOREWORD

This book, originally published early in the twentieth century, is still one of the best places for the interested reader to begin learning about the myths of the North American Indian tribes. It includes the customs and tales of the Algonquian, Iroquois, Sioux, Pawnee, and several Northern and Northwestern tribes, all related in an unornamented style that allows the simplicity of oral storytelling to shine through.

In this book, the myths are neither bowdlerized nor prettified, but are presented in a straightforward manner that displays to advantage the freshness of the stories themselves. These myths share many of the themes of myths of other cultures, yet their unique flavor, due perhaps to the American characters and landscapes, fills the reader with wonder.

There are many theories to account for the cross-cultural ideas found in many of the myths—from migrations of the human species from a common birthplace where all stories originated, to Jungian archetypes that express themselves similarly among all peoples because of the structure of the human mind. No one knows why, for example, the owl, in nature not particularly wise, is seen as the bird of wisdom by many Native American tribes as well as the creature most closely associated with the Greek goddess of wisdom, Athena, or her Roman counterpart, Minerva.

Unlike the classical myths, Native American tales were part of a living religion at the time of their collection. While the religious significance of the Greek, Roman, and Norse myths can only be surmised, it is known that the stories in this book were an integral part of a divinatory religion in which a state of trance was induced for the purpose of hearing stories related by supernatural beings. Many tales tell of tribal heroes who acquired "medicine" from such beings—through marriage to, or salvation by, one of them—and who then passed those rituals, dances, or fetishes on to their people.

The macabre humor of some of the tales is also striking. The Chinook trickster-hero Blue Jay, for example, journeys to the underworld and finds his sister married to a ghost. She introduces piles of bones as her relatives and explains that they turn back into human beings at various times, but loud voices make them turn into bones again. So Blue Jay entertains himself by doing just such transformations on his young brother-in-law while fishing. He also enjoys switching the skulls of a child and a man, to amuse himself when they become human again.

Today's readers are indebted to the author of this early anthology, Lewis Spence, and to the numerous story collectors who made it possible. It must also be noted, however, that while myths are eternal, mythologists are very much a product of their time. Reading now, with the hindsight of many years — years in which the world has changed and people have become politically sensitized to questions of race and gender — it is easy to laugh or take offense at the ethnocentricity of early scholars, with their talk of the "Red Man" and "his" myths. It should be kept in mind, though, that it was not too long before this book was originally published that the Native American was seen as having a culture hardly worth studying at all.

However, the ethnocentricity of the story collectors involved can't be denied. Many of them worked for the U.S. Department of Ethnology and had a stake in showing the beliefs of these people as barbaric compared with the more worthy Western concepts replacing them. It leaves a bitter taste to read about the "savagery" of the "Red Man" and his habit of scalping, knowing, as we now do, that scalping was brought to the New World by early

Europeans. Whatever violent acts are committed by Europeans the author sees as imitations of the Indian. But in viewing the author in the context of his own time, we can see that he showed open-mindedness in seeing that *any* acts of barbarism were committed by whites.

A late twentieth-century self-awareness enables us to see the observer in the process of observing. In the first part of this century, people didn't see themselves that way. The author relates, for example, the experience of one of the early story collectors who noted, regarding body-painting traditions, that some Sioux Indians were laughing at another because of the way he wore his feathers, shells, and paint, which struck them as comic. The collector was quick to point out the absurdity of this: the laughing Indians unable to see their own feathers, shells, or paint as absurd. What he couldn't see, of course, was that, to others, he might have strangely cut facial hair, a peculiar frock coat and top hat, or funny metal and jeweled ornaments.

Finally, despite such moments of condescension, the story collectors who made this anthology possible are to be commended for another reason. If the stories had not been gathered when they were, many of them would have been lost forever. The early researchers were dedicated enough to pursue myths in languages hardly known by anyone (sometimes only a handful of native speakers were left, after the decimation of their people), and to pursue these stories in areas of great deprivation, among people who regarded them with suspicion. Today, we can learn much from their work, as well as take pleasure in their accounts.

MARCIA GOLUB

New York
*1994*

# PREFACE TO THE FIRST EDITION

THE North American Indian has so long been an object of the deepest interest that the neglect of his picturesque and original mythologies and the tales to which they have given rise is difficult of comprehension. In boyhood we are wont to regard him as an instrument specially designed for the execution of tumultuous incident, wherewith heart-stirring fiction may be manufactured. In manhood we are too apt to consider him as only fit to be put aside with the matter of Faery and such evanescent stuff and relegated to the limbo of imagination. Satiated with his constant recurrence in the tales of our youth, we are perhaps but too ready to hearken credulously to accounts which picture him as a disreputable vagabond, getting a precarious living by petty theft or the manufacture of bead ornaments.

It is, indeed, surprising how vague a picture the North American Indian presents to the minds of most people in Europe when all that recent anthropological research has done on the subject is taken into account. As a matter of fact, few books have been published in England which furnish more than the scantiest details concerning the Red Race, and these are in general scarce, and, when obtained, of doubtful scientific value.

The primary object of this volume is to furnish the reader with a general view of the mythologies of the Red Man of North America, accompanied by such historical and ethnological information as will assist him in gauging the real conditions under which this most interesting section of humanity existed. The basic difference between the Indian and European mental outlook is insisted upon, because it is felt that no proper comprehension of American Indian myth or conditions of life can be attained when such a distinction is not recognized and allowed for. The difference between the view-point, mundane and spiritual, of the Red Man and that of the European is as vast as that which separates the conceptions and philosophies of the East and West. Nevertheless we shall find in the North American mythologies much that enters into the composition of the immortal tales of the older religions of the Eastern Hemisphere. All myth, Asiatic, European, or American, springs from similar natural conceptions, and if we discover in American mythology peculiarities which we do not observe in the systems of Greece, Rome, or Egypt, we may be certain that these arise from circumstances of environment and racial habit as modified by climate and kindred conditions alone.

In the last thirty years much has been accomplished in placing the study of the American aborigines on a sounder basis. The older school of ethnologists were for the most part obsessed with the wildest ideas concerning the origin of the Indians, and many of them believed the Red Man to be the degenerate descendant of the lost Ten Tribes of Israel or of early Phœnician adventurers. But these 'antiquaries' had perforce to give way to a new school of students well equipped with scientific knowledge, whose labours, under the admirable direction of the United States Bureau of Ethnology, have borne rich fruit. Many treatises of the utmost value on the ethnology, mythology, and tribal customs of the North American Indians have been issued by this conscientious and enterprising State department. These are written by men who possess first-hand knowledge of Indian life and languages, many of whom have faced great privations and hardships in order to collect the material they have published. The series is, indeed, a monument to that nobler type of heroism which science

# PREFACE

can kindle in the breast of the student, and the direct, unembellished verbiage of these volumes conceals many a life-story which for quiet, unassuming bravery and contempt for danger will match anything in the records of research and human endurance.

LEWIS SPENCE

# Myths of the
# North American
# Indians

# CHAPTER I : DIVISIONS, CUSTOMS, AND HISTORY OF THE RACE

### The First Indians in Europe

ALMOST immediately upon the discovery of the New World its inhabitants became a source of the greatest interest to all ranks and classes among the people of Europe. That this should have been so is not a little surprising when we remember the ignorance which prevailed regarding the discovery of the new hemisphere, and that in the popular imagination the people of the new-found lands were considered to be inhabitants of those eastern countries which European navigation had striven so long and so fruitlessly to reach. The very name 'Indian' bestowed upon the men from the islands of the far western ocean proves the ill-founded nature and falsity of the new conditions which through the discovery of Columbus were imposed upon the science of geography. Why all this intense and vivid interest in the strange beings whom the Genoese commander carried back with him as specimens of the population of the new-found isles ? The Spaniards were accustomed to the presence and sight of Orientals. They had for centuries dwelt side by side with a nation of Eastern speech and origin, and the things of the East held little of novelty for them. Is it not possible that the people, by reason of some natural motive difficult of comprehension, did not credit in their hearts the scientific conclusions of the day ? Something deeper and more primitive than science was at work in their minds, and some profound human instinct told them that the dusky and befeathered folk they beheld in the triumphal procession of the Discoverer were not the inhabitants of an Orient with which they were more or less familiar, but erstwhile dwellers in a mystic continent which had been isolated from the rest of mankind for countless centuries.

There are not wanting circumstances which go far to prove that instinct, brushing aside the conclusions of science, felt that it had rightly come upon the truth. The motto on the arms granted to Columbus is eloquent of the popular feeling when it states,

> To Castile and Leon
> Columbus gave a *new world*,

and the news was greeted in London with the pronouncement that it seemed "a thing more divine than human"—a conclusion which could scarcely have been arrived at if it was considered that the reaching of the farthest Orient point alone had been achieved.

The primitive and barbarous appearance of the Indians in the train of Columbus deeply impressed the people of Spain. The savage had before this event been merely "a legendary and heraldic animal like the griffin and the phœnix." In the person of the Indian he was presented for the first time to the astonished gaze of a European people, who were quick to distinguish the differences in feature and general appearance between the Red Man and the civilized Oriental—although his resemblance to the Tartar race was insisted upon by some early writers.

Popular interest, instead of abating, grew greater, and with each American discovery the 'Indian' became the subject of renewed controversy. Works on the origin and customs of the American aborigines, of ponderous erudition but doubtful conclusions, were eagerly perused and discussed. These were not any more extravagant, however, than many theories propounded at a much later date. In the early nineteenth century a school of enthusiastic antiquaries, perhaps the most distinguished of whom was Lord Kingsborough, determined upon proving the identity of the American aborigines with the lost Ten Tribes of Israel, and brought to bear upon the subject a perfect battery of erudition of the most extraordinary kind. His lordship's great work on the subject, *The Antiquities of Mexico*, absorbed a fortune of some fifty thousand pounds by its publication. The most absurd philological conclusions were arrived at in the course of these researches, examples of which it would but weary the reader to peruse. Only a shade less ridiculous were the deductions drawn from Indian customs where these bore a certain surface resemblance to Hebrew rite or priestly usage.

### Indians as Jews

As an example of this species of argument it will be sufficient to quote the following passage from a work published in 1879: [1]

"The Indian high-priest wears a breastplate made of a white conch-shell, and around his head either a wreath of swan feathers, or a long piece of swan skin doubled, so as to show only the snowy feathers on each side. These remind us of the breastplate and mitre of the Jewish high-priest. They have also a magic stone which is transparent, and which the medicine-men consult ; it is most jealously guarded, even from their own people, and Adair could never procure one. Is this an imitation of the Urim and Thummim ? Again, they have a feast of first-fruits, which they celebrate with songs and dances, repeating ' Halelu-Halelu-Haleluiah ' with great earnestness and fervour. They dance in three circles round the fire that cooks these fruits on a kind of altar, shouting the praises of

[1] *The Migration from Shinar*, by Captain G. Palmer (London).　3

Yo-He-Wah (Jehovah ?). These words are only used in their religious festivals."

To what tribe the writer alludes is not manifest from the context.

### Welsh-speaking Indians

An ethnological connexion has been traced for the Red Man of North America, with equal parade of erudition, to Phœnicians, Hittites, and South Sea Islanders. But one of the most amusing of these theories is that which attempts to substantiate his blood-relationship with the inhabitants of Wales ! The argument in favour of this theory is so quaint, and is such a capital example of the kind of learning under which American ethnology has groaned for generations, that it may be briefly examined. In the author's *Myths of Mexico and Peru* (p. 5) a short account is given of the legend of Madoc, son of Owen Gwyneth, a Welsh prince, who quitted his country in disgust at the manner in which his brothers had partitioned their father's territories. Sailing due west with several vessels, he arrived, says Sir Thomas Herbert in his *Travels* (1634), at the Gulf of Mexico, " not far from Florida," in the year 1170. After settling there he returned to Wales for reinforcements, and once more fared toward the dim West, never to be heard of more. But, says the chronicler, "though the Cambrian issue in the new found world may seeme extinct, the Language to this day used among these Canibals, together with their adoring the crosse, using Beades, Reliques of holy men and some other, noted in them of Acusano and other places, . . . points at our Madoc's former being there." The Cambrians, continued Sir Thomas, left in their American colony many names of "Birds, Rivers, Rocks, Beasts and the like,

4

some of which words are these : *Gwrando*, signifying
in the Cambrian speech to give eare unto or hearken.
*Pen-gwyn*, with us a white head, refered by the
Mexicans to a Bird so-called, and Rockes complying
with that Idiom. Some promontories had like de-
nominations, called so by the people to this day, tho'
estranged and concealed by the Spaniard. Such are
the Isles *Corroeso*. The Cape of *Brutaine* or *Brittaine*.
The floud *Gwyndowr* or white water, *Bara* bread,
*Mam* mother, *Tate* father, *Dowr* water, *Bryd* time, *Bu*
or *Buch* a Cow, *Clugar* a Heathcocke, *Llwynog* a Fox,
*Wy* an Egge, *Calaf* a Quill, *Trwyn* a Nose, *Nef* Heaven ;
and the like then used ; by which, in my conceit, none
save detracting Opinionatists can justly oppose such
worthy testimonies and proofes of what I wish were
generally allowed of."

### Antiquity of Man in America

To turn to more substantial conclusions concerning
the racial affinities of the Red Man, we find that it is only
within very recent times that anything like a reasoned
scientific argument has been arrived at. Founding
upon recently acquired geological, anthropological, and
linguistic knowledge, inquirers into the deeper realms of
American ethnology have solved the question of how the
Western Hemisphere was peopled, and the arguments
they adduce are so convincing in their nature as to
leave no doubt in the minds of unbiased persons.

It is now admitted that the presence of man in the
Old World dates from an epoch so far distant as to be
calculated only by reference to geological periods of
which we know the succession but not the duration,
and research has proved that the same holds good
of the Western Hemisphere. Although man undoubtedly found his way from the Old World to the

5

New, the period at which he did so is so remote that for all practical purposes he may be said to have peopled both hemispheres simultaneously. Indeed, "his relative antiquity in each has no bearing on the history of his advancement."

It is known that the American continent offers no example of the highly organized primates—for example, the larger apes—in which the Old World abounds, save man himself, and this circumstance is sufficient to prove that the human species must have reached America as strangers. Had man been native to the New World there would have been found side by side with him either existing or fossil representatives of the greater apes and other anthropoid animals which illustrate his pedigree in the Old World.

### The Great Miocene Bridge

Again, many careful observers have noticed the striking resemblance between the natives of America and Northern Asia. At Bering Strait the Old World and the New are separated by a narrow sea-passage only, and an elevation of the sea-bed of less than two hundred feet would provide a 'land-bridge' at least thirty miles in breadth between the two continents. It is a geological fact that Bering Strait has been formed since the Tertiary period, and that such a 'land-bridge' once existed, to which American geologists have given the name of 'the Miocene bridge.' By this 'bridge,' it is believed, man crossed from Asia to America, and its subsequent disappearance confined him to the Western Hemisphere.

### American Man in Glacial Times

That this migration occurred before the Glacial period is proved by the circumstance that chipped

6

flints and other implements have been discovered in ice-drift at points in Ohio, Indiana, and Minnesota, to which it is known that the southern margin of the ice-sheet extended. This proves that man was driven southward by the advancing ice, as were several Old World animal species which had migrated to America. However, it is difficult in many cases to accept what may seem to be evidence of the presence of prehistoric man in North America with any degree of confidence, and it will be well to confine ourselves to the most authentic instances. In the loess of the Mississippi at Natchez Dr. Dickson found side by side with the remains of the mylodon and megalonyx human bones blackened by time. But Sir Charles Lyell pointed out that these remains might have been carried by the action of water from the numerous Indian places of burial in the neighbourhood. In New Orleans, while trenches were being dug for gas-pipes, a skeleton was discovered sixteen feet from the surface, the skull of which was embedded beneath a gigantic cypress-tree. But the deposit in which the remains were found was subsequently stated to be of recent origin. A reed mat was discovered at Petit Anse, Louisiana, at a depth of from fifteen to twenty feet, among a deposit of salt near the tusks or bones of an elephant. In the bottom-lands of the Bourbeuse River, in Missouri, Dr. Koch discovered the remains of a mastodon. It had sunk in the mud of the marshes, and, borne down by its own ponderous bulk, had been unable to right itself. Espied by the hunters of that dim era, it had been attacked by them, and the signs of their onset—flint arrow-heads and pieces of rock—were found mingled with its bones. Unable to dispatch it with their comparatively puny weapons, they had built great fires round it, the cinder-heaps of which remain to the

7

height of six feet, and by this means they had presumably succeeded in suffocating it.

In Iowa and Nebraska Dr. Aughey found many evidences of the presence of early man in stone weapons mingled with the bones of the mastodon. In California, Colorado, and Wyoming scores of stone mortars, arrow-heads, and lance-points have been discovered in deposits which show no sign of displacement. Traces of ancient mining operations are also met with in California and the Lake Superior district, the skeletons of the primitive miners being found, stone hammer in hand, beneath the masses of rock which buried them in their fall. As the object of these searchers was evidently metal of some description, it may reasonably be inferred that the remains are of comparatively late date.

### The Calaveras Skull

In 1866 Professor J. D. Whitney discovered the famous 'Calaveras' skull at a depth of about a hundred and thirty feet in a bed of auriferous gravel on the western slope of the Sierra Nevada, California. The skull rested on a bed of lava, and was covered by several layers of lava and volcanic deposit. Many other remains were found in similar geological positions, and this was thought to prove that the Calaveras skull was not an isolated instance of the presence of man in America in Tertiary times. The skull resembles the Eskimo type, and chemical analysis discovered the presence of organic matter. These circumstances led to the conclusion that the great age claimed by Whitney for the relic was by no means proved, and this view was strengthened by the knowledge that displacements of the deposits in which it had been discovered had frequently been caused by volcanic agency.

## More Recent Finds

More recent finds have been summarized by an eminent authority connected with the United States Bureau of Ethnology as follows : " In a post-Glacial terrace on the south shore of Lake Ontario the remains of a hearth were discovered at a depth of twenty-two feet by Mr. Tomlinson in digging a well, apparently indicating early aboriginal occupancy of the St. Lawrence basin.   From the Glacial or immediately post-Glacial deposits of Ohio a number of articles of human workmanship have been reported : a grooved axe from a well twenty-two feet beneath the surface, near New London ; a chipped object of waster type at Newcomerstown, at a depth of sixteen feet in Glacial gravel; chipped stones in gravels, one at Madisonville at a depth of eight feet, and another at Loveland at a depth of thirty feet.   At Little Falls, Minn., flood-plain, deposits of sand and gravel are found to contain many artificial objects of quartz.   This flood-plain is believed by some to have been finally abandoned by the Mississippi well back toward the close of the Glacial period in the valley, but that these finds warrant definite conclusions as to time is seriously questioned by Chamberlain.   In a Missouri river-beach near Lansing, Kansas, portions of a human skeleton were recently found at a depth of twenty feet, but geologists are not agreed as to the age of the formation.   At Clayton, Mo., in a deposit believed to belong to the loess, at a depth of fourteen feet, a well-finished grooved axe was found.   In the Basin Range region, between the Rocky Mountains and the sierras, two discoveries that seem to bear on the antiquity of human occupancy have been reported : in a silt deposit in Walker River Valley, Nevada, believed to be

9

of Glacial age, an obsidian implement was obtained
at a depth of twenty-five feet; at Nampa, Idaho, a
clay image is reported to have been brought up by a
sand-pump from a depth of three hundred and twenty
feet in alternating beds of clay and quicksand underlying a lava flow of late Tertiary or early Glacial age.
Questions are raised by a number of geologists respecting
the value of these finds."

### Later Man in America

Whatever doubt attaches to the presence of man in
America during the Tertiary period—a doubt which is
not shared by most American archæologists—there is
none regarding his occupation of the entire continent
in times less remote, yet far distant from the dawn of
the earliest historical records of Asia or Europe. In
caves and 'kitchen-middens' or rubbish-heaps over
the entire length and breadth of the American continent numerous evidences of the presence of populous
centres have been discovered. Mingled with the shells
of molluscs and the bones of extinct animals human
remains, weapons, and implements are to be found,
with traces of fire, which prove that the men of those
early days had risen above the merely animal existence
led by the first-comers to American soil.

### Affinities with Siberian Peoples

As has already been indicated, careful observers
have repeatedly remarked upon the strong likeness
between the American races and those of North-
eastern Asia. This likeness is not only physical, but
extends to custom, and to some extent to religious
belief.

"The war-dances and medicine customs of the
Ostiaks resemble those of the Kolusches even to the

smallest details, and the myth of a heaven-climber, who ascends the sky from a lofty tree, lowering himself again to earth by a strip of leather, a rope of grass, a plait of hair, or the curling wreath of smoke from a hut, occurs not only among the Ugrian tribes, but among the Dogrib Indians. Such myths, it is contended, though insufficient to prove common descent, point to early communications between these distant stocks. Superstitious usages, on the other hand, it is argued, are scarcely likely to have been adopted in consequence of mere intercourse, and indicate a common origin. Thus, among the Itelmians of Kamchatka it is forbidden to carry a burning brand otherwise than in the fingers ; it must on no account be pierced for that purpose with the point of a knife. A similar superstition is cherished by the Dakota. Again, when the tribes of Hudson Bay slay a bear they daub the head with gay colours, and sing around it hymns having a religious character ; it is understood to symbolize the spirit of the deceased animal. A similar practice, it is said, prevails throughout Siberia, and is met with among the Gilyaks of the Amur, and the Ainu. The Ostiaks hang the skin of a bear on a tree, pay it the profoundest respect, and address it while imploring pardon of the spirit of the animal for having put it to death ; their usual oath, moreover, is ' by the bear,' as the polished Athenians habitually swore ' by the dog.' Earthen vessels, it is further urged, were manufactured not only by the Itelmians, but by the Aleutians and the Kolusches of the New World ; whereas the Assiniboins, settled farther to the southward, cooked their flesh in kettles of hide, into which red-hot stones were cast to heat the water." [1]

[1] Payne, *History of the New World*, ii. 87–88, summarizing the investigations of Peschel and Tylor.

# MYTHS OF THE AMERICAN INDIANS

## The Evidence of American Languages

The structure of the aboriginal languages of America corroborates the conclusion that the American race proceeded from one instead of several sources, and that it is an ethnological extension of North-eastern Asia. Not only does the 'machinery' of American speech closely resemble that of the neighbouring Asiatic races in the possession of a common basis of phonesis and strenuity, but the rejection of labial explodents, which extends from Northern Asia through the speech of the Aleutian Islands to North-western America, is good evidence of affinity.

## Evidences of Asiatic Intercourse

Evidences of Asiatic intercourse with America in recent and historical times are not wanting. It is a well-authenticated fact that the Russians had learned from the native Siberians of the whereabouts of America long before the discovery of the contiguity of the continents by Bering. Charlevoix, in his work on the origin of the Indians, states that Père Grellon, one of the French Jesuit Fathers, encountered a Huron woman on the plains of Tartary who had been sold from tribe to tribe until she had passed from Bering Strait into Central Asia. Slight though such incidents seem, it is by means of them that important truths may be gleaned. If one individual was exchanged in this manner, there were probably many similar cases.

## Later Migrations

There are theories in existence worthy of respect which would regard the North American Indians as the last and recent wave of many Asiatic migrations to

American soil. If credence can be extended to the
Norse sagas which describe the visits of tenth-century
Scandinavian voyagers to the eastern coasts of America,
the accounts given of the race encountered by these
early discoverers by no means tally with any possible
description of the Red Man. The viking seafarers
nicknamed the American natives *Skrælingr*, or 'Chips,'
because of their puny appearance, and the account
which they gave of them would seem to class them as
a folk possessing Eskimo affinities. Many remains discovered in the eastern States are of the Eskimo type,
and when one combines with this the Indian traditions
of a great migration—traditions which cannot have
survived for many generations—it will be seen that
the exact epoch of the entrance of the Red Man into
America is by no means finally settled.

### The Norsemen in America

As the visits of the Norsemen to America during
the tenth century have been alluded to, perhaps some
further reference to this absorbing subject may be
made, as it is undoubtedly germane to the question of
the identity of the pre-Indian inhabitants of eastern
North America. The Scandinavian colonization of
Iceland tempted the intrepid viking race to extend
their voyages into still more northerly waters, and this
resulted in the discovery of Greenland. Once settled
upon those dreary beaches, it was practically inevitable that the hardy seamen would speedily discover
American soil. Biarne Herjulfson, sailing from Iceland to Greenland without knowledge of the waters
he navigated, was caught in dense fog and shifting
wind, so that he knew not in what direction he sailed.
"Witless, methinks, is our forth-faring," laughed the
stout Norseman, "seeing that none of us has beheld

the Greenland sea." Holding doggedly on, however, the adventurers came at last in sight of land. But this was no country of lofty ice such as they had been told to expect. A land of gentle undulations covered with timber met their sea-sad eyes. Bearing away, they came to another land like the first. The wind fell, and the sailors proposed to disembark. But Biarne refused. Five days afterward they made Greenland. Biarne had, of course, got into that Arctic current which sets southward from the Polar Circle between Iceland and Greenland, and had been carried to the coasts of New England.[1]

### Leif the Lucky

Biarne did not care to pursue his discoveries, but at the court of Eric, Earl of Norway, to which he paid a visit, his neglect in following them up was much talked about. All Greenland, too, was agog with the news. Leif, surnamed 'the Lucky,' son of Eric the Red, the first colonizer of Greenland, purchased Biarne's ship, and, hiring a crew of thirty-five men, one of whom was a German named Tyrker (perhaps Tydsker, the Norse for 'German'), set sail for the land seen by Biarne. He soon espied it, and cast anchor, but it was a barren place; so they called it Hellu-land, or 'Land of Flat Stones,' and, leaving it, sailed southward again. Soon they came to another country, which they called Mark-land, or 'Wood-land,' for it was low and flat and well covered with trees. These shores also they left, and again put to sea.

### The Land of Wine

After sailing still farther south they came to a strait lying between an island and a promontory. Here they

[1] Rafn, *Antiquitates Americanæ*, xxix. 17-25.

landed and built huts. The air was warm after the sword-like winds of Greenland, and when the day was shortest the sun was above the horizon from half-past seven in the morning until half-past four in the afternoon. They divided into two bands to explore the land. One day Tyrker, the German, was missing. They searched for him, and found him at no great distance from the camp, in a state of much excitement. For he had discovered vines with grapes upon them—a boon to a man coming from a land of vines, who had beheld none for half a lifetime. They loaded the ship's boat with the grapes and felled timber to freight the ship, and in the spring sailed away from the new-found country, which they named 'Wine-land.'

It would seem that the name Hellu-land was applied to Newfoundland or Labrador, Mark-land to Nova Scotia, and Wine-land to New England, and that Leif wintered in some part of the state of Rhode Island.

### The Skrælingr

In the year 1002 Leif's brother Thorwald sailed to the new land in Biarne's ship. From the place where Leif had landed, which the Norsemen named 'Leif's Booths' (or huts), he explored the country southward and northward. But at a promontory in the neighbourhood of Boston he was attacked and slain by the Skrælingr who inhabited the country. These men are described as small and dwarfish in appearance and as possessing Eskimo characteristics. In 1007 a bold attempt was made to colonize the country from Greenland. Three ships, with a hundred and sixty men aboard, sailed to Wine-land, where they wintered, but the incessant attacks of the Skrælingr rendered colonization impossible, and the Norsemen took their departure. The extinction of the Scandinavian colonies

15

in Greenland put an end to all communication with America. But the last voyage from Greenland to American shores took place in 1347, only a hundred and forty-five years before Columbus discovered the West Indian Islands. In 1418 the Skrælingr of Greenland —the Eskimo—attacked and destroyed the Norse settlements there, and carried away the colonists into captivity. It is perhaps the descendants of these Norse folk who dared the world of ice and the ravening breakers of the Arctic sea who have been discovered by a recent Arctic explorer ![1]

The authenticity of the Norse discoveries is not to be questioned. No less than seventeen ancient Icelandic documents allude to them, and Adam of Bremen mentions the territory discovered by them as if referring to a widely known country.

### The Dighton Rock

A rock covered with inscriptions, known as the Dighton Writing Rock, situated on the banks of the Taunton River, in Massachusetts, was long pointed out as of Norse origin, and Rafn, the Danish antiquary, pronounced the script which it bore to be runic. With equal perspicacity Court de Gébelin and Dr. Styles saw in it a Phœnician inscription. It is, in fact, quite certain that the writing is of Indian origin, as similar rock-carvings occur over the length and breadth of the northern sub-continent. Almost as doubtful are the theories which would make the ' old mill ' at Newport a Norse ' biggin.' However authentic the Norse settlements in America may be, it is certain that the Norsemen left no traces of their occupation in that continent, and although the building at Newport distinctly resembles the remains of Norse architecture in

[1] See *Eric Rothens Saga*, in Mueller, *Sagenbibliothek*, p. 214.

Greenland, the district in which it is situated is quite out of the sphere of Norse settlement in North America.

## The Mound-Builders

The question of the antiquity of the Red Race in North America is bound up with an archæological problem which bristles with difficulties, but is quite as replete with interest. In the Mississippi basin and the Gulf States, chiefly from La Crosse, Wisconsin, to Natchez, Miss., and in the central and southern districts of Ohio, and in the adjoining portion of Indiana and South Wisconsin, are found great earthen mounds, the typical form of which is pyramidal. Some, however, are circular, and a few pentagonal. Others are terraced, extending outward from one or two sides, while some have roadways leading up to the level surface on the summit. These are not mere accumulations of *débris*, but works constructed on a definite plan, and obviously requiring a considerable amount of skill and labour for their accomplishment. " The form, except where worn down by the plough, is usually that of a low, broad, round-topped cone, varying in size from a scarcely perceptible swell in the ground to elevations of eighty or even a hundred feet, and from six to three hundred feet in diameter." [1]

## Mounds in Animal Form

Many of these structures represent animal forms, probably the totem or eponymous ancestor of the tribe which reared them. The chief centre for these singular erections seems to have been Wisconsin, where they are very numerous. The eagle, wolf, bear, turtle, and fox are represented, and even the human form has been

[1] *Bulletin 30*, Bureau of American Ethnology.

17

attempted. There are birds with outstretched wings, measuring more than thirty-two yards from tip to tip, and great mammalian forms sixty-five yards long. Reptilian forms are also numerous. These chiefly represent huge lizards. At least one mound in the form of a spider, whose body and legs cover an acre of ground, exists in Minnesota.

According to the classification of Squier, these structures were employed for burial, sacrifice, and observation, and as temple-sites. Other structures often found in connexion with them are obviously enclosures, and were probably used for defence. The conical mounds are usually built of earth and stones, and are for the most part places of sepulture. The flat-topped structures were probably employed as sites for buildings, such as temples, council-houses, and chiefs' dwellings. Burials were rarely made in the wall-like enclosures or effigy mounds. Many of the enclosures are of true geometrical figure, circular, square, or octagonal, and with few exceptions these are found in Ohio and the adjoining portions of Kentucky, Indiana, and West Virginia. They enclose an expanse varying from one to a hundred acres.

### What the Mounds Contain

In the sepulchral mounds a large number of objects have been found which throw some light on the habits of the folk who built them. Copper plates with stamped designs are frequent, and these are difficult to account for. In one mound were found no less than six hundred stone hatchet-blades, averaging seven inches long by four wide. Under another were exhumed two hundred calcined tobacco-pipes, and copper ornaments with a thin plating of silver; while from others were taken fragments of pottery, obsidian implements, ivory

18

and bone needles, and scroll-work cut out of very thin plates of mica. In several it was observed that cremation had been practised, but in others the bodies were found extended horizontally or else doubled up. In some instances the ashes of the dead had been placed carefully in skulls, perhaps those of the individuals whose bodies had been given to the flames. Implements, too, are numerous, and axes, awls, and other tools of copper have frequently been discovered.

### The Tomb of the Black Tortoise

A more detailed description of one of these groups of sepulchral mounds may furnish the reader with a clearer idea of the structures as a whole. The group in question was discovered in Minnesota, on the northern bank of St. Peter's River, about sixty miles from its junction with the Mississippi. It includes twenty-six mounds, placed at regular distances from each other, and forming together a large rectangle. The central mound represents a turtle forty feet long by twenty-seven feet wide and twelve feet high. It is almost entirely constructed of yellow clay, which is not found in the district, and therefore must have been brought from a distance. Two mounds of red earth of triangular form flank it north and south, and each of these is twenty-seven feet long by about six feet wide at one end, the opposite end tapering off until it scarcely rises above the level of the soil. At each corner rises a circular mound twelve feet high by twenty-five feet in diameter. East and west of the structure stand two elongated mounds sixty feet long, with a diameter of twelve feet. Two smaller mounds on the right and left of the turtle-shaped mound are each twelve feet long by four feet high, and consist of white sand mixed with numerous fragments of mica, covered with

19

a layer of clay and a second one of vegetable mould. Lastly, thirteen smaller mounds fill in the intervals in the group.

Conant gives an explanation of the whole group as follows : "The principal tomb would be the last home of a great chief, the Black Tortoise. The four mounds which form the corners of the quadrangle were also erected as a sign of the mourning of the tribe. The secondary mounds are the tombs of other chiefs, and the little mounds erected in the north and south corresponded with the number of bodies which had been deposited in them. The two pointed mounds indicate that the Black Tortoise was the last of his race, and the two large mounds the importance of that race and the dignity which had belonged to it. Lastly, the two mounds to the right and left of the royal tomb mark the burial-places of the prophets or soothsayers, who even to our own day play a great part among the Indian tribes. The fragments of mica found in their tombs would indicate their rank."[1]

### Who were the Mound-Builders?

It is not probable that the reader will agree with all the conclusions drawn in the paragraph quoted above, which would claim for these structures a hieroglyphic as well as a sepulchral significance. But such speculations cannot destroy the inherent interest of the subject, however much they may irritate those who desire to arrive at logical conclusions concerning it. Who then were the folk who raised the mounds of Ohio and the Mississippi and spread their culture from the Gulf states region to the Great Lakes? Needless to say, the 'antiquaries' of the last century stoutly maintained that they were strangers from over the sea,

[1] *Footprints of Vanished Races*, p. 18.

sun- and serpent-worshippers who had forsaken the cities of Egypt, Persia, and Phœnicia, and had settled in the West in order to pursue their strange religions undisturbed. But such a view by no means commends itself to modern science, which sees in the architects of these mounds and pyramids the ancestors of the present aborigines of North America. Many of the objects discovered in the mounds are of European manufacture, or prove contact with Europeans, which shows that the structures containing them are of comparatively modern origin. The articles discovered and the character of the various monuments indicate a culture stage similar to that noted among the more advanced tribes inhabiting the regions where the mounds occur at the period of the advent of the whites. Moreover, the statements of early writers on these regions, such as the members of De Soto's expedition, prove beyond question that some of the structures were erected by the Indians in post-Columbian times. "It is known that some of the tribes inhabiting the Gulf states, when De Soto passed through their territory in 1540–41, as the Yuchi, Creeks, Chickasaw, and Natchez, were still using and probably constructing mounds, and that the Quapaw of Arkansas were also using them. There is also documentary evidence that the ' Texas ' tribe still used mounds at the end of the seventeenth century, when a chief's house is described as being built on one. There is also sufficient evidence to justify the conclusion that the Cherokee and Shawnee were mound-builders. . . . According to Miss Fletcher, the Winnebago build miniature mounds in the lodge during certain ceremonies." [1]

Nothing has been found in the mounds to indicate

[1] *Bulletin 30,* Bureau of American Ethnology.

great antiquity, and the present tendency among archæologists is to assign to them a comparatively recent origin.

## The 'Nations' of North America

In order that the reader may be enabled the better
to comprehend the history and customs of the Red
Race in North America, it will be well at this juncture
to classify the various ethnic stocks of which it is
composed. Proceeding to do so on a linguistic basis—
the only possible guide in this instance—we find that
students of American languages, despite the diversity
of tongues exhibited in North America, have referred
all of these to ten or a dozen primitive stems.[1] Let us
first examine the geographical position of the ' nations '
of the American aborigines in the sixteenth century,
at the period of the advent of the white man, whilst
yet they occupied their ancestral territory.

The Athapascan stock extended in a broad band
across the continent from the Pacific to Hudson Bay,
and almost to the Great Lakes below. Tribes cognate
to it wandered far north to the mouth of the Mackenzie
River, and, southward, skirted the Rockies and the
coast of Oregon south of the estuary of the Columbia
River, and spreading over the plains of New Mexico,
as Apaches, Navahos, and Lipans, extended almost to
the tropics. The Athapascan is the most widely
distributed of all the Indian linguistic stocks of North
America, and covered a territory of more than forty
degrees of latitude and seventy-five degrees of longi-
tude. Its northern division was known as the Tinneh
or Déné, and consisted of three groups—eastern,
north-western, and south-western, dwelling near the
Rockies, in the interior of Alaska, and in the
mountain fastnesses of British America respectively.

[1] See the map, p. 361.

The Pacific division occupied many villages in a strip of territory about four hundred miles in length from Oregon to Eel River in California. The southern division occupied a large part of Arizona and New Mexico, the southern portion of Utah and Colorado, the western borders of Kansas, and the northern part of Mexico to lat. 25°. The social conditions and customs as well as the various dialects spoken by the several branches and offshoots of this great family differed considerably according to climate and environment. Extremely adaptable, the Athapascan stock appear to have adopted many of the customs and ceremonies of such tribes as they were brought into contact with, and do not seem to have had any impetus to frame a culture of their own. Their tribes had little cohesion, and were subdivided into family groups or loose bands, which recognized a sort of patriarchal government and descent. Their food-supply was for the most part precarious, as it consisted almost entirely of the proceeds of hunting expeditions, and the desperate and never-ending search for provender rendered this people somewhat narrow and material in outlook.

### The Iroquois

The Iroquois—Hurons, Tuscaroras, Susquehannocks, Nottoways, and others—occupied much of the country from the St. Lawrence River and Lake Ontario to the Roanoke. Several of their tribes banded themselves into a confederacy known as the 'Five Nations,' and these comprised the Cayugas, Mohawks, Oneidas, Onondagas, and Senecas. The Cherokees, dwelling in the valleys of East Tennessee, appear to have been one of the early offshoots of the Iroquois. A race of born warriors, they pursued their craft with an excess of cruelty which made them the terror of the white settler. It was with the

23

Iroquois that most of the early colonial wars were waged, and their name, which they borrowed from the Algonquins, and which signifies 'Real Adders,' was probably no misnomer. They possessed chiefs who, strangely enough, were nominated by the matrons of the tribe, whose decision was confirmed by the tribal and federal councils. The 'Five Nations' of the Iroquois made up the Iroquois Confederacy, which was created about the year 1570, as the last of a series of attempts to unite the tribes in question. The Mohawks, so conspicuous in colonial history, are one of their sub-tribes. Many of the Iroquoian tribes "have been settled by the Canadian Government on a reservation on Grand River, Ontario, where they still reside. . . . All the Iroquois [in the United States] are in reservations in New York, with the exception of the Oneida, who are settled in Green Bay, Wisconsin. The so-called Seneca, of Oklahoma, are composed of the remnants of many tribes . . . and of emigrants from all the tribes of the Iroquoian Confederation." In 1689 the Iroquois were estimated to number about twelve thousand, whereas in 1904 they numbered over sixteen thousand.

### The Algonquins

The Algonquian [1] family surrounded the Iroquois on every side, and extended westward toward the Rocky Mountains, where one of their famous offshoots, the Blackfeet, gained a notoriety which has rendered them the heroes of many a boyish tale. They were milder than the Iroquois, and less Spartan in habits. Their

---

[1] This name has been adopted to distinguish the *family* from the tribal name, 'Algonquin' or 'Algonkin,' but is not employed when speaking of individuals. Thus we speak of 'the Algonquian race,' but, on the other hand, of 'an Algonquin Indian.'

western division comprised the Blackfeet, Arapaho, and Cheyenne, situated near the eastern slope of the Rocky Mountains ; the northern division, situated for the most part to the north of the St. Lawrence, comprised the Chippeways and Crees ; the north-eastern division embraced the tribes inhabiting Quebec, the Maritime Provinces, and Maine, including the Montagnais and Micmacs ; the central division, dwelling in Illinois, Wisconsin, Indiana, Michigan, and Ohio, included the Foxes, Kickapoos, Menominees, and others ; and the eastern division embraced all the Algonquian tribes that dwelt along the Atlantic coast, the Abnaki, Narragansets, Nipmucs, Mohicans (or Mohegans), Shawnees, Delawares, and Powhatans.

The Algonquins were the first Indians to come into contact with the white man. As a rule their relations with the French were friendly, but they were frequently at war with the English settlers. The eastern branch of the race were quickly defeated and scattered, their remnants withdrawing to Canada and the Ohio valley. Of the smaller tribes of New England, Virginia, and other eastern states there are no living representatives, and even their languages are extinct, save for a few words and place-names. The Ohio valley tribes, with the Wyandots, formed themselves into a loose confederacy and attempted to preserve the Ohio as an Indian boundary ; but in 1794 they were finally defeated and forced to cede their territory. Tecumseh, an Algonquin chief, carried on a fierce war against the United States for a number of years, but by his defeat and death at Tippecanoe in 1811 the spirit of the Indians was broken, and the year 1815 saw the commencement of a series of Indian migrations westward, and a wholesale cession of Indian territory which continued over a period of about thirty years.

25

## A Sedentary People

The Algonquins had been for generations the victims of the Iroquois Confederacy, and only when the French had guaranteed them immunity from the attacks of their hereditary enemies did they set their faces to the east once more, to court repulse a second time at the hands of the English settlers. Tall and finely proportioned, the Algonquins were mainly a sedentary and agricultural people, growing maize and wild rice for their staple foods. Indeed, more than once were the colonists of New England saved from famine by these industrious folk. In 1792 Wayne's army found a continuous plantation along the entire length of the Maumee River from Fort Wayne to Lake Erie, and such evidence entirely shatters the popular fallacy that the Indian race were altogether lacking in the virtues of industry and domesticity. They employed fish-shells and ashes as fertilizers, and made use of spades and hoes. And it was the Algonquins who first instilled in the white settlers the knowledge of how to prepare those succulent dainties for which New England is famous—hominy, succotash, maple-sugar, and johnny-cake. They possessed the art of tanning deerskin to a delicate softness which rendered it a luxurious and delightful raiment, and, like the Aztecs, they manufactured mantles of feather-work. They had also elaborated a system of picture-writing. In short, they were the most intelligent and advanced of the eastern tribes, and had their civilization been permitted to proceed unhindered by white aggression and the recurring inroads of their hereditary enemies, the Iroquois, it would probably have evolved into something resembling that of the Nahua of Mexico, without, perhaps, exhibiting the sanguinary fanaticism of that people. The great weakness of the Algonquian culture was that it never achieved a degree of tribal organization and cohesion sufficient to enable them to withstand their foes.

### The Muskhogean Race

The Muskhogean race included the Choctaws, Chickasaws, Creeks, and Seminoles, who occupied territory in the Gulf states east of the Mississippi, possessing almost all of Mississippi and Alabama, and portions of Tennessee, Georgia, Florida, and South Carolina. Many early notices of this people are extant. They were met by Narvaez in Florida in 1528, and De Soto passed through their territory in 1540-41. By 1700 the entire Apalachee tribe had been civilized and Christianized, and had settled in seven large and well-built towns. But the tide of white settlement gradually pressed the Muskhogean tribes backward from the coast region, and though they fought stoutly to retain their patrimony, few of the race remain in their native area, the majority having been removed to the tribal reservation in Oklahoma before 1840. They were an agricultural and sedentary people, occupying villages of substantially built dwellings. A curious diversity, both physical and mental, existed among the several tribes of which the race was composed. They possessed a general council formed of representatives from each town, who met annually or as occasion required. Artificial deformation of the skull was practised by nearly all of the Muskhogean tribes, chiefly by the Choctaws, who were called by the settlers 'Flatheads.' The Muskhogean population at the period of its first contact with the whites has been estimated at some fifty thousand souls. In 1905 they numbered rather more, but this estimate included about fifteen thousand freedmen of negro blood.

27

# MYTHS OF THE AMERICAN INDIANS

## The Sioux

The Siouan or Dakota stock—Santees, Yanktons, Assiniboins, and Tetons—inhabited a territory extending from Saskatchewan to Louisiana. Their physical, mental, and moral attributes are the most admired of all the western tribes, and their courage is unquestioned. They dwelt in large bands or groups. "Personal fitness and popularity determined chieftainship. . . . The authority of the chief was limited by the band council, without whose approbation little or nothing could be accomplished. War parties were recruited by individuals who had acquired reputation as successful leaders, while the *shamans* formulated ceremonials and farewells for them. Polygamy was common. . . . Remains of the dead were usually, though not invariably, placed on scaffolds." [1]

## Caddoan Family

The Caddoan family comprises three geographic groups, the northern, represented by the Arikara, the middle, embracing the Pawnee Confederacy, once dwelling in Nebraska, and the southern group, including the Caddo, Kichai, and Wichita. Once numerous, this division of the Red Race is now represented by a few hundreds of individuals only, who are settled in Oklahoma and North Dakota. The Caddo tribes were cultivators of the soil as well as hunters, and practised the arts of pottery-making and tanning. They lacked political ability and were loosely confederated.

## The Shoshoneans

The Shoshoneans or 'Snake' family of Nevada, Utah, and Idaho comprise the Root-diggers, Comanches, and

[1] *Bulletin 30*, Bureau of American Ethnology.

other tribes. These people, said to be of low culture, speak a related dialect and partake in some measure of the same blood as the famous Aztec race who founded the empire of Anahuac, and raised architectural monuments rivalling the most famous structures of the ancient world."[1]

### Early Wars with the Whites

Numerous minor wars between the Indians and the colonists followed upon the settlement of Virginia, but on the whole the relations between them were peaceable until the general massacre of white women and children on March 22, 1622, while the men of the colony were working in the fields. Three hundred and forty-seven men, women, and children were slain in a single day. This holocaust was the signal for an Indian war which continued intermittently for many years and cost the colonists untold loss in blood and treasure. Inability to comprehend each other's point of view was of course a fertile source of irritation between the races, and even colonists who had ample opportunities for observing and studying the Indians during a long course of years appear to have been incapable of understanding their outlook and true character. The dishonesty of white traders, on the other hand, aroused the Indian to a frenzy of childish indignation. It was a native saying that "One pays for another," and when an Indian was slain his nearest blood-relation considered that he had consummated a righteous revenge by murdering the first white man whom he met or waylaid. Each race accused the other of treachery and unfairness. Probably the colonists, despite their

[1] Brinton, *Myths of the New World.*

veneer of civilization, were only a little less ignorant than, and as vindictively cruel as, the barbarians with whom they strove. The Indian regarded the colonist as an interloper who had come to despoil him of the land of his fathers, while the Virginian Puritan considered himself the salt of the earth and the Indian as a heathen or 'Ishmaelite' sent by the Powers of Darkness for his discomfiture, whom it was an act of both religion and policy to destroy. Vengeful ferocity was exhibited on both sides. Another horrible massacre of five hundred whites in 1644 was followed by the defeat of the Indians who had butchered the colonists. Shortly before that event the Pequot tribe in Connecticut had a feud with the English traders, and tortured such of them as they could lay hands on. The men of Connecticut, headed by John Mason, a military veteran, marched into the Pequot country, surrounded the village of Sassacus, the Pequot chief, gave it to the flames, and slaughtered six hundred of its inhabitants. The tribe was broken up, and the example of their fate so terrified the other Indian peoples that New England enjoyed peace for many years after.

### King Philip's War

The Dutch of New York were at one period almost overwhelmed by the Indians in their neighbourhood, and in 1656 the Virginians suffered a severe defeat in a battle with the aborigines at the spot where Richmond now stands. In 1675 there broke out in New England the great Indian war known as King Philip's War. Philip, an Indian chief, complained bitterly that those of his subjects who had been converted to Christianity were withdrawn from his control, and he made vigorous war on the settlers, laying many of their towns in ashes. But victory was with the colonists at the battle called the 'Swamp Fight,' and Philip and his men were scattered.

Captain Benjamin Church it was who first taught the colonists to fight the Indians in their own manner. He moved as stealthily as the savages themselves, and, to avoid an alarm, never allowed an Indian to be shot who could be reached with the hatchet. The Indians who were captured were sold into slavery in the West India Islands, where the hard labour and change of climate were usually instrumental in speedily putting an end to their servitude.

Step by step the Red Man was driven westward until he vanished from the vicinity of the earlier settlements altogether. From that period the history of his conflicts with the whites is bound up with the records of their western extension.

## The Reservations

The necessity of bringing the Indian tribes under the complete control of the United States Government and confining them to definite limits for the better preservation of order was responsible for the policy of placing them on tracts of territory of their own called 'reservations.' This step led the natives to realize the benefits of a settled existence and to depend on their own industry for a livelihood rather than upon the more precarious products of the chase. An Act of Congress was passed in 1887 which put a period to the existence of the Indian tribes as separate communities, and permitted all tribal lands and reservations to be so divided that each individual member of a tribe might possess a separate holding. Many of these holdings are of considerable value, and the possessors are by no means poorly endowed with this world's goods. On the whole the policy of the United States toward the Indians has been dictated by justice and humanity, but instances have not been wanting in which arid lands have been foisted upon the Indians, and the pressure of white settlers has frequently forced the Government to dispossess the Red Man of the land that had originally been granted to him.

### The Story of Pocahontas

Many romantic stories are told concerning the relations of the early white settlers with the Indians. Among the most interesting is that of Pocahontas, the daughter of the renowned Indian chief Powhatan, the erstwhile implacable enemy of the whites. Pocahontas, who as a child had often played with the young colonists, was visiting a certain chief named Japazaws, when an English captain named Argall bribed him with a copper kettle to betray her into his hands. Argall took her a captive to Jamestown. Here a white man by the name of John Rolfe married her, after she had received Christian baptism. This marriage brought about a peace between Powhatan and the English settlers in Virginia.

When Dale went back to England in 1616 he took with him some of the Indians. Pocahontas, who was now called 'the Lady Rebecca,' and her husband accompanied the party. Pocahontas was called a princess in England, and received much attention. But when about to return to the colony she died, leaving a little son.

The quaint version of Captain Nathaniel Powell, which retains all the known facts of Pocahontas' story, states that "During this time, the Lady Rebecca, *alias* Pocahontas, daughter to Powhatan, by the diligent care of Master John Rolfe her husband, and his friends, was taught to speak such English as might well be understood, well instructed in Christianity, and was become very formal and civil after our English manner ; she had also by him a child which she loved most dearly, and the Treasurer and Company took order both for the maintenance of her and it, besides there were divers persons of great rank and quality had been kind to her ; and before she arrived at London, Captain Smith, to deserve her former courtesies, made her qualities known to the Queen's most excellent Majesty and her Court, and wrote a little book to this effect to the Queen : An abstract whereof follows :

" ' *To the Most High and Virtuous Princess, Queen Anne of Great Britain*

" ' MOST ADMIRED QUEEN,

" ' The love I bear my God, my King and Country, hath so oft emboldened me in the worst of extreme dangers, that now honesty doth constrain me to presume thus far beyond myself, to present your Majesty this short discourse : if ingratitude be a deadly poison to all honest virtues, I must be guilty of that crime if I should omit any means to be thankful.

" ' So it is,

" ' That some ten years ago being in Virginia, and taken prisoner by the power of Powhatan their chief King, I received from this great savage exceeding great courtesy, especially from his son Nantaquaus, the most manliest, comeliest, boldest spirit I ever saw in a savage, and his sister Pocahontas, the King's most dear and well-beloved daughter, being but a child of twelve or thirteen years of age, whose compassionate pitiful heart, of my desperate estate, gave me much cause to respect her ; I being the first Christian this proud King and his grim attendants ever saw : and thus enthralled in their barbarous power, I cannot say I felt the

33

least occasion of want that was in the power of these my mortal foes to prevent, notwithstanding all their threats. After some six weeks fatting among these savage courtiers, at the minute of my execution, she hazarded the beating out of her own brains to save mine ; and not only that, but so prevailed with her father, that I was safely conveyed to Jamestown : where I found about eight and thirty miserable poor and sick creatures, to keep possession of all those large territories of Virginia ; such was the weakness of this poor Commonwealth, as had the savages not fed us, we directly had starved. And this relief, most gracious Queen, was commonly brought us by this Lady Pocahontas.

" ' Notwithstanding all these passages, when inconstant Fortune turned our peace to war, this tender virgin would still not spare to dare to visit us, and by her our jars have been oft appeased, and our wants still supplied. Were it the policy of her father thus to employ her, or the ordinance of God thus to make her His instrument, or her extraordinary affection to our nation, I know not ; but of this I am sure : when her father, with the utmost of his policy and power, sought to surprise me, having but eighteen with me, the dark night could not affright her from coming through the irksome woods, and with watered eyes gave me intelligence, with her best advice to escape his fury ; which had he known, he had surely slain her.

" ' Jamestown with her wild train she as freely frequented as her father's habitation ; and during the time of two or three years [1608–9] she, next under God, was still the instrument to preserve this Colony from death, famine and utter confusion ; which if in those times it had once been dissolved, Virginia might have lain as it was at our first arrival to this day.

" ' Since then, this business having been turned and

varied by many accidents from that I left it at : it is most certain, after a long and troublesome war after my departure, betwixt her father and our Colony, all which time she was not heard of ;

"'About two years after she herself was taken prisoner, being so detained near two years longer, the Colony by that means was relieved, peace concluded ; and at last rejecting her barbarous condition, she was married to an English gentleman, with whom at this present she is in England ; the first Christian ever of that nation, the first Virginian ever spoke English, or had a child in marriage by an Englishman : a matter surely, if my meaning be truly considered and well understood, worthy a prince's understanding.

"'Thus, most gracious Lady, I have related to your Majesty, what at your best leisure our approved Histories will account you at large, and done in the time of your Majesty's life ; and however this might be presented you from a more worthy pen, it cannot from a more honest heart, as yet I never begged anything of the state, or any : and it is my want of ability and her exceeding desert ; your birth, means and authority ; her birth, virtue, want and simplicity, doth make me thus bold, humbly to beseech your Majesty to take this knowledge of her, though it be from one so unworthy to be the reporter, as myself, her husband's estate not being able to make her fit to attend your Majesty. The most and least I can do is to tell you this, because none so oft has tried it as myself, and the rather being of so great a spirit, however her stature : if she should not be well received, seeing this kingdom may rightly have a kingdom by her means ; her present love to us and Christianity might turn to such scorn and fury, as to divert all this good to the worst of evil : whereas finding so great a Queen should do her some honour more than she can imagine, for being so kind to your servants and subjects, would so ravish her with content, as endear her dearest blood to effect that, your Majesty and all the King's honest subjects most earnestly desire.'"

Captain Powell continues :

"The small time I staid in London, divers courtiers and others, my acquaintances, have gone with me to see her, that generally concluded, they did think God had had a great hand in her conversion, and they have seen many English Ladies worse favoured, proportioned, and behavioured; and as since I have heard, it pleased both the King and Queen's Majesty honourably to esteem her, accompanied with that honourable Lady the Lady de la Ware, and that honourable Lord her husband, and divers other persons of good qualities, both publicly at the masques and otherwise, to her great satisfaction and content, which doubtless she would have deserved, had she lived to arrive in Virginia.

"The Treasurer, Council and Company, having well furnished Captain Samuel Argall, the Lady Pocahontas alias Rebecca, with her husband and others, in the good ship called the *George*; it pleased God at Gravesend to take this young Lady to His mercy, where she made not more sorrow for her unexpected death, than joy to the beholders to hear and see her make so religious and godly an end. Her little child Thomas Rolfe, therefore, was left at Plymouth with Sir Lewis Stukly, that desired the keeping of it."

### Indian Kidnapping

Many are the tales of how Indians raiding a white settlement have kidnapped and adopted into their families the children of the slain whites, but none is more enthralling than that of Frances Slocum, who was carried away from home by a party of Delawares when but five years of age, and who lived with them until her death in 1847. When discovered by the whites she was an old woman of over seventy years of age. The story is told by the writer of a local history as follows :

"The Slocums came from Warwick, Rhode Island, and Jonathan Slocum, the father of the far-famed captive girl, emigrated, in 1777, with a wife and nine children. They located near one of the forts, upon a spot of ground which is at present covered by the city of Wilkes-Barre.

" The early training of the family had been on principles averse to war, and Jonathan was loath to mix with the tumult of the valley. A son by the name of Giles, of a fiery spirit, could not brook the evident intentions of the Torys and British, and consequently he shouldered his musket, and was one to take part in the battle of July 3, 1778.

"The prowling clans of savages and bushwhacking Torys which continued to harass the valley occasioned much mischief in different parts, and in the month of November following the battle it was the misfortune of the Slocum family to be visited by a party of these Delawares, who approached the cabin, in front of which two Kingsley boys were engaged at a grindstone sharpening a knife. The elder had on a Continental coat, which aroused the ire of the savages, and he was shot down without warning and scalped by the very knife which he had put edge to.

" The report roused the inmates of the house, and Mrs. Slocum had reached the door in time sufficient to see the boy of her neighbour scalped.

" An elder daughter seized a young child two years old, and flew with terror to the woods. It is said that

37

her impetuosity in escaping caused the Indians to roar with laughter. They were about to take away a boy when Mrs. Slocum pointed to a lame foot, exclaiming : 'The child is lame ; he can do thee no good.' They dropped the boy and discovered little Frances hidden away under the staircase. It was but the act of a moment to secure her, and when they bore her away the tender child could but look over the Indian's shoulder and scream 'Mamma ! '

"The alarm soon spread, but the elasticity of a Delaware's step had carried the party away into the mountains.

"Mr. Slocum was absent at the time of the capture, and upon returning at night learned the sad news.

"The family's trials did not end here. Miner, who is ever in sympathy with the early annals of Wyoming, thus depicts the scenes which occurred afterwards :

"'The cup of vengeance was not yet full. December 16th, Mr. Slocum and Isaac Tripp, his father-in-law, an aged man, with William Slocum, a youth of nineteen or twenty, were feeding cattle from a stack in the meadow, in sight of the fort, when they were fired upon by Indians. Mr. Slocum was shot dead ; Mr. Tripp wounded, speared, and tomahawked ; both were scalped. William, wounded by a spent ball in the heel, escaped and gave the alarm, but the alert and wily foe had retreated to his hiding-place in the mountain. This deed, bold as it was cruel, was perpetrated within the town plot, in the centre of which the fortress was located. Thus, in little more than a month, Mrs. Slocum had lost a beloved child, carried into captivity ; the doorway had been drenched in blood by the murder of a member of the family ; two others of the household had been taken away prisoners ; and now her husband and father were both stricken down to the

38

grave, murdered and mangled by the merciless Indians. Verily, the annals of Indian atrocities, written in blood, record few instances of desolation and woe equal to this.' "

" In 1784, after peace had settled upon the country, two of the Slocum brothers visited Niagara, in hopes of learning something of the whereabouts of the lost sister, but to no purpose. Large rewards were offered, but money will not extract a confession from an Indian.

" Little Frances all this time was widely known by many tribes of Indians, but she had become one of them, hence the mystery which shrouded her fate.

" The efforts of the family were untiring. Several trips were made westward, and each resulted in vain. A large number of Indians of different tribes were convened, in 1789, at Tioga Point, to effect a treaty with Colonel Proctor. This opportunity seemed to be the fitting one, for one visit could reach several tribes, but Mrs. Slocum, after spending weeks of inquiry among them, was again obliged to return home in sorrow, and almost despair.

" The brothers took a journey in 1797, occupying nearly the whole summer, in traversing the wilderness and Indian settlements of the west, but to no purpose. Once, indeed, a ray of hope seemed to glimmer upon the domestic darkness, for a female captive responded to the many and urgent inquiries, but Mrs. Slocum discovered at once that it was not her Frances. The mother of the lost child went down to the grave, having never heard from her daughter since she was carried away captive.

" In 1826, Mr. Joseph Slocum, hearing of a prominent Wyandot chief who had a white woman for a wife, repaired to Sandusky, but was disappointed when he beheld the woman, who he knew to a certainty could

39

not be Frances. Hope had become almost abandoned, and the family was allowing the memory of the lost girl to sink into forgetfulness, when one of those strange freaks of circumstances which seem so mysterious to humanity, but which are the ordinary actions of Infinity, brought to light the history and the person of the captive girl of Wyoming.

"Colonel Ewing, who was connected with Indian service, had occasion to rest with a tribe on the Wabash, when he discovered a woman whose outlines and texture convinced him that she must be a white woman, though her face was as red as any squaw's could be. He made inquiries, and she admitted that she had been taken from her parents when she was young, that her name was Slocum, and that she was now so old that she had no objections to having her relations know of her whereabouts.

"The Colonel knew full well how anxious many eastern hearts were to hear of the lost one of earlier days, and thinking that he would do a charitable service, he addressed the following letter to the Postmaster of Lancaster, Pennsylvania:

"'LOGANSPORT, INDIANA: *January* 20, 1835

"'DEAR SIR,—

"' In the hope that some good may result from it, I have taken this means of giving to your fellow-citizens—say the descendants of the early settlers of Susquehanna—the following information : and if there be any now living whose name is Slocum, to them, I hope, the following may be communicated through the public prints of your place.

"' There is now living near this place, among the Miami tribe of Indians, an aged white woman, who a few days ago told me, while I lodged in the camp

40

one night, that she was taken away from her father's house, on or near the Susquehanna River, when she was very young—say from five to eight years old, as she thinks—by the Delaware Indians, who were then hostile toward the whites. She says her father's name was Slocum ; that he was a Quaker, rather small in stature, and wore a large-brimmed hat ; was of sandy hair and light complexion, and much freckled ; that he lived about a half a mile from a town where there was a fort ; that they lived in a wooden house of two stories high, and had a spring near the house. She says three Delawares came to the house in the daytime, when all were absent but herself, and perhaps two other children : her father and brothers were absent making hay. The Indians carried her off, and she was adopted into a family of Delawares, who raised her and treated her as their own child. They died about forty years ago, somewhere in Ohio. She was then married to a Miami, by whom she had four children ; two of them are now living—they are both daughters— and she lives with them. Her husband is dead ; she is old and feeble, and thinks she will not live long.

"'These considerations induced her to give the present history of herself, which she would never do before, fearing that her kindred would come and force her away. She has lived long and happy as an Indian, and, but for her colour, would not be suspected of being anything else but such. She is very respectable and wealthy, sober and honest. Her name is without reproach. She says her father had a large family, say eight children in all—six older than herself, one younger, as well as she can recollect ; and she doubts not that there are still living many of their descendants, but seems to think that all her brothers and sisters must be dead, as she is very old herself, not far from

41

the age of eighty. She thinks she was taken prisoner before the last two wars, which must mean the Revolutionary war, as Wayne's war and the late war have been since that one. She has entirely lost her mother tongue, and speaks only in Indian, which I also understand, and she gave me a full history of herself.

" 'Her own Christian name she has forgotten, but says her father's name was Slocum, and he was a Quaker. She also recollects that it was on the Susquehanna River that they lived. I have thought that from this letter you might cause something to be inserted in the newspapers of your county that might possibly catch the eye of some of the descendants of the Slocum family, who have knowledge of a girl having been carried off by the Indians some seventy years ago. This they might know from family tradition. If so, and they will come here, I will carry them where they may see the object of my letter alive and happy, though old and far advanced in life.

" 'I can form no idea whereabouts on the Susquehanna River this family could have lived at that early period, namely, about the time of the Revolutionary war, but perhaps you can ascertain more about it. If so, I hope you will interest yourself, and, if possible, let her brothers and sisters, if any be alive—if not, their children—know where they may once more see a relative whose fate has been wrapped in mystery for seventy years, and for whom her bereaved and afflicted parents doubtless shed many a bitter tear. They have long since found their graves, though their lost child they never found. I have been much affected with the disclosure, and hope the surviving friends may obtain, through your goodness, the information I desire for them. If I can be of any service to them, they may command me. In the meantime, I hope you will

42

excuse me for the freedom I have taken with you, a total stranger, and believe me to be, Sir, with much respect, your obedient servant,

" ' GEO. W. EWING.'

" This letter met the fate of many others of importance—it was flung away as a wild story.

" The Postmaster died, and had been in his grave time sufficient to allow his wife an opportunity of straightening his affairs. She was in the act of overhauling a mass of papers belonging to her husband's business when she encountered the letter of Colonel Ewing. A woman's perceptions are keen and quick, and the tender emotions which were begotten in her mind were but the responses of her better nature. Her sympathy yearned for one of her own sex, and she could do no more than proclaim the story to the world. Accordingly she sent the letter to the editor of the Lancaster *Intelligence*, and therein it was published.

"Newspapers of limited circulation may not revolutionize matters of great importance, but they have their sphere in detail, and when the aggregate is summed they accomplish more than the mighty engines of larger mediums.

" It was so in this case—the Lancaster paper was about issuing an extra for temperance purposes, and this letter happened to go into the forme to help ' fill up,' as poor printers sometimes express it. The Lancaster office was not poor, but the foreman did ' fill up ' with the Ewing letter. Rev. Samuel Bowman, of Wilkes-Barre, by chance saw a copy. He knew the Slocums, and the entire history of the valley as it was given by tradition.

" He was not present in the valley at the time, but

his heart warmed for the scenes and associations of early times in Wyoming. He mailed one of the papers to a Slocum, a brother of the captive girl, and the effect produced was as if by magic. Everybody was acquainted with the history of Frances, and all were interested in her fate. Sixty years had gone by since she was carried away, an innocent girl, and now the world had found the lost one.

"There was one mark which could not be mistaken —little Frances when a child had played with a brother in the blacksmith's shop, and by a careless blow from the latter a finger was crushed in such a manner that it never regained its original form.

"Mr. Isaac Slocum, accompanied by a sister and brother, sought an interview with the tanned woman, through the aid of an interpreter, and the first question asked, after an examination of the finger, was : 'How came that finger jambed ?' The reply was convincing and conclusive : 'My brother struck it with a hammer in the shop, a long time ago, before I was carried away.'

"Here then at last, by this unmistakable token, the lost was found. Her memory proved to be unerring ; the details of events sixty years old were perfect, and given in such a manner as to awaken in the hearts of the Slocum family warm emotions for the withered old woman. Her life, although rude, had been a happy one, and no inducements were strong enough to persuade her to leave the camp-fires of her adoption.

"By Act of Congress, Ma-con-a-qua, the Indian title of Frances Slocum, was granted one mile square of the reservation which was appointed to the Indians of Indiana, west of the Mississippi—to be held by herself during her life, and to revert to her heirs forever. She died March 9th, 1847, and was given Christian burial in a beautiful spot where the romantic waters of the Missisinewa and Wabash rivers join their ripples on the way to the sea.

"The story of the captive girl of Wyoming has been breathed around the hearths of the entire Christian world as one of the most fruitful in romance and song."

### Dwellings

The habitations of the Indians of North America may be classed as community houses (using the term 'community' in the sense of comprising more than one family) and single or family dwellings. "The house architecture of the northern tribes is of little importance, in itself considered ; but as an outcome of their social condition, and for comparison with that of the southern village Indians, is highly important. The typical community houses, as those of the Iroquois tribes, were 50 to 100 feet long by 16 to 18 wide, with frame of poles, and with sides and triangular roof covered with bark, usually of the elm. The interior was divided into compartments, and a smoke-hole was left in the roof. A Mohican house, similar in form, 14 by 60 feet, had the sides and roof made of rushes and chestnut bark, with an opening along the top of the roof from end to end. The Mandan circular community house was usually about 14 feet in diameter. It was supported by two series of posts and cross-beams, and the wide roof and sloping sides were covered with willow or brush matting and earth. The fireplace was in the centre. Morgan thinks that the oblong, round-roof houses of the Virginia and North Carolina tribes, seen and described by Captain John Smith and drawn by John White, were of the community order. That some of them housed a number of families is distinctly stated. Morgan includes also in the community class the circular, dome-shaped earth lodges of Sacramento Valley and the L-form, tent-shaped, thatched lodges of the higher areas of California ; but the leading examples of community houses are the large, sometimes massive, many-celled clusters of stone or adobe in New Mexico and Arizona known as *pueblos*. These dwellings vary in form, some of those built in prehistoric times being semicircular, others oblong, around or enclosing a court or *plaza*. These buildings were constructed usually in terrace form, the lower having a one-story tier of apartments, the next two stories, and so on to the uppermost tier, which sometimes constituted a seventh story. The masonry consisted usually of small flat stones laid in adobe mortar and chinked with spalls ; but sometimes large balls of adobe were used as building stones, or a double row of wattling was erected and filled in with grout, solidly tamped. By the latter method, known as *pisé* construction, walls 5 to 7 feet thick were sometimes built. The outer walls of the lowest story were pierced only by small openings, access to the interior being gained by means of ladders, which could be drawn up if necessary, and of a hatchway in the roof. It is possible that some of the elaborate structures of Mexico were developed from such hive-like buildings as those of the typical *pueblos*, the cells increasing in size toward the south, as suggested by Bandelier. Chimneys appear to have been unknown in North America until after contact of the natives with Europeans, the hatchway in the roof serving the double purpose of entrance and flue. Other forms, some 'community' and others not, are the following : The Tlingit, Haida, and some other tribes build substantial rectangular houses, with sides and ends formed of planks, and with the fronts elaborately carved and

46

painted with symbolic figures. Directly in front of the house a totem pole is placed, and near by a memorial pole is erected. These houses are sometimes 40 by 100 feet in the Nootka and Salish regions, and are occupied by a number of families. Formerly some of the Haida houses are said to have been built on platforms supported by posts. Some of these seen by such early navigators as Vancouver were 25 or 30 feet above ground, access being had by notched logs serving as ladders. Among the north-western Indian tribes, as the Nez Percés, the dwelling was a frame of poles covered with rush matting or with buffalo or elk skins. The houses of the Californian tribes were rectangular or circular; of the latter, some were conical, others dome-shaped. There was also formerly in use in various parts of California, and to some extent on the interior plateaus, a semi-subterranean earth-covered lodge known amongst the Maidu as *kum*. The most primitive abodes were those of the Paiute and the Cocopa, consisting simply of brush shelters for summer, and for winter of a framework of poles bent together at the top and covered with brush, bark, and earth. Somewhat similar structures are erected by the Pueblos as farm shelters, and more elaborate houses of the same general type are built by the Apache of Arizona. As indicated by archæological researches, the circular wigwam, with sides of bark or mats, built over a shallow excavation in the soil, and with earth thrown against the base, appears to have been the usual form of dwelling in the Ohio valley and the immediate valley of the Mississippi in prehistoric and early historic times. Another kind of dwelling, in use in Arkansas before the Discovery, was a rectangular structure with two rooms in front and one in the rear; the walls were of upright posts thickly plastered with clay on a sort of

47

wattle. With the exception of the *pueblo* structures, buildings of stone or adobe were unknown until recent times. The dwellings of some of the tribes of the plains, such as the Sioux, Arapaho, Comanche, and Kiowa, were generally portable skin tents or *tipis*, but those of the Omaha, Osage, and some others were more substantial. The dwellings of the Omaha, according to Miss Fletcher, 'are built by setting carefully selected and prepared posts together in a circle, and binding firmly with willows, then backing them with dried grass, and covering the entire structure with closely packed sods. The roof is made in the same manner, having an additional support of an inner circle of posts, with crochets to hold the cross-logs which act as beams to the dome-shaped roof. A circular opening in the centre serves as a chimney, and also to give light to the interior of the dwelling ; a sort of sail is rigged and fastened outside of this opening to guide the smoke and prevent it from annoying the occupants of the lodge. The entrance passage-way, which usually faces eastward, is from 6 to 10 feet long, and is built in the same manner as the lodge.' An important type is the Wichita grass hut, circular dome-shaped with conical top. The frame is built somewhat in panels formed by ribs and cross-bars ; these are covered with grass tied on shingle fashion. These grass lodges vary in diameter from 40 to 50 feet. The early Florida houses, according to Le Moyne's illustrations published by De Bry, were either circular with dome-like roof, or oblong with rounded roof, like those of Secotan in North Carolina, as shown in John White's figures. The frame was of poles covered with bark, or the latter was sometimes thatched. The Chippeway usually constructed a conical or hemispherical framework of poles, covered with bark. Formerly caves and rock-shelters were used in some sections as abodes, and in the Pueblo region houses were formerly constructed in natural recesses or shelters in the cliffs, whence the designation cliff-dwellings. Similar habitations are still in use to some extent by the Tarahumare of Chihuahua, Mexico. Cavate houses with several rooms were also hewn in the sides of soft volcanic cliffs; so numerous are these in Verde Valley, Arizona, and the Jemez plateau, New Mexico, that for miles the cliff-face is honeycombed with them. As a rule the women were the builders of the houses where wood was the structural material, but the men assisted with the heavier work. In the southern states it was a common custom to erect mounds as foundations for council-houses, for the chief's dwelling, or for structures designed for other official uses. The erection of houses, especially those of a permanent character, was usually attended with great ceremony, particularly when the time for dedication came. The construction of the Navaho *hogan*, for example, was done in accordance with fixed rules, as was the cutting and sewing of the *tipi* among the Plains tribes, while the new houses erected during the year were usually dedicated with ceremony and feasting. Although the better types of houses were symmetrical and well-proportioned, their builders had not learned the use of the square or the plumb-line. The unit of measure was also apparently unknown, and even in the best types of ancient *pueblo* masonry the joints of the stonework were not ' broken.' The Indian names for some of their structures, as *tipi*, *wigwam*, *wickiup*, *hogan*, have come into use to a great extent by English-speaking people." [1]

[1] *Bulletin 30*, Bureau of American Ethnology.

## Tribal Law and Custom

There is but little exact data available respecting the social polity of the Red Race of North America. Kinship appears to have been the basis of government among most of the tribes, and descent was traced both through the male and female line, according to locality. In most tribes military and civil functions were carefully distinguished from each other, the civil government being lodged in the hands of chiefs of varying grades. These chiefs were elected by a tribal council, and were not by virtue of their office military leaders. Every village or group was represented in the general council by a head-man, who was sometimes chosen by the priests. Secret societies exercised a powerful sway.

## Hunting

Hunting was almost the sole occupation of the males of the Indian tribes. So much were they dependent on the produce of the chase for their livelihood that they developed the pursuit of game into an art. In commerce they confined themselves to trading in skins and furs ; but they disposed of these only when their personal or tribal requirements had been fully satisfied. When the tribe had returned from its summer hunting expedition, and after the spoils of the chase had been faithfully distributed among its members—a tribal custom which was rigorously adhered to—ceremonial rites were engaged in and certain sacred formulæ were observed. In hunting game the Indians usually erected pens or enclosures, into which the beasts were driven and slaughtered. Early writers believed that they fired the prairie grass and pressed in upon the panic-stricken herd ; but this is contradicted by the Indians themselves, who assert that fire would be injurious to the fur of the animals hunted. Indeed, such an act, causing a herd to scatter, was punishable by death. In exceptional cases, however, the practice might be resorted to in order to drive the animals into the woods. In pursuing their prey it was customary for the tribe to form a circle, and thus prevent escape. The most favourable months for hunting were June, July, and August, when the animals were fat and the fur of rich quality. To the hunter who had slain the animal the tribe awarded the skin and part of the carcass. The other portions were usually divided among the inhabitants of the village. As a result of this method of sharing there was very little waste. The flesh, which was cut into thin slices, was hung up to dry in the sun on long poles, and rolled up and stored for winter use. The pelts were used in the making of clothing, shields, and bags. Ropes, tents, and other articles were also prepared from the skins. Bowstrings and sewing-thread were made from the sinews, and drinking-cups were shaped out of the larger bones.

Among the methods employed in capturing game was the setting of traps, into which the animal was decoyed. A more primitive method of taking animals by the hand was largely in use. The hunter would steal upon his prey in the dead of night, using the utmost cunning and agility, and seize upon the unwary bird or sleeping animal. The Indians were skilled in climbing and diving, and, employing the art of mimicry, in which they attained great proficiency, they would surround a herd of animals and drive them into a narrow gorge out of which they could not escape. Their edged weapons, fashioned from stone, bones, and reeds, and used with great skill, assisted them effectually when brought to close quarters with their prey. Dogs, although not regularly trained, they found of much value in the hunt, especially for tracking down the more swift and savage beasts. With the assistance of fire the hunter's conquest over the animal became assured. His prey would be driven out of its hiding-place by smoke, or the torch would dazzle it. Drugging animals with poisonous roots and polluting streams to capture fish were largely practised. The use of nets and scoops for taking animals from the water and the fashioning of rakes for securing worms from the earth were other methods employed to obtain food. The use of the canoe gave rise to the invention of the harpoon.

The wandering habits of their game and the construction of fences were obstacles which strengthened their perception and gave excellent training for the hunt. The variety of circumstances with which they had to meet caused them to prepare or devise the many weapons and snares to which they resorted. Certain periods or seasons of the year were observed for the hunting of particular animals, each of which figured as a token or heraldic symbol of a tribe or *gens*.

Schoolcraft, in an accurate and entertaining account of Indian hunting in his *Historical and Statistical Information respecting the Indian Tribes*, says :

"The simplest of all species of hunting is perhaps the art of hunting the deer. This animal, it is known, is endowed with the fatal curiosity of stopping in its flight to turn round and look at the object that disturbed it ; and as this is generally done within rifle-range, the habit is indulged at the cost of its life ; whereas, if it trusted unwaveringly to its heels, it would escape.

"One of the most ingenious modes of hunting the

deer is that of *fire-hunting*, which is done by descending
a stream in a canoe at night with a flambeau. In the
latter part of spring and summer the Indian hunters on
the small interior rivers take the bark of the elm or
cedar, peeling it off whole, for five or six feet in length,
and, turning it inside out, paint the outer surface black
with charcoal. It is then pierced with an orifice to fit
it on the bow of the canoe, so as to hide the sitter ; then
a light or torch is made by small rolls, two or three
feet long, of twisted birch bark (which is very inflam-
mable), and this is placed on the extreme bow of the
boat, a little in front of the bark screen, in which
position it throws its rays strongly forward, leaving
all behind in darkness. The deer, whose eyes are fixed
on the light as it floats down, is thus brought within
range of the gun. Swans are hunted in the same
way.

"The mazes of the forest are, however, the Indian
hunter's peculiar field of action. No footprint can be impressed there with which he is not familiar. In his tem-
porary journeys in the search after game he generally
encamps early, and sallies out at the first peep of day on
his hunting tour. If he is in a forest country he chooses
his ambush in valleys, for the plain reason that all
animals, as night approaches, come into the valleys. In
ascending these he is very careful to take that side of a
stream which throws a shadow from it, so that he may
have a clear view of all that passes on the opposite side,
while he is himself screened by the shadow. But he is
particularly on the alert to take this precaution if he is
apprehensive of lurking foes. The tracks of an animal
are the subject of the minutest observation ; they tell
him at a glance the species of animal that has passed,
the time that has elapsed, and the course it has pursued.
If the surface of the earth be moist, the indications are

53

plain ; if it be hard or rocky, they are drawn from less palpable but scarcely less unmistakable signs.

"One of the largest and most varied days' hunt of which we are apprised was by a noted Chippeway hunter, named Nokay, on the upper Mississippi, who, tradition asserts, in one day, near the mouth of the Crow Wing River, killed sixteen elk, four buffaloes, five deer, three bears, one lynx, and a porcupine. This feat has doubtless been exceeded in the buffalo ranges of the south-west, where the bow and arrow is known to have been so dexterously and rapidly applied in respect to that animal ; but it is seldom that the chase in forest districts is as successful as in this instance.

"On one occasion the celebrated chief Wabojeeg went out early in the morning, near the banks of Lake Superior, to set martin-traps. He had set about forty, and was returning to his wigwam, armed with his hatchet and knife only, when he encountered a buck moose. He sheltered himself behind trees, retreating ; but as the animal pursued, he picked up a pole, and, unfastening his moccasin-strings, tied the knife firmly to the pole. He then took a favourable position behind a tree and stabbed the animal several times in the throat and breast. At length it fell, and he cut out and carried home the tongue as a trophy of his prowess.

"In 1808, Gitshe Iawba, of Kewywenon, Lake Superior, killed a three-year-old moose of three hundred pounds weight. It was in the month of February, and the snow was so soft, from a partial thaw, that the *agim*, or snow-shoes, sank deep at every step. After cutting up the animal and drawing out the blood, he wrapped the flesh in the skin, and, putting himself under it, rose up erect. Finding he could bear the weight, he then took a litter of nine pups in a blanket upon his right arm, threw his wallet on top of his head, and, putting his gun over his left shoulder, walked six miles to his wigwam. This was the strongest man that has appeared in the Chippeway nation in modern times.

"In 1827, Annimikens, of Red River of the North, was one day quite engrossed in looking out a path for his camp to pass, when he was startled by the sharp snorting of a grizzly bear. He immediately presented his gun and attempted to fire ; but, the priming not igniting, he was knocked by the animal, the next instant, several steps backward, and his gun driven full fifteen feet through the air. The bear then struck him on one cheek and tore away a part of it. The little consciousness he had left told him to be passive, and manifest no signs of life. Fortunately, the beast had satiated his appetite on the carcass of a buffalo near by. Having clawed his victim at pleasure, he then took him by the neck, dragged him into the bushes, and there left him. Yet from such a wound the Indian recovered, though a disfigured man, and lived to tell me the story with his own lips.

"Relations of such hunting exploits and adventures are vividly repeated in the Indian country, and constitute a species of renown which is eagerly sought by the young."

## Costume

The picturesque costume of the Red Man is so original in character as to deserve more than passing mention. An authority on Indian costume, writing in *Bulletin 30* of the Bureau of American Ethnology, says :

"The tribes of Northern America belong in general to the wholly clothed peoples, the exceptions being those inhabiting the warmer regions of the southern

United States and the Pacific coast, who were semi-clothed. Tanned skin of the deer family was generally the material for clothing throughout the greater part of the country. The hide of the buffalo was worn for robes by tribes of the plains, and even for dresses and leggings by older people, but the leather was too harsh for clothing generally, while elk- or moose-skin, although soft, was too thick. Fabrics of bark, hair, fur, mountain-sheep wool, and feathers were made in the North Pacific, Pueblo, and southern regions, and cotton has been woven by the Hopi from ancient times. Climate, environment, elevation, and oceanic currents determined the materials used for clothing as well as the demand for clothing. Sinew from the tendons of the larger animals was the usual sewing material, but fibres of plants, especially the agave, were also employed. Bone awls were used in sewing ; bone needles were rarely employed and were too large for fine work. The older needlework is of exceptionally good character and shows great skill with the awl. Unlike many other arts, sewing was practised by both sexes, and each sex usually made its own clothing. The typical and more familiar costume of the Indian man was of tanned buck-skin, and consisted of a shirt, a breech-cloth, leggings tied to a belt or waist-strap, and low moccasins. The shirt, which hung free over the hips, was provided with sleeves and was designed to be drawn over the head. The woman's costume differed from that of the man in the length of the shirt, which had short sleeves hanging loosely over the upper arm, and in the absence of the breech-cloth. Women also wore the belt to confine the garment at the waist. Robes of skin, woven fabrics, or of feathers were also worn, but blankets were substituted for these later. The costume presented tribal differences in cut, colour, and ornamentation. The free edges were generally fringed, and quill embroidery and beadwork, painting, scalp-locks, tails of animals, feathers, claws, hoofs, shells, etc., were applied as ornaments or charms. The typical dress of the Pueblo Indians is generally similar to that of the Plains tribes, except that it is made largely of woven fabrics.

"Among the Pacific coast tribes, and those along the Mexican border, the Gulf, and the Atlantic coast, the customary garment of women was a fringe-like skirt of bark, cord, strung seeds, or peltry, worn around the loins. In certain seasons or during special occupations only the loin-band was worn. For occasional use in cooler weather a skin robe or cape was thrown about the shoulders, or, under exceptional conditions, a large robe woven of strips of rabbit-skin. Ceremonial costume was much more elaborate than that for ordinary wear. Moccasins and leggings were worn throughout much of this area, but in the warmer parts and in California their use was unusual. Some tribes near the Mexican boundary wear sandals, and sandal-wearing tribes once ranged widely in the south-west. These have also been found in Kentucky caverns. Hats, usually of basketry, were worn by many Pacific coast tribes. Mittens were used by the Eskimo and other tribes of the far north. Belts of various materials and ornamentation not only confined the clothing, but supported pouches, trinket-bags, paint-bags, etc. Larger pouches and pipe-bags of fur or deer-skin, beaded or ornamented with quill-work, and of plain skin, netting, or woven stuff, were slung from the shoulder. Necklaces, earrings, charms, and bracelets in infinite variety formed a part of the clothing, and the wrist-guard to protect the arm from the recoil of the bowstring was general.

" Shortly after the advent of whites Indian costume

57

was profoundly modified over a vast area of America by the copying of European dress and the use of traders' stuffs. Knowledge of prehistoric and early historic primitive textile fabrics has been derived from impressions of fabrics on pottery, and from fabrics themselves that have been preserved by charring in fire, contact with copper, or protection from the elements in caves.

"A synopsis of the costumes worn by tribes living in the several geographical regions of northern America follows. The list is necessarily incomplete, for on account of the abandonment of tribal costumes the data are chiefly historical.

"ATHAPASCAN. *Mackenzie and Yukon*—Men : Shirt-coat, legging-moccasins, breech-cloth, hat and hood. Women : Long shirt-coat, legging-moccasins, belt.

"ALGONQUIAN-IROQUOIS. *Northern*—Men : Robe, shirt-coat, long-coat, trousers, leggings, moccasins, breech-cloth, turban. *Virginia*—Men and women : Cloak, waist-garment, moccasins, sandals (?), breech-cloth (?). *Western*—Men : Robe, long dress-shirt, long leggings, moccasins, bandolier-bag. Women : Long dress-shirt, short leggings, moccasins, belt. *Arctic*—Men : Long coat, open in front, short breeches, leggings, moccasins, gloves or mittens, cap or headdress. Women : Robe, shirt-dress, leggings, moccasins, belt, cap, and sometimes a shoulder-mantle.

"SOUTHERN or MUSKHOGEAN. *Seminole*—Men : Shirt, over-shirt, leggings, moccasins, breech-cloth, belt, turban. Formerly the Gulf tribes wore robe, waist-garment, and occasionally moccasins.

"PLAINS. Men : Buffalo robe, shirt to knees or longer, breech-cloth, thigh-leggings, moccasins, headdress. Women : Long shirt-dress with short ample cape sleeves, belt, leggings to the knees, moccasins.

"NORTH PACIFIC. *Chilkat*—Men : Blanket or bark mat robe, shirt-coat (rare), legging-moccasins, basket hat. Women : Tanned skin shoulder-robe, shirt-dress with sleeves, fringed apron, leggings (?), moccasins, breech-cloth (?).

"WASHINGTON-COLUMBIA. *Salish*—Men : Robe, head-band, and, rarely, shirt-coat, leggings, moccasins, breech-cloth. Women : Long shirt-dress, apron, and, rarely, leggings, breech-cloth, moccasins.

" Shoshonean. Same as the Plains tribes.

" California-Oregon. *Hupa*—Men : Robe, and waist-garment on occasion, moccasins (rarely) ; men frequently and old men generally went entirely naked. Women : Waist-garment and narrow aprons ; occasionally robe-cape, like Pueblo, over shoulders or under arms, over breast ; basket cap ; sometimes moccasins. *Central California*—Men : Usually naked ; robe, network cap, moccasins, and breech-cloth occasionally. Women : Waist-skirt of vegetal fibre or buckskin, and basketry cap ; robe and moccasins on occasion.

" South-western. *Pueblo*—Men : Blanket or rabbit-skin or feather robe, shirt with sleeves, short breeches partly open on outer sides, breech-cloth, leggings to knees, moccasins, hair-tape, and head-band. Women : Blanket fastened over one shoulder, extending to knees ; small calico shawl over blanket thrown over shoulders ; legging-moccasins, belt. Sandals formerly worn in this area. Snow-moccasins of fur sometimes worn in winter. *Apache*—Men : Same as on plains. Women : Same, except legging-moccasins with shield toe. *Navaho*—Now like Pueblo ; formerly like Plains tribes.

" Gila-Sonora. *Cocopa and Mohave*—Men : Breech-cloth, sandals, sometimes head-band. Women : Waist-garments, usually of fringed bark, front and rear. *Pima*—Same as Plains ; formerly cotton robe, waist-cloth and sandals."

## Face-Painting

A first-hand account of how the Indian brave decorated his face cannot but prove of interest. Says a writer who dwelt for some time among the Sioux : [1]

" Daily, when I had the opportunity, I drew the patterns their faces displayed, and at length obtained a collection, whose variety even astonished myself. The strange combinations produced in the kaleidoscope may be termed weak when compared to what an Indian's imagination produces on his forehead, nose, and cheek. I will try to give some account of them as far as words will reach. Two things struck me most in their arrangement of colour. First, the fact that they did not trouble themselves at all about the natural divisions

[1] J. G. Kohl, *Kitchi-gami* (1860).

of the face; and, secondly, the extraordinary mixture of the graceful and the grotesque. At times, it is true, they did observe those natural divisions produced by nose, eyes, mouth, etc. The eyes were surrounded with regular coloured circles; yellow or black stripes issued harmoniously and equidistant from the mouth; over the cheeks ran a semicircle of green dots, the ears forming the centre. At times, too, the forehead was traversed by lines running parallel to the natural contour of that feature; this always looked somewhat human, so to speak, because the fundamental character of the face was unaltered. Usually, however, these regular patterns do not suit the taste of the Indians. They like contrasts, and frequently divide the face into two halves, which undergo different treatment; one will be dark—say black or blue—but the other quite light, yellow, bright red, or white: one will be crossed by thick lines made by the forefingers, while the other is arabesque, with extremely fine lines, produced by the aid of a brush.

"This division is produced in two different ways. The line of demarcation sometimes runs down the nose, so that the right cheek and side are buried in gloom, while the left looks like a flower-bed in the sunshine. At times, though, they draw the line across the nose, so that the eyes glisten out of the dark colour, while all beneath the nose is bright and lustrous. It seems as if they wished to represent on their faces the different phases of the moon. I frequently inquired whether there was any significance in these various patterns, but was assured it was a mere matter of taste. They were simple arabesques, like their squaws' work on the moccasins, girdles, tobacco-pouches, etc.

"Still there is a certain symbolism in the use of the colours. Thus, red generally typifies joy and festivity;

and black mourning. When any very melancholy death takes place, they rub a handful of charcoal over the entire face. If the deceased is only a distant relative, a mere trellis-work of black lines is painted on the face ; they have also a half-mourning, and only paint half the face black. Red is not only their joy, but also their favourite colour. They generally cover their face with a coating of bright red, on which the other colours are laid ; for this purpose they employ vermilion, which comes from China, and is brought them by the Indian traders. However, this red is by no means *de rigueur*. Frequently the ground colour is a bright yellow, for which they employ chrome-yellow, obtained from the trader.

"They are also very partial to Prussian blue, and employ this colour not only on their faces, but as a type of peace on their pipes ; and as the hue of the sky, on their graves. It is a very curious fact, by the way, that hardly any Indian can distinguish blue from green. I have seen the sky which they represent on their graves by a round arch, as frequently of one colour as the other. In the Sioux language *toya* signifies both green and blue; and a much-travelled Jesuit Father told me that among many Indian tribes the same confusion prevails. I have also been told that tribes have their favourite colours, and I am inclined to believe it, although I was not able to recognize any such rule. Generally all Indians seem to hold their own native copper skin in special affection, and heighten it with vermilion when it does not seem to them sufficiently red.

"I discovered during a journey I took among the Sioux that there is a certain national style in this face-painting. They were talking of a poor Indian who had gone mad, and when I asked some of his countrymen present in what way he displayed his insanity, they said, 'Oh, he dresses himself up so funnily with feathers and shells; he paints his face so comically that it is enough to make one die of laughing.' This was said to me by persons so overladen with feathers, shells, green and vermilion, Prussian blue, and chrome-yellow, that I could hardly refrain from smiling. Still, I drew the conclusion from it that there must be something conventional and typical in their variegated style which might be easily infringed."

## Indian Art

If the Red Race of North America did not produce artistic work of an exalted order it at least evolved a distinctive and peculiar type of art. Some of the drawings and paintings on the walls of the brick erections of the southern tribes and the heraldic and religious symbols painted on the skin-covered lodges of the Plains people are intricate and rhythmic in plan and brilliant in colouring. The houses of the north-west coast tribes, built entirely of wood, are supported by pillars elaborately carved and embellished to represent the totem or tribal symbol of the owner. On both the interior and exterior walls brilliantly coloured designs, usually scenes from Indian mythology, are found.

The decoration of earthenware was and is common to most of the tribes of North America, and is effected both by carving and stamping. It is in the art of carving that the Indian race appears to have achieved its greatest æsthetic triumph. Many carved objects are exceedingly elaborate and intricate in design, and some of the work on stone pipes, masks, and household utensils and ornaments has won the highest admiration of European masters of the art. Indeed, many of the pipes and claystone carvings of the Chimpseyans and Clallams of Vancouver, and the Chippeways and Babeens, are by no means inferior to the best specimens of European mediæval carved work.

In the potter's art the Indian people often exhibit great taste, and the tribes of the Mississippi valley and the Pueblo Indians had made exceptional progress in plaster design. As has already been mentioned, the mound-builders displayed considerable skill in metalwork, and the stamped plates of copper taken from the earthen pyramids which they raised strikingly illustrate the fact that Indian art is the growth and outcome of centuries of native effort and by no means a thing of yesterday.

In weaving, needlework of all kinds, bead-work, and feather-work the Indians show great taste. Most of the designs they employ are geometric in plan. In feather-work especially the aboriginal peoples of the whole American continent excel. Rank was indicated among the Plains tribes either by the variety and number of feathers worn or by the manner of mounting or notching them.

The aboriginal art of North America is in the highest degree symbolic and mythologic. It is thus entirely removed from any taint of materialism, and had it been permitted to evolve upon its own peculiar lines it might have developed a great measure of idealistic excellence.

### Warfare

In the art of guerrilla warfare the Indians have always shown exceptional skill. Armed with bow and arrow, a war-club, or a tomahawk, they carried on a fierce resistance to the incursions of the white man. These weapons were artistically shaped and moulded, and

63

were eminently suited to their owner's mode of fighting.
But as they came more into contact with the whites
the natives displayed a particular keenness to obtain
firearms and gunpowder, steel knives and hatchets.
They dispensed with their own rude if effective implements of war, and, obtaining the coveted weapons
by making successful raids upon the camps of their
enemies, they set themselves to learn how to use them.
So mysterious did gunpowder appear to them that
they believed it to possess the property of reproduc-
tion, and planted it in the earth in the hope that it
would yield a supply for their future needs. In
attacking the settlers they used many ingenious arti-
fices to entrap or ambuscade them. These methods,
naturally, proved successful against the whites, who
had yet to learn Indian war-craft, but soon the settlers
learned to adopt the same devices. The Indian would
imitate the cry of the wild goose to attract the white
hunter into the woods, where he would spring upon
him. He would also reverse his snow-shoes in winter,
to make it appear to the settler that he was retreating.
Covering themselves with twigs to look like a bush
was another method adopted by Indian spies. Occasionally they would approach the white man apparently
in a spirit of friendliness, only to commit some act
of treachery. Block-houses were built by the settlers
as a means of defence against Indian nocturnal sur-
prises, and into these the women and children were
hurried for safety. But the perseverance of the white
man and the declining birth-rate of the Indian tribes
began to create a new situation. Driven repeatedly
from one part of the country to another, and confined
to a limited territory in which to live, hunt, and
cultivate the soil, the Indians finally adopted a less
aggressive attitude to those whom they at first, and

for some time after their settlement, regarded with suspicion and resentment.

Although the methods of warfare differed with the various tribes, the general scheme of operations was usually dictated by the council of chiefs, in whose hands the making of peace and war also lay. The campaign was generally prefaced by many eloquent harangues from the leaders, who gradually wrought the braves into a fury of resentment against their enemies. The ceremony of the war-dance was then proceeded with. Ranged in a circle, the warriors executed a kind of shuffle, occasionally slowly gyrating, with gestures and movements obviously intended to imitate those of some bird or beast,[1] and grunting, clucking, and snarling the while. This ceremony was always undertaken in full panoply of war-paint and feathers. Subsequently the braves betook themselves to the 'war-path.' If the campaign was undertaken in wooded country, they marched in single file.[2] The most minute attention was paid to their surroundings to prevent ambuscade. The slightest sound, even the snapping of a twig, was sufficient to arrest their attention and cause them to halt. Alert, suspicious, and with every nerve strung to the highest point of tension, they proceeded with such exceeding caution that to surprise them was almost impossible. Should a warrior become isolated from the main body and be attacked and fatally wounded, he regarded it as essential to the safety of his comrades to utter a piercing shriek, which reverberated far through the forest ways and placed the rest of the band on their guard. This was known as the 'death-whoop.'

When the campaign was undertaken in prairie or open

[1] Perhaps their personal or tribal totems. See "Totemism," pp. 80–86.

[2] Hence the expression ' Indian file.'

country, the method usually employed was that of night attack ; but if for any reason this could not be successfully made, a large circle was drawn round the place to be assailed, and gradually narrowed, the warriors who composed it creeping and wriggling through the grass, and when sufficiently near rising and rushing the camp or fort with wild war-cries.  If a stout defence with firearms was anticipated, the warriors would surround the objective of attack on horseback, and ride round and round the fated position, gradually picking off the defenders with their rifles or arrows as the opportunity presented itself. Once the place was stormed the Indian brave neither asked nor gave quarter, at least so far as its male defenders were concerned.  These were at once slain and scalped, the latter sanguinary process being effected by the brave placing his knees on his enemy's shoulders, describing a rapid circle with his knife in the centre of the victim's head, seizing the portion of the scalp thus loosened, and quickly detaching it.

Schoolcraft, dealing with the subject of Indian warfare, a matter upon which he was well qualified to speak, writes : [1]

" Success in war is to the Indian the acme of glory, and to learn its arts the object of his highest attainment. The boys and youths acquire the accomplishment at an early period of dancing the war-dance ; and although they are not permitted to join its fascinating circle till they assume the envied rank of actual warriors, still their early sports and mimic pastimes are imitations of its various movements and postures.  The envied eagle's feather is the prize.  For this the Indian's talent, subtlety, endurance, bravery, persevering fasts, and what may be called religious penances and observances are made.

[1] *Historical and Statistical Information respecting the Indian Tribes.*

# WARFARE

"The war-path is taken by youths at an early age. That age may be stated, for general comparison, to be sixteen; but, without respect to exact time, it is always after the primary fast, during which the youth chooses his personal guardian or *monedo*—an age when he first assumes the duties of manhood. It is the period of the assumption of the three-pointed blanket, the true toga of the North American Indian.

"The whole force of public opinion, in our Indian communities, is concentrated on this point; its early lodge teachings (such as the recital of adventures of bravery), its dances, its religious rites, the harangues of prominent actors, made at public assemblages (such as is called 'striking the post'), all, in fact, that serves to awaken and fire ambition in the mind of the savage, is clustered about the idea of future distinction in war.

". . . The Indian has but one prime honour to grasp; it is triumph in the war-path; it is rushing upon his enemy, tearing the scalp reeking from his head, and then uttering his terrific *sa-sa-kuon* (death-whoop). For this crowning act he is permitted to mount the honoured feather of the war-eagle—the king of carnivorous birds. By this mark he is publicly known, and his honours recognized by all his tribe, and by the surrounding tribes whose customs assimilate.

"When the scalp of an enemy has been won, very great pains are taken to exhibit it. For this purpose it is stretched on a hoop and mounted on a pole. The inner part is painted red, and the hair adjusted to hang in its natural manner. If it be the scalp of a male, eagle's feathers are attached to denote *that* fact. If a female, a comb or scissors is hung on the frame. In this condition it is placed in the hands of an old woman, who bears it about in the scalp-dance, while opprobrious epithets are uttered against the tribe from which it was taken. Amidst these wild rejoicings the war-cry is vociferated, and the general sentiment with old and young is : ' Thus shall it be done to our enemies.'

" The feather of the eagle is the highest honour that a warrior can wear, and a very extravagant sum is sometimes given to procure one. The value of a horse has been known to be paid. The mode in which a feather is to be cut and worn is important to be noticed.

" The scale of honour with the several tribes may vary, but the essential features are the same. Among the Dakota tribes an eagle's feather with a red spot denotes that the wearer has killed an enemy, a notch cut in it and edges of the feather painted red indicates that the throat of an enemy has been cut. Small consecutive notches on the front side of the feather, without paint, denote that the wearer is the third person that has touched the dead body ; both edges notched, that he is the fourth person who has touched it ; and the feather partly denuded that he is the fifth person that has touched the slain.

" On the blanket or buffalo robe worn by the Dakota Indian a red or black hand is often seen painted. The red hand indicates that the wearer has been wounded by his enemy, the black hand that he has slain his enemy.

" The warlike tribe of the Chippeways, on the sources of the Mississippi, who, from a national act in their history, bear the distinctive name of Pillagers, award a successful warrior who shoots down and scalps his enemy three feathers ; and for the still more dangerous act of taking a wounded prisoner on the field, five— for they conceive that a wounded enemy is desperate, and will generally reserve his fire for a last act of vengeance, if he die the moment after. Those of the war-party who come up immediately and strike the enemy, so as to get marks of blood on their weapons, receive two feathers ; for it is customary for as many as can to perform this act. . . . Those who have been of the war-party, and merely *see* the fight, although they may have no blood-marks of which to boast as honours, and may even have lacked promptness in following the leader closely, are yet allowed to mount *one* feather. These honours are publicly awarded ; no one dares to assume them without authority, and there are instances where the feathers falsely assumed have been pulled violently from their heads in a public assemblage of the Indians. They never, however, blame each other for personal acts denoting cowardice or any species of timidity while on the war-path, hoping by this elevated course to encourage the young men to do better on another occasion.

" All war-parties consist of volunteers. The leader, or war-captain, who attempts to raise one must have some reputation to start on. His appeals, at the assemblages for dancing the preliminary war-dance, are to the principles of bravery and nationality. They are brief and to the point. He is careful to be thought to act under the guidance of the Great Spirit, of whose secret will he affects to be apprised in dreams, or by some rites.

"The principle of enlistment is sufficiently well preserved. For this purpose, the leader who proposes to raise the war-party takes the war-club in his hands, smeared with vermilion, to symbolize blood, and begins his war-song. I have witnessed several such scenes. The songs are brief, wild repetitions of sentiments of heroic deeds, or incitements to patriotic or military ardour. They are accompanied by the drum and rattle, and by the voice of one or more choristers. They are repeated slowly, sententiously, and with a measured cadence, to which the most exact time is kept. The warrior stamps the ground as if he could shake the universe. His language is often highly figurative, and he deals with the machinery of the clouds, the flight of carnivorous birds, and the influence of spiritual agencies, as if the region of space were at his command. He imagines his voice to be heard in the clouds; and while he stamps the ground with well-feigned fury, he fancies himself to take hold of the 'circle of the sky' with his hands. Every few moments he stops abruptly in his circular path, and utters the piercing war-cry.

"He must be a cold listener who can sit unmoved by these appeals. The ideas thrown out succeed each other with the impetuosity of a torrent. They are suggestive of heroic frames of mind, of strong will, of burning sentiment.

> "'Hear my voice, ye warlike birds!
> I prepare a feast for you to batten on;
> I see you cross the enemy's lines;
> Like you I shall go.
> I wish the swiftness of your wings;
> I wish the vengeance of your claws;
> I muster my friends;
> I follow your flight.
> Ho, ye young men that are warriors,
> Look with wrath on the battlefield!'

"Each warrior that rises and joins the war-dance thereby becomes a volunteer for the trip. He arms and equips himself; he provides his own sustenance; and when he steps out into the ring and dances, he chants his own song, and is greeted with redoubling yells. These ceremonies are tantamount to 'enlistment,' and no young man who thus comes forward can honourably withdraw.

"The sentiments of the following song were uttered by the celebrated Wabojeeg, as the leader of the

# WARFARE

Chippeways, after a victory over the combined Sioux
and Sauks and Foxes, at the Falls of St. Croix, during
the latter part of the seventeenth century :

### I

"'Hear my voice, ye heroes !
On that day when our warriors sprang
With shouts on the dastardly foe,
Just vengeance my heart burned to take
On the cruel and treacherous breed,
The Bwoin—the Fox—the Sauk.

### II

"'And here, on my breast, have I bled !
See—see ! my battle scars !
Ye mountains, tremble at my yell !
I strike for life.

### III

"'But who are my foes ?  They shall die,
They shall fly o'er the plains like a fox ;
They shall shake like a leaf in the storm.
Perfidious dogs ! they roast our sons with fire !

### IV

"'Five winters in hunting we'll spend,
While mourning our warriors slain,
Till our youth grown to men
For the battle-path trained,
Our days like our fathers we'll end.

### V

"'Ye are dead, noble men ! ye are gone,
My brother—my fellow—my friend !
On the death-path where brave men must go
But we live to revenge you !  We haste
To die as our forefathers died.'

"In 1824, Bwoinais, a Chippeway warrior of Lake
Superior, repeated to me, with the appropriate tunes,
the following war-songs, which had been uttered

during the existing war between that nation and the Dakotas :

### I

    " ' Oshawanung undossewug
      Penasewug ka baimwaidungig.'
      [From the south—they come, the warlike
          birds—
      Hark ! to their passing screams.]

### II

    " ' Todotobi penaise
      Ka dow Wiawwiaun.'
      [I wish to have the body of the fiercest
          bird,
      As swift—as cruel—as strong.]

### III

    " ' Ne wawaıbena, neowai
      Kagait ne minwaindum
      Nebunaikumig tshebaibewishenaun.'
      [I cast my body to the chance of battle.
      Full happy am I, to lie on the field—
      On the field over the enemy's line.] "

## The Indian Wife and Mother

The position of women among the North American Indians is distinctly favourable, when the general circumstances of their environment are considered. As with most barbarian people, the main burden of the work of the community falls upon them. But in most cases the bulk of the food-supply is provided by the men, who have often to face long and arduous hunting expeditions in the search for provender. The labour of planting and digging seed, of hoeing, harvesting, and storing crops, is invariably borne by the women. In the more accessible Indian territory of North America, however, the practice of agriculture is falling into desuetude, and the aborigines are becoming accustomed to rely to a great extent on a supply of cereals from outside sources.

In the art of weaving Indian women were and are extremely skilful. In the southern regions the Hopi women have woven cotton garments from time immemorial.

Among the various tribes the institution of marriage greatly depends for its circumstances upon the system of totemism, a custom which will be found fully described in the chapter which deals with the mythology of the Red Race. This system places a taboo upon marriages between members of the same clan or other division of a tribe. The nature of the ceremony itself differs with locality and race. Among the Plains Indians polygamy was common, and the essential feature of the ceremony was the presentation of gifts to the bride's father. In some tribes the husband had absolute power, and separation and divorce were common. But other Plains people were free from the purchase system, and the wishes of their women were consulted. East of the Mississippi the Iroquoian, Algonquian (except in the north and west), and Muskhogean tribes retained descent of name and property in the female line. Exchange of gifts preceded marriage with these peoples. Among the Hurons a council of mothers arranged the unions of the members of the tribe. Monogamy, on the whole, prevailed throughout the continent ; and, generally speaking, the marriage bond was regarded rather loosely.

### Indian Child-Life

One of the most pleasing features in Indian life is the great affection and solicitude bestowed by the parents upon their children. As a close student of Indian custom and habit avers, " The relation of parent to child brings out all the highest traits of Indian character." Withal, infant mortality is extraordinarily high, owing to the lack of sanitary measures. The father prepares the wooden cradle which is to be the infant's portable bed until it is able to walk. The *papoose* has first a child-name, which later gives place to the appellation which it will use through life. Children of both sexes have toys and games, the boys amusing themselves with riding and marksmanship, while the girls play with dolls and imitate their mothers 'keeping wigwam.' In warm weather a great deal of the children's time is spent in swimming and paddling. They are exceedingly fond of pets, particularly puppies, which they frequently dress and carry upon their backs like babies. Among some of the southern peoples small figures representing the various tribal deities are distributed as dolls to the children at certain ceremonies, and the sacred traditions of the race are thus impressed upon them in tangible form. It is a mistake to think that the Indian child receives no higher instruction. This, however, is effected by moral suasion alone, and physical punishment is extremely rare. Great good-humour prevails among the children, and fighting and quarrelling are practically unknown.

At about fifteen years of age the Indian boy undertakes a solitary fast and vigil, during which his totem or medicine spirit is supposed to instruct him regarding his future career. At about thirteen years of age the girl undergoes a like test, which signalizes her entrance into womanhood.

### Adventure with a Totem

An account of the manner in which a young Indian beheld his totem states that the lad's father sent him to a mountain-top to look for Utonagan, the female guardian spirit of his ancestors. At noon, on his arrival at the mountain, he heard the howls of the totem spirit, and commenced to ascend the slope, chilled by fear as the yells grew louder. He climbed a tree, and still heard the cries, and the rustle of the spirit in the branches below. Then terror overcame him, and he fled. Utonagan pursued him. She gained upon him, howling so that his knees gave way beneath him and he might not turn. Then he bethought him of one of his guardian spirits, and, with a fresh access of courage, he left his pursuer far behind. He cast away his blanket; Utonagan reached it, and, after snuffing at it, took up the chase once more. Then he thought of his guardian spirit the wolf, and again new strength came to him. Still in great terror, he looked back. Utonagan followed with a wolf-like lope.. Then he thought of his guardian spirit the bitch, and once more he gained ground. At length, exhausted by his exertions, he sank to the earth in a fainting condition, and fell asleep. Through the eyes of sleep he saw the spirit as a wolf. She said to him : " I am she whom your family and the Indians call Utonagan. You are dear to me. Look at me, Indian." He looked, and lost his sense of fear. When he awoke the sun was high in the sky. He bathed in the creek and returned home.

### An Indian Girl's Vigil

Another story is told of an Indian girl's vigil. Catherine Wabose, when about thirteen years of age, left her mother's lodge and built a small one for herself. After a fast of four days she was visited by her mother, who gave her a little snow-water to drink. On the eve of the sixth day, while still fasting, she was conscious of a superhuman voice, which invited her to walk along a shining path, which led forward and upward. There she first met the 'Everlasting Standing Woman,' who gave her her 'supernatural' name. She next met the 'Little Man Spirit,' who told her that his name would be the name of her first son. She was next addressed by the 'Bright Blue Sky,' who endowed her with the gift of life. She was then encircled by bright points of light and by sharp, painless instruments, but, mounting upon a fish-like animal, she swam through the air back to her lodge. On the sixth day she experienced a repetition of the vision. On the seventh day she was fed with a little pounded corn in snow-water. After the seventh day she beheld a large round object like a stone descend from the sky and enter the lodge. It conferred upon her the gift of prophecy, and by virtue of this she assumed the rank of a prophetess upon her return to the tribe.

It is not difficult to suppose that the minds of these unfortunate children were temporarily deranged by the sustained fasts they had been forced to undertake.

### Picture-Writing

Most of the tribes of North America had evolved a rude system of picture-writing. This consisted, for the most part, of figures of natural objects connected by symbols having arbitrary or fixed meanings. Thus the system was both ideographic and pictographic; that is, it represented to some extent abstract ideas as well as concrete objects. These scripts possessed so many arbitrary characters, and again so many symbols which possessed different meanings under varying circumstances, that to interpret them is a task of the greatest complexity. They were usually employed in the compilation of the seasonal calendars, and sometimes the records of the tribe were preserved by their means.

Perhaps the best known specimen of Indian script is the Dakota ' Lone-dog Winter-count,' supposed to have been painted originally on a buffalo-robe. It is said to be a chronicle covering a period of seventy-one years from the beginning of the nineteenth century. Similar chronicles are the *Wallum-Olum*, which are painted records of the Leni-Lenâpé, an Algonquian people, and the calendar history of the Kiowa. The former consists of several series, one of which records the doings of the tribes down to the time of the arrival of the European colonists at the beginning of the seventeenth century. We append an extract from the *Wallum-Olum* as a specimen of genuine aboriginal composition. The translation is that made by the late Professor Brinton.

> After the rushing waters had subsided, the Lenâpé of the Turtle were close together, in hollow houses, living together there.

> It freezes where they abode : it snows where they abode : it storms where they abode: it is cold where they abode.

> At this northern place, they speak favourably of mild, cool lands, with many deer and buffaloes.

> As they journeyed, some being strong, some rich, they separated into house-builders and hunters :

> The strongest, the most united, the purest were the hunters.

> The hunters showed themselves at the north, at the east, atthe south, at the west.

> In that ancient country, in that northern country, in that Turtle country, the best of Lenâpé were the Turtle-men. [That is, probably, men of the Turtle totem.]

> All the cabin fires of that land were disquieted, and all said to their priest: "Let us go."

77

To the Snake land, to the east, they went forth, going away, earnestly grieving.

Split asunder, weak, trembling, their land burned: they went, torn and broken, to the Snake Island.

Those from the north being free, without care, went forth from the land of snow, in different directions.

The fathers of the Bald Eagle and the White Wolf remain along the sea, rich in fish and strength.

Floating up the streams in their canoes, our fathers were rich, they were in the light, when they were at those islands.

Head Beaver and Big Bird said: "Let us go to Snake Island," they said.

All say they will go along to destroy all the land.

Those of the north agreed,
Those of the east agreed.
Over the water, the frozen sea,
They went to enjoy it.

On the wonderful slippery water,
On the stone-hard water all went,
On the great tidal sea, the muscle-bearing sea.

Ten thousand at night,
All in one night,
To the Snake Island, to the east, at night,
They walk and walk, all of them.

The men from the north, the east, the south:
The Eagle clan, the Beaver clan, the Wolf clan,
The best men, the rich men, the head men,
Those with wives, those with daughters, those with dogs.

They all come, they tarry at the land of the spruce-pines:
Those from the west come with hesitation,
Esteeming highly their old home at the Turtle land.

There was no rain, and no corn, so they moved farther seaward.

At the place of caves, in the Buffalo land, they at last had food, on a pleasant plain.

## Modern Education and Culture

After the establishment of the United States Government a number of Christian and lay bodies undertook the education and enlightenment of the aborigines. Until 1870 all Government aid for this object passed through the hands of missionaries, but in 1875 a committee on Indian affairs had been appointed by Congress, which voted funds to support Indian students at Dartmouth and Princeton Colleges. Many day-schools were provided for the Indians, and these aimed at fitting them for citizenship by inculcating in them the social manners and ethical ideas of the whites. The school established by Captain R. H. Pratt at Carlisle, Pa., for the purpose of educating Indian boys and girls has turned out many useful members of society. About 100 students receive higher instruction in Hampton Institute. There are now 253 Government schools for the education of Indian youth, involving an annual expenditure of five million dollars, and the patient efforts of the United States Government may be said to be crowned with triumph and success when the list of cultured Indian men and women who have attended these seminaries is perused. Many of these have achieved conspicuous success in industrial pursuits and in the higher walks of life.

# CHAPTER II : THE MYTHOLOGIES OF THE NORTH AMERICAN INDIANS

## Animism

ALL mythological systems spring from the same fundamental basis. The gods are the children of reverence and necessity. But their genealogy stretches still farther back. Savage man, unable to distinguish between the animate and inanimate, imagines every surrounding object to be, like himself, instinct with life. Trees, the winds, the river (which he names " the Long Person "), all possess life and consciousness in his eyes. The trees moan and rustle, therefore they speak, or are, perchance, the dwelling-place of powerful spirits. The winds are full of words, sighings, warnings, threats, the noises, without doubt, of wandering powers, friendly or unfriendly beings. The water moves, articulates, prophesies, as, for example, did the Peruvian Rimac and Ipurimac—' the Oracles,' ' the Prophesiers.' Even abstract qualities were supposed to possess the attributes of living things. Light and darkness, heat and cold, were regarded as active and alert agencies. The sky was looked upon as the All-Father from whose co-operation with the Mother Earth all living things had sprung. This condition of belief is known as ' animism.'

## Totemism

If inanimate objects and natural phenomena were endowed by savage imagination with the qualities of life and thought, the creatures of the animal world were placed upon a still higher level. The Indian, brought into contact with the denizens of the forest and prairie, conceived a high opinion of their qualities and instinctive abilities. He observed that they possessed greater cunning in forest-craft than himself, that their hunting instinct was much more sure, that they seldom suffered from lack of provisions, that they were more swift of foot. In short, he considered them to be his superiors in those faculties which he most coveted and admired. Various human attributes and characteristics became personified and even exaggerated in some of his neighbours of wood and plain. The fox was proverbial for craft, the wild cat for stealth, the bear for a wrong-headed stupidity, the owl for a cryptic wisdom, the deer for swiftness. In each of these attributes the several animals to whom they belonged appeared to the savage as more gifted than himself, and so deeply was he influenced by this seeming superiority that if he coveted a certain quality he would place himself under the protection of the animal or bird which symbolized it. Again, if a tribe or clan possessed any special characteristic, such as fierceness or cunning, it was usually called by its neighbours after the bird or beast which symbolized its character. A tribe would learn its nickname from captives taken in war ; or it might even bestow such an appellation upon itself. After the lapse of a few generations the members of a tribe would regard the animal whose qualities they were supposed to possess as their direct ancestor, and would consider that all the members of his species were their blood-relations. This belief is known as totemism, and its adoption was the means of laying the foundation of a widespread system of tribal rule and custom, by which marriage and many of the affairs of life were and are wholly governed. Probably all European and Asiatic peoples have passed through this stage, and its remains are to be found deeply embedded in our present social system.

## Totemic Law and Custom

Few generations would elapse before the sense of ancestral devotion to the totem or eponymous fore-father of the tribe would become so strong as to be exalted into a fully developed system of worship of him as a deity. That the totem develops into the god is proved by the animal likeness and attributes of many deities in lands widely separate. It accounts for the jackal- and ibis-headed gods of Egypt, the bull-like deities of Assyria, the bestial gods of Hindustan—possibly even for the owl which accompanied the Grecian Pallas, for does not Homer speak of her as 'owl-eyed'? May not this goddess have developed from an owl totem, and may not the attendant bird of night which perches on her shoulder have been per-mitted to remain as a sop to her devotees in her more ancient form, who objected to her portrayal as a human being, and desired that some reminder of her former shape might be preserved? That our British ancestors possessed a totemic system is undoubted. Were not the clan Chattan of the Scottish Highlands the "sons of the cat"? In the *Dean of Lismore's Book* we read of a tribe included under the "sons to the king of Rualay" one battalion of whom was 'cat-headed,' or wore the totem crest of the cat. The swine-gods and other animal deities possessed by the British Celts assist this theory, as do the remains of many folk-customs in England and Scotland. Our crests are but so many family symbols which have come down to us from the distant days when our forefathers painted them upon their shields or wore them upon their helmets as the badge of their tribe, and thus of its supposed beast-progenitor or protector.

As has been said, a vast and intricate system of tribal

law and custom arose from the adoption of totemism. The animal from which the tribe took its name might not be killed or eaten, because of its blood-kinship with the clan. Descent from this ancestor postulated kinship between the various members of the tribe, male and female ; therefore the female members were not eligible for marriage with the males, who had perforce to seek for wives elsewhere. This often led to the partial adoption of another tribe or family in the vicinity, and of its totem, in order that a suitable exchange of women might be made as occasion required, and thus to the inclusion of two *gentes* or divisions within the tribe, each with its different totem-name, yet each regarding itself as a division of the tribal family. Thus a member of the ' Fox ' *gens* might not marry a woman of his own division, but must seek a bride from the ' Bears,' and similarly a ' Bear ' tribesman must find a wife from among the ' Foxes.'

### Severity of Totemic Rule

The utmost severity attached to the observation of totemic law and custom, to break which was regarded as a serious crime. Indeed, no one ever thought of infringing it, so powerful are habit and the force of association. It is not necessary to specify here the numerous customs which may be regarded as the outcome of the totemic system, for many of these have little in common with mythology proper. It will suffice to say that they were observed with a rigour beside which the rules of the religions of civilized peoples appear lax and indulgent. As this system exercised such a powerful influence on Indian life and thought, the following passage from the pen of a high authority on Indian totemism may be quoted with advantage : [1]

[1] J. R. Swanton, in *Handbook of the North American Indians.*

# MYTHS OF THE AMERICAN INDIANS

"The native American Indian, holding peculiar self-centred views as to the unity and continuity of all life and the consequent inevitable interrelations of the several bodies and beings in nature, especially of man to the beings and bodies of his experience and environment, to whom were imputed by him various anthropomorphic attributes and functions in addition to those naturally inherent in them, has developed certain fundamentally important cults, based on those views, that deeply affect his social, religious, and civil institutions. One of these doctrines is that persons and organizations of persons are one and all under the protecting and fostering tutelage of some imaginary being or spirit. These tutelary or patron beings may be grouped, by the mode and motive of their acquirement and their functions, into two fairly well defined groups or classes : (1) those which protect individuals only, and (2) those which protect organizations of persons. But with these two classes of tutelary beings is not infrequently confounded another class of protective imaginary beings, commonly called fetishes, which are regarded as powerful spiritual allies of their possessors. Each of these several classes of guardian beings has its own peculiar traditions, beliefs, and appropriate cult. The modes of the acquirement and the motives for the acquisition of these several classes of guardian beings differ in some fundamental and essential respects. The exact method of acquiring the clan or gentile group patrons or tutelaries is still an unsolved problem, although several plausible theories have been advanced by astute students to explain the probable mode of obtaining them. With respect to the personal tutelary and the fetish, the data are sufficiently clear and full to permit a satisfactory description and definition of these two classes of tutelary and auxiliary beings. From the available data bearing

84

on this subject, it would seem that much confusion regarding the use and acquirement of personal and communal tutelaries or patron beings has arisen by regarding certain social, political, and religious activities as due primarily to the influence of these guardian deities, when in fact those features were factors in the social organization on which has been later imposed the cult of the patron or guardian spirit. Exogamy, names and class names, and various taboos exist where 'totems' and 'totemism,' the cults of the guardian spirits, do not exist.

" Some profess to regard the clan or gentile group patron or tutelary as a mere development of the personal guardian, but from the available but insufficient data bearing on the question it appears to be, in some of its aspects, more closely connected in origin, or rather in the method of its acquisition, with the fetish, the Iroquois *otchina' ken'da*, ' an effective agency of sorcery,' than with any form of the personal tutelary. This patron spirit of course concerns the group regarded as a body, for with regard to each person of the group, the clan or gentile guardian is inherited, or rather acquired by birth, and it may not be changed at will. On the other hand, the personal tutelary is obtained through the rite of vision in a dream or a trance, and it must be preserved at all hazards as one of the most precious possessions. The fetish is acquired by personal choice, by purchase, or by inheritance, or from some chance circumstance or emergency, and it can be sold or discarded at the will of the possessor in most cases ; the exception is where a person has entered into a compact with some evil spirit or being that, in consideration of human or other sacrifices in its honour at stated periods, the said spirit undertakes to perform certain obligations to this man or woman, and in default of which the person forfeits his right to live.

" 'Totemism' is a purely philosophical term which modern anthropological literature has burdened with a great mass of needless controversial speculation and opinion. The doctrine and use of tutelary or patron guardian spirits by individuals and by organized bodies of persons are defined by Powell as 'a method of naming,' and as 'the doctrine and system of naming.' But the motive underlying the acquisition and use of guardian or tutelary spirits, whether by an individual or by an organized body of persons, is always the same— namely, to obtain welfare and to avoid ill-fare. So it appears to be erroneous to define this cult as 'the doctrine and system of naming.' It is rather the recognition, exploitation, and adjustment of the imaginary mystic relation of the individual or of the body of organized persons to the postulated *orendas*, mystic powers, surrounding each of these units of native society. With but few exceptions, the recognized relation between the clan or *gens* and its patron deity is not one of descent or source, but rather that of protection, guardianship, and support. The relationship as to source between these two classes of superior beings is not yet determined; so to avoid confusion in concepts, it is better to use distinctive names for them, until their connexion, if any, has been definitely ascertained : this question must not be prejudged. The hypothetic inclusion of these several classes in a general one, branded with the rubric 'totem' or its equivalent, has led to needless confusion. The native tongues have separate names for these objects, and until the native classification can be truthfully shown to be erroneous it would seem to be advisable to designate them by distinctive names. Notwithstanding the great amount of study of the literature of the social features of aboriginal American society, there are many data relative to this subject that have been overlooked or disregarded."

## Fetishism

Side by side with animism and totemism flourishes a third type of primitive belief, known as 'fetishism.' This word is derived from the Portuguese *feitiço*, 'a charm,' 'something made by art,' and is applied to any object, large or small, natural or artificial, regarded as possessing consciousness, volition, and supernatural qualities, and especially *orenda*, or magic power.

As has been said, the Indian intelligence regards all things, animals, water, the earth, trees, stones, the heavenly bodies, even night and day, and such properties as light and darkness, as possessing animation and the power of volition. It is, however, the general Indian belief that many of these are under some spell or potent enchantment. The rocks and trees are confidently believed by the Indian to be the living tombs of imprisoned spirits, resembling the dryads of Greek folk-lore, so that it is not difficult for him to conceive an intelligence, more or less potent, in any object, no matter how uncommon—indeed, the more uncommon the greater the probability of its being the abode of some powerful intelligence, incarcerated for revenge or some similar motive by the spell of a mighty enchanter.

The fetish is, in short, a mascot—a luck-bringer. The civilized person who attaches a four-leaf-clover charm to his watch-chain or her bangle is unconsciously following in the footsteps of many pagan ancestors; but with this difference, that the idea that 'luck' resides in the trinket is weak in the civilized mind, whereas in the savage belief the 'luck' resident in the fetish is a powerful and living thing—an intelligence

87

which must be placated with prayer, feast, and sacrifice. Fetishes which lose their reputations as bringers of good-fortune usually degenerate into mere amulets or talismanic ornaments, and their places are taken by others. The fetish differs from the class of tutelary or 'household' gods in that it may be sold or bartered, whereas tutelary or domestic deities are never to be purchased, or even loaned.

## Fetish Objects

Nearly all the belongings of a *shaman*, or medicine-man, are classed as fetishes by the North American Indians. These usually consist of the skins of beasts, birds, and serpents, roots, bark, powder, and numberless other objects. But the fetish must be altogether divorced from the idea of religion proper, with which it has little or no connexion, being found side by side with religious phases of many types. The fetish may be a bone, a feather, an arrow-head, a stick, carved or painted, a fossil, a tuft of hair, a necklace of fingers, a stuffed skin, the hand of an enemy, anything which might be suggested to the original possessor in a dream or a flight of imagination. It is sometimes fastened to the scalp-lock, to the dress, to the bridle, concealed between the layers of a shield, or specially deposited in a shrine in the wigwam. The idea in the mind of the original maker is usually symbolic, and is revealed only to one formally chosen as heir to the magical possession, and pledged in his turn to a similar secrecy.

Notwithstanding that the cult of fetishism is not, strictly speaking, a department of religious activity, a point exists at which the fetish begins to evolve into a god. This happens when the object survives the test of experience and achieves a more than personal or tribal popularity. Nevertheless the fetish partakes more of the nature of those spirits which are subservient to man (for example, the Arabian *jinn*) than of gods proper, and if it is prayed and sacrificed to on occasion, the 'prayers' are rather of the nature of a magical invocation, and the 'sacrifices' no more than would be accorded to any other assisting agent. Thus sharply must we differentiate between a fetish or captive spirit and a god. But it must be further borne in mind that a fetish is not necessarily a piece of personal property. It may belong collectively to an entire community. It is not necessarily a small article, but may possess all the appearances of a full-blown idol. An idol, however, is the abode of a god—the image into which a deity may materialize. A fetish, on the other hand, is *the place of imprisonment of a subservient spirit,* which cannot escape, and, if it would gain the rank of godhead, must do so by a long series of luck-bringing, or at least by the performance of a number of marvels of a protective or fortune-making nature. It is not unlikely that a belief exists in the Indian mind that there are many wandering spirits who, in return for food and other comforts, are willing to materialize in the shape the savage provides for them, and to assist him in the chase and other pursuits of life.

### Apache Fetishes

Among the Athapascan Indians the Apaches, both male and female, wear fetishes which they call *tzi-daltai*, manufactured from lightning-riven wood, generally pine or cedar, or fir from the mountains. These are highly valued, and are never sold. They are shaved very thin, rudely carved in the semblance of the human form, and decorated with incised lines representing the lightning. They are small in size, and few of them are painted.

Bourke describes one that an Apache chief carried about with him, which was made of a piece of lath, unpainted, having a figure in yellow drawn upon it, with a narrow black band and three snake's heads with white eyes. It was further decorated with pearl buttons and small eagle-down feathers. The reverse and obverse were identical.

Many of the Apaches attached a piece of malachite to their guns and bows to make them shoot accurately. Bourke mentions a class of fetishes which he terms 'phylacteries.' These are pieces of buckskin or other material upon which are inscribed certain characters or symbols of a religious or 'medicine' nature, and they are worn attached to the person who seeks benefit from them. They differ from the ordinary fetish in that they are concealed from the public gaze. These 'phylacteries,' Bourke says, "themselves medicine," may be employed to enwrap other 'medicine,' and "thus augment their own potentialities." He describes several of these objects. One worn by an Indian named Ta-ul-tzu-je "was tightly rolled in at least half a mile of saddler's silk, and when brought to light was found to consist of a small piece of buckskin two inches square, upon which were drawn red and yellow crooked lines, which represented the red and yellow snake. Inside were a piece of malachite and a small cross of lightning-riven pine, and two very small perforated shells. The cross they designated 'the black mind.'" Another 'phylactery' consisted of a tiny bag of hoddentin, holding a small quartz crystal and four feathers of eagle-down. This charm, it was explained by an Indian, contained not merely the 'medicine' of the crystal and the eagle, but also that of the black bear, the white lion, and the yellow snake.

# FETISHISM AMONG THE ALGONQUINS

## Iroquoian Fetishes

Things that seem at all unusual are accepted by the Hurons, a tribe of the Iroquois, as *oky*, or supernatural, and therefore it is accounted lucky to find them. In hunting, if they find a stone or other object in the entrails of an animal they at once make a fetish of it. Any object of a peculiar shape they treasure for the same reason. They greatly fear that demons or evil spirits will purloin their fetishes, which they esteem so highly as to propitiate them in feasts and invoke them in song. The highest type of fetish obtainable by a Huron was a piece of the onniont, or great armoured serpent, a mythological animal revered by many North American tribes.

## Fetishism among the Algonquins

Hoffmann states that at the 'medicine' lodges of some Algonquian tribes there are preserved fetishes or amulets worn above the elbows, consisting of strands of bead-work, metal bands, or skunk skins, while bracelets of shells, buckskin, or metal are also worn. A great tribal fetish of the Cheyenne was their 'medicine' arrow, which was taken from them by the Pawnees in battle. The head of this arrow projects from the bag which contains it, and it is covered with delicate waved or spiral lines, which denote its sacred character. It was, indeed, the palladium of the tribe. A peculiar type of fetish consisted of a mantle made from the skin of a deer and covered with feathers mixed with beadings. It was made and used by the medicine-men as a mantle of invisibility, or charmed covering to enable spies to traverse an enemy's country in security. In this instance the fetishistic power depended upon the devices drawn upon the article. The principal fetishes among the Hidatsa tribe of the Sioux are the skins of foxes and wolves, the favourite worn fetish being the stripe from the back of a wolf-skin with the tail hanging down the shoulders. A slit is made in the skin, through which the warrior puts his head, so that the skin of the wolf's head hangs down upon his breast. The most common tribal fetishes of the Sioux are, or were, buffalo heads, the neck-bones of which they preserve in the belief that the buffalo herds will thereby be prevented from removing to too great a distance. At certain periods they perform a ceremony with these bones, which consists in taking a potsherd filled with embers, throwing sweet-smelling grease upon it, and fumigating the bones with the smoke. There are certain trees and stones which are regarded as fetishes. To these offerings of red cloth, red paint, and other articles are made. Each individual has his personal fetish, and it is carried in all hunting and warlike excursions. It usually consists of a head, claws, stuffed skin, or other representative feature of the fetish animal. Even the horses are provided with fetishes, in the shape of a deer's horn, to ensure their swiftness. The rodent teeth of the beaver are regarded as potent charms, and are worn by little girls round their necks to make them industrious.

At Sikyatki, in Arizona, a territorial nucleus of the Hopi Indians, Mr. Fewkes had opportunities of inspecting many interesting fetish forms. A number of these discovered in native graves were pebbles with a polished surface, or having a fancied resemblance to some animal shape. Many of the personal fetishes of the Hopi consist of fossils, some of which attain the rank of tribal fetishes and are wrapped up in sacred bundles, which are highly venerated. In one grave was found a single large fetish in the shape of a mountain lion, made of sandstone, in which legs, ears, tail, and eyes are represented, the mouth still showing the red pigment with which it had been coloured. This is almost identical with some fetishes used by the Hopi at the present day.

## Totemism and Fetishism Meet

Fetishism among the Zuñi Indians of the south arose from an idea they entertained that they were kin with animals; in other words, their fetishes were totemistic. Totemism and fetishism were by no means incompatible with one another, but often flourished side by side. Fetishism of the Zuñi description is, indeed, the natural concomitant of a totemic system. Zuñi fetishes are usually concretions of lime or objects in which a natural resemblance to animals has been heightened by artificial means. Ancient fetishes are much valued by these people, and are often found by them in the vicinity of villages inhabited by their ancestors, and as tribal possessions are handed down from one generation to another. The medicine-men believe them to be the actual petrifactions of the animals they represent.

## The Sun-Children

The Zuñi philosophy of the fetish is given in the "Tale of the Two Sun-Children" as follows : " Now that the surface of the earth was hardened even the animals of prey, powerful and like the fathers [gods] themselves, would have devoured the children of men, and the two thought it was not well that they should all be permitted to live, for, said they, 'Alike the children of men and the children of the animals of prey multiply themselves. The animals of prey are provided with talons and teeth ; men are but poor, the finished beings of earth, therefore the weaker.'

93

Whenever they came across the pathway of one of these animals, were he a great mountain lion or but a mere mole, they struck him with the fire of lightning which they carried on their magic shields. *Thlu!* and instantly he was shrivelled and turned into stone. Then said they to the animals that they had changed into stone, 'That ye may not be evil unto man, but that ye may be a great good unto them, have we changed you into rock everlasting. By the magic breath of prey, by the heart that shall endure for ever within you, shall ye be made to serve instead of to devour mankind.' Thus was the surface of the earth hardened and scorched, and many of all kinds of beings changed to stone. Thus, too, it happens that we find here and there throughout the world their forms, sometimes large, like the beings themselves, sometimes shrivelled and distorted, and we often see among the rocks the forms of many beings that live no longer, which shows us that all was different in the 'days of the new.' Of these petrifactions, which are, of course, mere concretions or strangely shaped rock-forms, the Zuñi say : 'Whomsoever of us may be met with the light of such great good-fortune may see them, and should treasure them for the sake of the sacred [magic] power which was given them in the days of the new.' " [1]

## The Prey-Gods

This tradition furnishes additional evidence relative to the preceding statement, and is supposed to enlighten the Zuñi Indian as to wherein lies the power of fetishes. It is thought that the hearts of the great animals of prey are infused with a 'medicinal' or magic influence over the hearts of the animals they prey upon, and

[1] Cushing's *Zuñi Fetiches* (1883).

that they overcome them with their breath, piercing their hearts and quite numbing them. Moreover, their roar is fatal to the senses of the lower beasts. The mountain lion absorbs the blood of the game animals, therefore he possesses their acute senses. Again, those powers, as derived from his heart, are preserved in his fetish, since his heart still lives, even although his body be changed to stone. It happens, therefore, that the use of these fetishes is chiefly connected with the chase. But there are exceptions. The great animals of the chase, although fetishistic, are also regarded as supernatural beings, the mythological position of which is absolutely defined. In the City of the Mists lives Po-shai-an-K'ia, father of the 'medicine' societies, a culture-hero deity, whose abode is guarded by six beings known as the 'Prey-Gods,' and it is their counterfeit presentments that are made use of as fetishes. To the north of the City of the Mists dwells the Mountain Lion prey-god, to the west the Bear, to the south the Badger, to the east the Wolf, above the Eagle, below the Mole. These animals possess not only the guardianship of the six regions, but also the mastership of the 'medicine' or magic powers which emanate from them. They are the mediators between Po-shai-an-K'ia and man. The prey-gods, as 'Makers of the Path of Life,' are given high rank among the gods, but notwithstanding this their fetishes are " held as in captivity " by the priests of the various 'medicine' orders, and greatly venerated by them as mediators between themselves and the animals they represent. In this character they are exhorted with elaborate prayers, rituals, and ceremonials, and sometimes placated with sacrifices of the prey-gods of the hunt (*we-ma-a-ha-i*). Their special priests are the members of the Great Coyote

95

People—that is, they consist of eleven members of the Eagle and Coyote clans and of the Prey Brothers priesthood. These prey-gods appear to be almost unique, and may be indicated as an instance of fetishism becoming allied with religious belief. They depict, with two exceptions, the same species of prey animals as those supposed to guard the six regions, the exceptions being the coyote and the wild cat. These six prey animals are subdivided into six varieties. They are, strictly speaking, the property of the priests, and members and priests of the sacred societies are required to deposit their fetishes, when not in use, with the Keeper of the Medicine of the Deer. These 'medicines' or memberships alone can perfect the shape of the fetishes and worship them.

### The Council of Fetishes

The Day of the Council of the Fetishes takes place a little before or after the winter solstice or national New Year. The fetishes are taken from their places of deposit, and arranged according to species and colour in the form of a symbolic altar, quadrupeds being placed upright and birds suspended from the roof. The fetishes are prayed to, and prayer-meal is scattered over them. Chants are intoned, and a dance performed in which the cries of the fetish beasts are imitated. A prayer with responses follows. Finally all assemble round the altar and repeat the great invocation.

### The Fetish in Hunting

The use of fetishes in hunting among the Zuñi is extremely curious and involved in its nature. The hunter goes to the house of the Deer Medicine, where the vessel containing the fetish is brought out and placed before him. He sprinkles meal over the sacred vessel in the direction in which he intends to hunt, chooses a fetish from it, and presses it to his lips with an inspiration. He then places the fetish in a buckskin bag over his heart. Proceeding to the hunt, he deposits a spider-knot of yucca leaves where an animal has rested, imitates its cry, and is supposed by this means to confine its movements within a narrow circle. He then inspires deeply from the nostrils of the fetish, as though inhaling the magic breath of the god of prey, and then puffs the breath long and loudly in the direction whence the beast's tracks trend, in the belief that the breath he has borrowed from the prey-god will stiffen the limbs of the animal he hunts. When the beast is caught and killed he inhales its suspiring breath, which he breathes into the nostrils of the fetish. He then dips the fetish in the blood of the slain quarry, sips the blood himself, and devours the liver, in order that he may partake of the animal's qualities. The fetish is then placed in the sun to dry, and lastly replaced in the buckskin pouch with a blessing, afterward being duly returned to the Keeper of the Deer Medicine.

### Indian Theology

The late Professor Brinton, writing on the Indian attitude toward the eternal verities, says : [1]

"Nature, to the heathen, is no harmonious whole swayed by eternal principles, but a chaos of causeless effects, the meaningless play of capricious ghosts. He investigates not, because he doubts not. All events are to him miracles. Therefore his faith knows no bounds, and those who teach him that doubt is sinful must contemplate him with admiration. . . .

"Natural religions rarely offer more than this negative opposition to reason. They are tolerant to

[1] *Myths of the New World.*

97

a degree. The savage, void of any clear conception of a supreme deity, sets up no claim that his is the only true church. If he is conquered in battle he imagines that it is owing to the inferiority of his own gods to those of his victor, and he rarely, therefore, requires any other reasons to make him a convert.

"In this view of the relative powers of deities lay a potent corrective to the doctrine that the fate of man was dependent on the caprices of the gods. For no belief was more universal than that which assigned to each individual a guardian spirit. This invisible monitor was an ever-present help in trouble. He suggested expedients, gave advice and warning in dreams, protected in danger, and stood ready to foil the machinations of enemies, divine or human.

" With unlimited faith in this protector, attributing to him the devices suggested by his own quick wits and the fortunate chances of life, the savage escaped the oppressive thought that he was the slave of demoniac forces, and dared the dangers of the forest and the war-path without anxiety.

"By far the darkest side of such a religion is that which it presents to morality. The religious sense is by no means the voice of conscience. The Takahli Indian when sick makes a full and free confession of sins, but a murder, however unnatural and unprovoked, he does not mention, not counting it a crime. Scenes of licentiousness were approved and sustained throughout the continent as acts of worship; maidenhood was in many parts freely offered up or claimed by the priests as a right; in Central America twins were slain for religious motives; human sacrifice was common throughout the tropics, and was not unusual in higher latitudes; cannibalism was often enjoined; and in Peru, Florida, and Central America it was not uncommon for parents to slay their own children at the behest of a priest.

" The philosophical moralist contemplating such spectacles has thought to recognize in them one consoling trait. All history, it has been said, shows man living under an irritated God, and seeking to appease him by sacrifice of blood; the essence of all religion, it has been added, lies in that of which sacrifice is the symbol—namely, in the offering up of self, in the rendering up of our will to the will of God.

" But sacrifice, when not a token of gratitude, cannot be thus explained. It is not a rendering up, but a *substitution* of our will for God's will. A deity is angered by neglect of his dues ; he will revenge, certainly, terribly, we know not how or when. But as punishment is all he desires, if we punish ourselves he will be satisfied ; and far better is such self-inflicted torture than a fearful looking-for of judgment to come. Craven fear, not without some dim sense of the implacability of nature's laws, is at its roots.

" Looking only at this side of religion, the ancient philosopher averred that the gods existed solely in the apprehensions of their votaries, and the moderns have asserted that ' fear is the father of religion, love her late-born daughter '; that ' the first form of religious belief is nothing else but a horror of the unknown,' and that ' no natural religion appears to have been able to develop from a germ within itself anything whatever of real advantage to civilization.'

" Looking around for other standards wherewith to measure the progress of the knowledge of divinity in the New World, *prayer* suggests itself as one of the least deceptive. ' Prayer,' to quote the words of Novalis, ' is in religion what thought is in philosophy. The religious sense prays, as the reason thinks.' Guizot, carrying the analysis farther, thinks that it is prompted by a painful conviction of the inability of our will to conform to the dictates of reason.

"Originally it was connected with the belief that divine caprice, not divine law, governs the universe, and that material benefits rather than spiritual gifts are to be desired. The gradual recognition of its limitations and proper objects marks religious advancement. The Lord's Prayer contains seven petitions, only one of which is for a temporal advantage, and it the least that can be asked for.

"What immeasurable interval between it and the prayer of the Nootka Indian preparing for war :

"'Great Quahootze, let me live, not be sick, find the enemy, not fear him, find him asleep, and kill a great many of him.'

"Or, again, between it and a petition of a Huron to a local god, heard by Father Brébeuf :

"'Oki, thou who liveth in this spot, I offer thee tobacco. Help us, save us from shipwreck, defend us from our enemies, give us a good trade and bring us back safe and sound to our villages.'

"This is a fair specimen of the supplications of the lowest religions. Another equally authentic is given by Father Allouez. In 1670 he penetrated to an outlying Algonkin village, never before visited by a white man. The inhabitants, startled by his pale face and long black gown, took him for a divinity. They invited him to the council lodge, a circle of old men gathered round him, and one of them, approaching him with a double handful of tobacco, thus addressed him, the others grunting approval :

"'This indeed is well, Blackrobe, that thou dost visit us. Have mercy upon us. Thou art a Manito. We give thee to smoke.

"'The Naudowessies and Iroquois are devouring us. Have mercy upon us.

"'We are often sick ; our children die ; we are hungry. Have mercy upon us. Hear me, O Manito, I give thee to smoke.

"'Let the earth yield us corn ; the rivers give us fish ; sickness not slay us ; nor hunger so torment us. Hear us, O Manito, we give thee to smoke.'

"In this rude but touching petition, wrung from the heart of a miserable people, nothing but their wretchedness is visible. Not the faintest trace of an aspiration for spiritual enlightenment cheers the eye of the philanthropist, not the remotest conception that through suffering we are purified can be detected."

### The Indian Idea of God

The mythologies of the several stocks of the Red Race differ widely in conception and detail, and this has led many hasty investigators to form the conclusion that they were therefore of separate origin. But careful study has proved that they accord with all great mythological systems in their fundamental principles, and therefore with each other. The idea of God, often strange and grotesque perhaps, was nevertheless powerfully expressed in the Indian mythologies. Each division of the race possessed its own word to signify 'spirit.' Some of these words meant 'that which is above,' 'the higher one,' 'the invisible,' and these attributes accorded to deity show that the original Indian conception of it was practically the same as those which obtained among the primitive peoples of Europe and Asia. The idea of God was that of a great prevailing force who resided "in the sky." Savage or primitive man observes that all brightness emanates from the firmament above him. His eyes are dazzled by its splendour. Therefore he concludes that it must be the abode of the source of all life, of all spiritual excellence.

## 'Good' and 'Bad'

Before man has discovered the uses of that higher machinery of reason, philosophy, and has learned to marshal his theological ideas by its light, such deities as he worships conform very much to his own ethical standard. They mirror his morality, or lack of it. They are, like himself, savage, cruel, insatiable in their appetites. Very likely, too, the bestial attributes of the totemic gods cling to those deities who have been evolved out of that system. Among savage people ideas of good and evil as we conceive them are non-existent. To them 'good' merely implies everything which is to their advantage, 'evil' that which injures or distresses them. It is only when such a system as totemism, with its intricate taboos and stringent laws bearing on the various relationships of life, comes to be adopted that a 'moral' order arises. Slaughter of the totem animal becomes a 'crime'—sacrilege. Slaughter of a member of the totem clan, of a blood-brother, must be atoned for because he is of the totem blood. Marriage with a woman of the same totem blood becomes an offence. Neglect to pay fitting homage and sacrifice to the gods or totem is regarded with severity, especially when the evolution of a priestly caste has been achieved. As the totem is an ancestor, so all ancestors are looked upon with reverence, and deference to living progenitors becomes a virtue. In such ways a code of 'morality' is slowly but certainly produced.

## No 'Good' or 'Bad' Gods

But, oddly enough, the gods are usually exempt from these laws by which their worshippers are bound.

We find them murderous, unfilial, immoral, poly-
gamous, and often irreverent. This may be accounted
for by the circumstance that their general outlines were
filled in before totemism had become a fully developed
system, or it may mean that the savage did not believe
that divine beings could be fettered by such laws as he
felt himself bound to obey. However that may be,
we find the American gods neither better nor worse
than those of other mythological systems. Some of
them are prone to a sort of Puckish trickery and
are fond of practical joking : they had not reached
the exalted nobility of the pantheon of Olympus. But
what is more remarkable—and this applies to the deities
of all primitive races—we find that they possess no
ideas of good and evil. We find them occasionally
worshipping gods of their own—usually the creative
deities—and that may perhaps be accounted unto them
for righteousness. But they are only ' good ' to their
worshippers inasmuch as they ensure them abundant
crops or game, and only 'bad' when they cease to do
so. They are not worshipped because they are the
founts of truth and justice, but for the more immediately
cogent reason that, unless placated by the steam of
sacrifice, they will cease to provide an adequate food-
supply to man, and may malevolently send destruction
upon their neglectful worshippers. In the relations
between god and man among early peoples a specific
contract is implied : " Sacrifice unto us, provide us
with those offerings the steam of which is our food,
continue to do so, and we will see to it that you do
not lack crops and game and the essentials of life.
Fail to observe these customs and you perish." Under
such a system it will readily be granted that such horrors
as human sacrifice were only undertaken because they
were thought to be absolutely necessary to the existence

of the race as a whole, and were not prompted by any mere wanton delight in bloodshed.

Dealing with this point, the late Professor Brinton says in his *Myths of the New World* :

"The confusion of these distinct ideas [monotheism and polytheism] has led to much misconception of the native creeds. But another and more fatal error was that which distorted them into a dualistic form, ranging on one hand the good spirit with his legion of angels, on the other the evil one with his swarm of fiends, representing the world as the scene of their unending conflict, man as the unlucky football who gets all the blows.

"This notion, which has its historical origin among the Parsees of ancient Iran, is unknown to savage nations. 'The Hidatsa,' says Dr. Matthews, 'believe neither in a hell nor a devil.' 'The idea of the devil,' justly observes Jacob Grimm, 'is foreign to all primitive religions.' Yet Professor Mueller, in his voluminous work on those of America, after approvingly quoting this saying, complacently proceeds to classify the deities as good or bad spirits !

"This view, which has obtained without question in earlier works on the native religions of America, has arisen partly from habits of thought difficult to break, partly from mistranslations of native words, partly from the foolish axiom of the early missionaries, 'The gods of the Gentiles are devils.' Yet their own writings furnish conclusive proof that no such distinction existed out of their own fancies. The same word (*otkon*) which Father Bruyas employs to translate into Iroquois the term 'devil,' in the passage 'The devil took upon himself the figure of a serpent,' he is obliged to use for 'spirit' in the phrase, 'At the resurrection we shall be spirits,' which is a rather amusing illustration how impossible it was by any native word to convey the idea of the spirit of evil.

" When, in 1570, Father Rogel commenced his labours among the tribes near the Savannah River, he told them that the deity they adored was a demon who loved all evil things, and they must hate him ; whereas his auditors replied, that so far from this being the case, he whom he called a wicked being was the power that sent them all good things, and indignantly left the missionary to preach to the winds.

" A passage often quoted in support of this mistaken view is one in Winslow's *Good News from New England*, written in 1622. The author says that the Indians worship a good power called Kiehtan, and another ' who, as farre as wee can conceive, is the Devill,' named Hobbamock, or Hobbamoqui. The former of these names is merely the word ' great,' in their dialect of Algonkin, with a final *n*, and is probably an abbreviation of Kittanitowit, the great Manitou, a vague term mentioned by Roger Williams and other early writers, manufactured probably by them and not the appellation of any personified deity. The latter, so far from corresponding to the power of evil, was, according to Winslow's own statement, the kindly god who cured diseases, aided them in the chase, and appeared to them in dreams as their protector. Therefore, with great justice, Dr. Jarvis has explained it to mean ' the *oke* or tutelary deity which each Indian worships,' as the word itself signifies.

" So in many instances it turns out that what has been reported to be the evil divinity of a nation, to whom they pray to the neglect of a better one, is in reality the highest power they recognize."

# MYTHS OF THE AMERICAN INDIANS

## Creation-Myths

The mythologies of the Red Man are infinitely more rich in creative and deluge myths than those of any other race in the two hemispheres. Tales which deal with the origin of man are exceedingly frequent, and exhibit every phase of the type of creative story. Although many of these are similar to European and Asiatic myths of the same class, others show great originality, and strikingly present to our minds the characteristics of American aboriginal thought.

The creation-myths of the various Indian tribes differ as much from one another as do those of Europe and Asia. In some we find the great gods moulding the universe, in others we find them merely discovering it. Still others lead their people from subterranean depths to the upper earth. In many Indian myths we find the world produced by the All-Father sun, who thickens the clouds into water, which becomes the sea. In the Zuñi record of creation Awonawilona, the creator, fecundates the sea with his own flesh, and hatches it with his own heat. From this green scums are formed, which become the fourfold mother Earth and the all-covering father Sky, from whom sprang all creatures. "Then from the nethermost of the four caves of the world the seed of men and the creatures took form and grew ; even as with eggs in warm places worms quickly form and appear, and, growing, soon burst their shells and there emerge, as may happen, birds, tadpoles, or serpents : so man and all creatures grew manifoldly and multiplied in many kinds. Thus did the lowermost world-cave become overfilled with living things, full of unfinished creatures, crawling like reptiles over one another in black darkness, thickly crowding together and treading one on another, one spitting on another and doing other indecency, in such manner that the murmurings and lamentations became loud, and many amidst the growing confusion sought to escape, growing wiser and more manlike. Then Po-shai-an-K'ia, the foremost and the wisest of men, arising from the nethermost sea, came among men and the living things, and pitying them, obtained egress from that first world-cave through such a dark and narrow path that some seeing somewhat, crowding after, could not follow him, so eager mightily did they strive one with another. Alone then did Po-shai-an-K'ia come from one cave to another into this world, then island-like, lying amidst the world-waters, vast, wet, and unstable. He sought and found the Sun-Father, and besought him to deliver the men and the creatures from that nethermost world." [1]

## Algonquian Creation-Myth

In many other Indian mythologies we find the wind brooding over the primeval ocean in the form of a bird. In some creation-myths amphibious animals dive into the waters and bring up sufficient mud with them to form a beginning of the new earth. In a number of these tales no actual act of creation is recorded, but a reconstruction of matter only. The Algonquins relate that their great god Michabo, when hunting one day with wolves for dogs, was surprised to see the animals enter a great lake and disappear. He followed them into the waters with the object of rescuing them, but as he did so the lake suddenly overflowed and submerged the entire earth. Michabo despatched a raven with directions to find a piece of earth which might serve as a nucleus for a new world, but the bird returned from its quest unsuccessful. Then the god sent an

[1] Cushing, *13th Report*, Bureau of American Ethnology.

otter on a like errand, but it too failed to bring back the needful terrestrial germ. At last a musk-rat was sent on the same mission, and it returned with sufficient earth to enable Michabo to recreate the solid land. The trees had become denuded of their branches, so the god discharged arrows at them, which provided them with new boughs. After this Michabo married the musk-rat, and from their union sprang the human race.

### The Muskhogean Creation-Story

The Muskhogean Indians believe that in the beginning the primeval waste of waters alone was visible. Over the dreary expanse two pigeons or doves flew hither and thither, and in course of time observed a single blade of grass spring above the surface. The solid earth followed gradually, and the terrestrial sphere took its present shape. A great hill, Nunne Chaha, rose in the midst, and in the centre of this was the house of the deity Esaugetuh Emissee, the 'Master of Breath.' He took the clay which surrounded his abode, and from it moulded the first men, and as the waters still covered the earth he was compelled to build a great wall upon which to dry the folk he had made. Gradually the soft mud became transformed into bone and flesh, and Esaugetuh was successful in directing the waters into their proper channels, reserving the dry land for the men he had created.

This myth closely resembles the story in the Book of Genesis. The pigeons appear analogous to the brooding creative Spirit, and the manufacture of the men out of mud is also striking. So far is the resemblance carried that we are almost forced to conclude that this is one of the instances in which Gospel conceptions have been engrafted on a native legend.

# BIRD- AND SERPENT-WORSHIP

## Siouan Cosmology

The Mandan tribes of the Sioux possess a type of creation-myth which is common to several American peoples. They suppose that their nation lived in a subterranean village near a vast lake. Hard by the roots of a great grape-vine penetrated from the earth above, and, clambering up these, several of them got a sight of the upper world, which they found to be rich and well stocked with both animal and vegetable food. Those of them who had seen the new-found world above returned to their home bringing such glowing accounts of its wealth and pleasantness that the others resolved to forsake their dreary underground dwelling for the delights of the sunny sphere above. The entire population set out, and started to climb up the roots of the vine, but no more than half the tribe had ascended when the plant broke owing to the weight of a corpulent woman. The Mandans imagine that after death they will return to the underground world in which they originally dwelt, the worthy reaching the village by way of the lake, the bad having to abandon the passage by reason of the weight of their sins.

The Minnetarees believed that their original ancestor emerged from the waters of a lake bearing in his hand an ear of corn, and the Mandans possessed a myth very similar to that of the Muskhogees concerning the origin of the world.

## Bird- and Serpent-Worship and Symbols

The serpent and the bird appear sometimes separately, sometimes in strange combination, in North American mythology. The bird is always incomprehensible to the savage. Its power of flight, its appearance in the heavens where dwell the gods, and its musical song

109

combine to render it in his sight a being of mystery, possessing capabilities far above his own. From it he conceives the idea of the winged spirit or god, and he frequently regards it as a messenger from the bright regions of the sun or the sky deity. The flight and song of birds have always been carefully observed by primitive people as omens of grave import. These superstitions prevailed among the Red Race no less than among our own early ancestors. Many tribes imagined that birds were the visible spirits of the deceased. Thus the Powhatans of Virginia believed that the feathered race received the souls of their chiefs at death, and they were careful to do them no harm, accordingly. The Algonquins believed that birds caused the phenomenon of wind, that they created water-spouts, and that the clouds were the spreading and agitation of their wings. The Navaho thought that a great white swan sat at each of the four points of the compass and conjured up the blasts which came therefrom, while the Dakotas believed that in the west was the home of the Wakinyjan, 'the Flyers,' the breezes that send the storms. The thunder, too, is regarded by some Indian peoples as the flapping of the pinions of a great bird, whose tracks are seen in the lightning, "like the sparks which the buffalo scatters when he scours over a stony plain." Many of the tribes of the north-west coast hold the same belief, and imagine the lightning to be the flash of the thunder-bird's eye.

### Eagle-Worship

The eagle appears to have been regarded with extreme veneration by the Red Man of the north. "Its feathers composed the war-flag of the Creeks, and its image carved in wood or its stuffed skin sur-

Clasping her in his arms, he bore her to his village.
*Algonquian Myths and Legends*
*Page 154*

The hunter poised his spear and struck.
*Algonquian Myths and Legends*
*Page 179*

He suddenly assumed the shape of a gigantic porcupine.
*Iroquois Myths and Legends*
*Page 221*

She smiled at him and sang a strange, sweet song.
*Iroquois Myths and Legends*
*Page 259*

He leaned his shoulder against the rock.
*Sioux Myths and Legends*
*Page 277*

They arrived at the abode of the Water-god.
*Sioux Myths and Legends*
*Page 286*

He emerged in his own country.
*Sioux Myths and Legends*
*Page 295*

He seized hold of the hair.
*Myths and Legends of the Northern and Northwestern Indians*
*Page 317*

mounted their council lodges. None but an approved warrior dared wear it among the Cherokees, and the Dakotas allowed such an honour only to him who had first touched the corpse of the common foe."[1] The Natchez and other tribes esteemed it almost as a deity. The Zuñi of New Mexico employed four of its feathers to represent the four winds when invoking the rain-god. Indeed, it was venerated by practically every tribe in North America. The owl, too, was employed as a symbol of wisdom, and sometimes, as by the Algonquins, was represented as the attendant of the Lord of the Dead. The Creek medicine-men carried a stuffed owl-skin as the badge of their fraternity and a symbol of their wisdom, and the Cherokees placed one above the 'medicine' stone in their council lodge. The dove also appears to have been looked upon as sacred by the Hurons and Mandans.

### The Serpent and the Sun

Some Indian tribes adopted the serpent as a symbol of time. They reckoned by 'suns,' and as the outline of the sun, a circle, corresponds to nothing in nature so much as a serpent with its tail in its mouth, devouring itself, so to speak, this may have been the origin of the symbol. Some writers think that the serpent symbolized the Indian idea of eternity, but it is unlikely that such a recondite conception would appeal to a primitive folk.

### The Lightning Serpent

Among the Indians the serpent also typified the lightning. The rapidity and sinuosity of its motions, its quick spring and sharp recoil, prove the aptness of the illustration. The brilliancy of the serpent's basilisk

[1] Brinton, *Myths of the New World.*

glance and the general intelligence of its habits would speedily give it a reputation for wisdom, and therefore as the possessor of *orenda*, or magic power. These two conceptions would shortly become fused. The serpent as the type of the lightning, the symbol of the spear of the war-god, would lead to the idea that that deity also had power over the crops or summer vegetation, for it is at the time of year when lightning is most prevalent that these come to fruition. Again, the serpent would through this association with the war-god attain a significance in the eye of warriors, who would regard it as powerful war-physic. Thus, the horn of the great Prince of Serpents, which was supposed to dwell in the Great Lakes, was thought to be the most potent war-charm obtainable, and priests or medicine-men professed to have in their possession fragments of this mighty talisman.

The Algonquins believed that the lightning was an immense serpent vomited by the Manito, or creator, and said that he leaves serpentine twists and folds on the trees that he strikes. The Pawnees called the thunder "the hissing of the great snake."

In snake-charming as a proof of magical proficiency, as typifying the lightning, which, as the serpent-spear of the war-god, brings victory in battle, and in its agricultural connexion, lies most of the secret of the potency of the serpent symbol. As the emblem of the fertilizing summer showers the lightning serpent was the god of fruitfulness; but as the forerunner of floods and disastrous rains it was feared and dreaded.

## Serpent-Worship

Probably more ponderous nonsense has been written about the worship of reptiles ('ophiolatry,' as the mythologists of half a century ago termed it) than upon any other allied subject. But, this notwithstanding, there is no question that the serpent still holds a high place in the superstitious regard of many peoples, Asiatic and American. As we have already seen, it frequently represents the orb of day, and this is especially the case among the Zuñi and other tribes of the southern portions of North America, where sun-worship is more usual than in the less genial regions. With the Red Man also it commonly typified water. The sinuous motion of the reptile sufficiently accounts for its adoption as the symbol for this element. And it would be no difficult feat of imagination for the savage to regard the serpent as a water-god, bearing in mind as he would the resemblance between its movement and the winding course of a river. Kennebec, the name of a stream in Maine, means 'snake,' and Antietam, a creek in Maryland, has the same significance in the Iroquois dialect. Both Algonquins and Iroquois believed in the mighty serpent of the Great Lakes. The wrath of this deity was greatly to be feared, and it was thought that, unless duly placated, he vented his irascible temper upon the foolhardy adventurers who dared to approach his domain by raising a tempest or breaking the ice beneath their feet and dragging them down to his dismal fastnesses beneath.

### The Rattlesnake

The rattlesnake was the serpent almost exclusively honoured by the Red Race. It is slow to attack, but venomous in the extreme, and possesses the power of the basilisk to attract within reach of its spring small birds and squirrels. "It has the same strange susceptibility to the influence of rhythmic sounds as the vipers, in which lies the secret of snake-charming. Most of the Indian magicians were familiar with this singularity. They employed it with telling effect to put beyond question their intercourse with the unseen powers, and to vindicate the potency of their own guardian spirits who thus enabled them to handle with impunity the most venomous of reptiles. The well-known antipathy of these serpents to certain plants, for instance the hazel, which, bound around the ankles, is an alleged protection against their attacks, and perhaps some antidote to their poison used by the magicians, led to their frequent introduction in religious ceremonies. Such exhibitions must have made a profound impression on the spectators and redounded in a corresponding degree to the glory of the performer. 'Who is a *manito*?' asks the mystic Meda Chant of the Algonkins. 'He,' is the reply, 'he who walketh with a serpent, walking on the ground; he is a *manito*.' The intimate alliance of this symbol with the mysteries of religion, the darkest riddles of the Unknown, is reflected in their language, and also in that of their neighbours, the Dakotas, in both of which the same words *manito*, *wakan*, which express the supernatural in its broadest sense, are also used as terms for this species of animals! The pious founder of the Moravian Brotherhood, the Count of Zinzendorf, owed his life on one occasion to this deeply rooted superstition. He was visiting a missionary station among the Shawnees, in the Wyoming valley. Recent quarrels with the whites had unusually irritated this unruly folk, and they resolved to make him their first victim. After he had retired to his secluded hut, several of the braves crept upon him, and, cautiously lifting the corner of the lodge, peered in. The venerable man was seated before a little fire, a volume of the Scriptures on his knees, lost in the perusal of the sacred words. While they gazed, a huge rattlesnake, unnoticed by him, trailed across his feet, and rolled itself into a coil in the comfortable warmth of the fire. Immediately the would-be murderers forsook their purpose and noiselessly retired, convinced that this was indeed a man of God." [1]

### The Sacred Origin of Smoking

Smoking is, of course, originally an American custom, and with the Indians of North America possesses a sacred origin. Says an authority upon the barbarian use of tobacco: [2]

" Of the sacred origin of tobacco the Indian has no doubt, although scarcely two tribes exactly agree in the details of the way in which the invaluable boon was conferred on man. In substance, however, the legend is the same with all. Ages ago, at the time when spirits considered the world yet good enough for their occasional residence, a very great and powerful spirit lay down by the side of his fire to sleep in the forest. While so lying, his arch-enemy came that way, and thought it would be a good chance for mischief; so, gently approaching the sleeper, he rolled him over toward the fire, till his head rested among the glowing embers, and his hair was set ablaze. The roaring of the fire in his ears roused the good spirit, and, leaping to his feet, he rushed in a fright through the forest, and as he did so the wind caught his singed hair as it flew off, and, carrying it away, sowed it broadcast over the earth, into which it sank and took root, and grew up tobacco.

" If anything exceeds the savage's belief in tobacco, it is that which attaches to his pipe. In life it is his dearest companion, and in death is inseparable; for

[1] Brinton, *Myths of the New World*, pp. 131–133.
[2] Schoolcraft, *op. cit.*

whatever else may be forgotten at his funeral obsequies, his pipe is laid in the grave with him to solace him on his journey to the 'happy hunting-ground.' 'The first pipe' is among the most sacred of their traditions; as well it may be, when it is sincerely believed that no other than the Great Spirit himself was the original smoker.

"Many years ago the Great Spirit called all his people together, and, standing on the precipice of the Red Pipe-stone Rock, he broke a piece from the wall, and, kneading it in his hands, made a huge pipe, which he smoked over them, and to the north, south, east, and west. He told them that this stone was red, that it was their flesh, that of it they might make their pipes of peace; but it belonged equally to all; and the war-club and the scalping-knife must not be raised on this ground. And he smoked his pipe and talked to them till the last whiff, and then his head disappeared in a cloud; and immediately the whole surface of the rock for several miles was melted and glazed. Two great ovens were opened beneath, and two women (guardian spirits of the place) entered them in a blaze of fire; and they are heard there yet, and answer to the invocation of the priests, or medicine-men, who consult them on their visits to this sacred place.

"The 'sacred place' here mentioned is the site of the world-renowned 'Pipe-stone Quarry.' From this place has the North American Indian ever obtained material for his pipe, and from no other spot. Catlin asserts that in every tribe he has visited (numbering about forty, and extending over thousands of miles of country) the pipes have all been made of this red pipe-stone. Clarke, the great American traveller, relates that in his intercourse with many tribes who as yet had had but little intercourse with the whites he learned that almost every adult had made the pilgrimage to the sacred rock and drawn from thence his pipe-stone. So peculiar is this 'quarry' that Catlin has been at the pains to describe it very fully and graphically, and from his account the following is taken :

" ' Our approach to it was from the east, and the ascent, for the distance of fifty miles, over a continued succession of slopes and terraces, almost imperceptibly rising one above another, that seemed to lift us to a great height. There is not a tree or bush to be seen from the highest summit of the ridge, though the eye may range east and west, almost to a boundless extent, over a surface covered with a short grass, that is green at one's feet, and about him, but changing to blue in distance, like nothing but the blue and vastness of the ocean.

" ' On the very top of this mound or ridge we found the far-famed quarry or fountain of the Red Pipe, which is truly an anomaly in nature. The principal and most striking feature of this place is a perpendicular wall of close-grained, compact quartz, of twenty-five and thirty feet in elevation, running nearly north and south, with its face to the west, exhibiting a front of nearly two miles in length, when it disappears at both ends, by running under the prairie, which becomes there a little more elevated, and probably covers it for many miles, both to the north and south. The de-pression of the brow of the ridge at this place has been caused by the wash of a little stream, produced by several springs at the top, a little back from the wall, which has gradually carried away the superincumbent earth, and having bared the wall for the distance of two miles, is now left to glide for some distance over a perfectly level surface of quartz rock ; and then to leap from the top of the wall into a deep basin below, and thence seek its course to the Missouri, forming the extreme source of a noted and powerful tributary, called the " Big Sioux."

" ' At the base of this wall there is a level prairie, of half a mile in width, running parallel to it, in any, and in all parts of which, the Indians procure the red stone for their pipes, by digging through the soil and several slaty layers of the red stone to the depth of four or five feet. From the very numerous marks of ancient and modern diggings or excavations, it would appear that this place has been for many centuries resorted to for the red stone ; and from the great number of graves and remains of ancient fortifications in the vicinity, it would seem, as well as from their actual traditions, that the Indian tribes have long held this place in high superstitious estimation ; and also that it has been the resort of different tribes, who have made their regular pilgrimages here to renew their pipes.'

" As far as may be gathered from the various and slightly conflicting accounts of Indian smoking observances, it would seem that to every tribe, or, if it be an extensive one, to every detachment of a tribe, belongs a potent instrument known as 'medicine pipe-stem.' It is nothing more than a tobacco-pipe, splendidly adorned with savage trappings, yet it is regarded as a sacred thing to be used only on the most solemn occasions, or in the transaction of such important business as among us could only be concluded by the sanction of a Cabinet Council, and affixing the royal signature."

### The Gods of the Red Man

Most of the North American stocks possessed a regular pantheon of deities. Of these, having regard to their numbers, it will be impossible to speak in any detail, and it will be sufficient if we confine ourselves to some account of the more outstanding figures. As in all mythologies, godhead is often attached to the conception of the bringer of culture, the sapient being who first instructs mankind in the arts of life, agriculture, and religion. American mythologies possess many such hero-gods, and it is not always easy to say whether they belong to history or mythology. Of course, the circumstances surrounding the conception of some of these beings prove that they can be nothing else than mythological, but without doubt some of them were originally mere mortal heroes.

## Michabo

We discover one of the first class in Michabo, the Great Hare, the principal deity of the Algonquins. In the accounts of the older travellers we find him described as the ruler of the winds, the inventor of picture-writing, and even the creator and preserver of the world. Taking a grain of sand from the bed of the ocean, he made from it an island which he launched in the primeval waters. This island speedily grew to a great size; indeed, so extensive did it become that a young wolf which managed to find a footing on it and attempted to cross it died of old age before he completed his journey. A great 'medicine' society, called Meda, was supposed to have been founded by Michabo. Many were his inventions. Observing the spider spread its web, he devised the art of knitting nets to catch fish. He furnished the hunter with many signs and charms for use in the chase. In the autumn, ere he takes his winter sleep, he fills his great pipe and smokes, and the smoke which arises is seen in the clouds which fill the air with the haze of the Indian summer.

Some uncertainty prevailed among the various Algonquian tribes as to where Michabo resided, some of them believing that he dwelt on an island in Lake Superior, others on an iceberg in the Arctic Ocean, and still others in the firmament, but the prevalent idea seems to have been that his home was in the east, where the sun rises on the shores of the great river Ocean that surrounds the dry land.

That a being possessing such qualities should be conceived of as taking the name and form of a timid animal like the hare is indeed curious, and there is little doubt that the original root from which the name Michabo has been formed does not signify 'hare.' In fact, the root *wab*, which is the initial syllable of the Algonquian word for 'hare,' means also 'white,' and from it are derived the words for 'east,' 'dawn,' 'light,' and 'day.' Their names proceeding from the same root, the idea of the hare and the dawn became confused, and the more tangible object became the symbol of the god. Michabo was therefore the spirit of light, and, as the dawn, the bringer of winds. As lord of light he is also wielder of the lightning. He is in constant strife, nevertheless, with his father the West Wind, and in this combat we can see the diurnal struggle between east and west, light and darkness, common to so many mythologies.

Modern Indian tales concerning Michabo make him a mere tricksy spirit, a malicious buffoon, but in these we can see his character in process of deterioration under the stress of modern conditions impinging upon Indian life. It is in the tales of the old travellers and missionaries that we find him in his true colours as a great culture-hero, Lord of the Day and bringer of light and civilization.

# AHSONNUTLI

## The Battle of the Twin-Gods

Among the Iroquois we find a similar myth. It tells of two brothers, Ioskeha and Tawiscara, or the White One and the Dark One, twins, whose grandmother was the moon. When they grew up they quarrelled violently with one another, and finally came to blows. Ioskeha took as his weapon the horns of a stag, while Tawiscara seized a wild rose to defend himself. The latter proved but a puny weapon, and, sorely wounded, Tawiscara turned to fly. The drops of blood which fell from him became flint stones. Ioskeha later built for himself a lodge in the far east, and became the father of mankind and principal deity of the Iroquois, slaying the monsters which infested the earth, stocking the woods with game, teaching the Indians how to grow crops and make fires, and instructing them in many of the other arts of life. This myth appears to have been accepted later by the Mohawks and Tuscaroras.

## Awonawilona

We have already alluded in the Zuñi creation-myth to the native deity Awonawilona. This god stands out as one of the most perfect examples of deity in its constructive aspect to be found in the mythologies of America. He seems in some measure to be identified with the sun, and from the remote allusions regarding him and the manner in which he is spoken of as an architect of the universe we gather that he was not exactly in close touch with mankind.

## Ahsonnutli

Closely resembling him was Ahsonnutli, the principal deity of the Navaho Indians of New Mexico, who was regarded as the creator of the heavens and earth. He was supposed to have placed twelve men at each of the cardinal points to uphold the heavens. He was believed to possess the qualities of both sexes, and is entitled the Turquoise Man-woman.

## Atíus Tiráwa

Atíus Tiráwa was the great god of the Pawnees. He also was a creative deity, and ordered the courses of the sun, moon, and stars. As known to-day he is regarded as omnipotent and intangible ; but how far this conception of him has been coloured by missionary influence it would be difficult to say. We find, however, in other Indian mythologies which we know have not been sophisticated by Christian belief many references to deities who possess such attributes, and there is no reason why we should infer that Atíus Tiráwa is any other than a purely aboriginal conception.

## Esaugetuh Emissee

The great life-giving god of the Creeks and other Muskhogeans was Esaugetuh Emissee, whose name signifies, 'Master of Breath.' The sound of the name represents the emission of breath from the mouth. He was the god of wind, and, like many another divinity in American mythology, his rule over that element was allied with his power over the breath of life—one of the forms of wind or air. Savage man regards the wind as the great source of breath and life. Indeed, in many tongues the words ' wind,' ' soul,' and ' breath ' have a common origin. We find a like conception in the Aztec wind-god Tezcatlipoca, who was looked upon as the primary source of existence.[1]

[1] See the author's *Myths of Mexico and Peru,* in this series.

## The Coyote God

Among the people of the far west, the Californians and Chinooks, an outstanding deity is, strangely enough, the Coyote. But whereas among the Chinooks he was thought to be a benign being, the Maidu and other Californian tribes pictured him as mischievous, cunning, and destructive. Kodoyanpe, the Maidu creator, discovered the world along with Coyote, and with his aid rendered it habitable for mankind. The pair fashioned men out of small wooden images, as the gods of the Kiche of Central America are related to have done in the myth in the *Popol Vuh*. But the mannikins proved unsuitable to their purpose, and they turned them into animals. Kodoyanpe's intentions were beneficent, and as matters appeared to be going but ill, he concluded that Coyote was at the bottom of the mischief. In this he was correct, and on consideration he resolved to destroy Coyote. On the side of the disturber was a formidable array of monsters and other evil agencies. But Kodoyanpe received powerful assistance from a being called the Conqueror, who rid the universe of many monsters and wicked spir ts which might have proved unfriendly to the life of man, as yet unborn. The combat raged fiercely over a protracted period, but at last the beneficent Kodoyanpe was defeated by the crafty Coyote. Kodoyanpe had buried many of the wooden mannikins whom he had at first created, and they now sprang from their places and became the Indian race.

This is, of course, a day-and-night or light-and-darkness myth. Kodoyanpe is the sun, the spirit of day, who after a diurnal struggle with the forces of darkness flies toward the west for refuge. Coyote is the spirit of night, typified by an animal of nocturnal habits which slinks forth from its den as the shades of dusk fall on the land. We find a similar conception in Egyptian mythology, where Anubis, the jackal-headed, swallows his father Osiris, the brilliant god of day, as the night swallows up the sun.

Another version of the Coyote myth current in California describes how in the beginning there was only the primeval waste of waters, upon which Kodoyanpe and Coyote dropped in a canoe. Coyote willed that the surf beneath them should become sand.

"Coyote was coming. He came to Got'at. There he met a heavy surf. He was afraid that he might be drifted away, and went up to the spruce-trees. He stayed there a long time. Then he took some sand and threw it upon that surf: 'This shall be a prairie and no surf. The future generations shall walk on this prairie!' Thus Clatsop became a prairie. The surf became a prairie." [1]

But among other tribes as well as among the Chinooks Italapas, the Coyote, is a beneficent deity. Thus in the myths of the Shushwap and Kutenai Indians of British Columbia he figures as the creative agency, and in the folk-tales of the Ashochimi of California he appears after the deluge and plants in the earth the feathers of various birds, which according to their colour become the several Indian tribes.

## Blue Jay

Another mischievous deity of the Chinooks and other western peoples is Blue Jay. He is a turbulent braggart, schemer, and mischief-maker. He is the very clown of gods, and invariably in trouble himself if he is not manufacturing it for others. He has the shape of a jay-bird, which was given him by the Super-

[1] Boas, *Chinook Texts.*

natural People because he lost to them in an archery contest. They placed a curse upon him, telling him the note he used as a bird would gain an unenviable notoriety as a bad omen. Blue Jay has an elder brother, the Robin, who is continually upbraiding him for his mischievous conduct in sententious phraseology. The story of the many tricks and pranks played by Blue Jay, not only on the long-suffering members of his tribe, but also upon the denizens of the supernatural world, must have afforded intense amusement around many an Indian camp-fire. Even the proverbial gravity of the Red Man could scarcely hold out against the comical adventures of this American Owlglass.

## Thunder-Gods

North America is rich in thunder-gods. Of these a typical example is Haokah, the god of the Sioux. The countenance of this divinity was divided into halves, one of which expressed grief and the other cheerfulness—that is, on occasion he could either weep with the rain or smile with the sun. Heat affected him as cold, and cold was to him as heat. He beat the tattoo of the thunder on his great drum, using the wind as a drum-stick. In some phases he is reminiscent of Jupiter, for he hurls the lightning to earth in the shape of thunderbolts. He wears a pair of horns, perhaps to typify his connexion with the lightning, or else with the chase, for many American thunder-gods are mighty hunters. This double conception arises from their possession of the lightning-spear, or arrow, which also gives them in some cases the character of a war-god. Strangely enough, such gods of the chase often resembled in appearance the animals they hunted. For example, Tsul 'Kalu (Slanting Eyes), a hunter-god of the Cherokee Indians, seems to resemble a deer. He is of giant proportions, and dwells in a great mountain of the Blue Ridge Range, in North-western Virginia. He appears to have possessed all the game in the district as his private property. A Cherokee thunder-god is Asgaya Gigagei (Red Man). The facts that he is described as being of a red colour, thus typifying the lightning, and that the Cherokees were originally a mountain people, leave little room for doubt that he is a thunder-god, for it is around the mountain peaks that the heavy thunder-clouds gather, and the red lightning flashing from their depths looks like the moving limbs of the half-hidden deity. We also find occasionally invoked in the Cherokee religious formulæ a pair of twin deities known as the 'Little Men,' or 'Thunder-boys.' This reminds us that in Peru twins were always regarded as sacred to the lightning, since they were emblematic of the thunder-and-lightning twins, Apocatequil and Piguerao. All these thunder-gods are analogous to the Aztec Tlaloc, the Kiche Hurakan, and the Otomi Mixcoatl.[1] A well-known instance of the thunder- or hunter-god who possesses animal characteristics will occur to those who are familiar with the old English legend of Herne the Hunter, with his deer's head and antlers.

The Dakota Indians worshipped a deity whom they addressed as Waukheon (Thunder-bird). This being was engaged in constant strife with the water-god, Unktahe, who was a cunning sorcerer, and a controller of dreams and witchcraft. Their conflict probably symbolizes the atmospheric changes which accompany the different seasons.

[1] See *Myths of Mexico and Peru.*

### Idea of a Future Life

The idea of a future life was very widely disseminated among the tribes of North America. The general conception of such an existence was that it was merely a shadowy extension of terrestrial life, in which the same round of hunting and kindred pursuits was engaged in. The Indian idea of eternal bliss seems to have been an existence in the Land of the Sun, to which, however, only those famed in war were usually admitted.

That the Indians possessed a firm belief in a future state of existence is proved by their statements to the early Moravian missionaries, to whom they said : " We Indians shall not for ever die. Even the grains of corn we put under the earth grow up and become living things." The old missionary adds: " They conceive that when the soul has been awhile with God it can, if it chooses, return to earth and be born again." This idea of rebirth, however, appears to have meant that the soul would return to the bones, that these would clothe themselves with flesh, and that the man would rejoin his tribe. By what process of reasoning they arrived at such a conclusion it would be difficult to ascertain, but the almost universal practice which obtained among the Indians both of North and South America of preserving the bones of the deceased plainly indicates that they possessed some strong religious reason for this belief. Many tribes which dwelt east of the Mississippi once in every decade collected the bones of those who had died within that period, carefully cleaned them, and placed them in a tomb lined with beautiful flowers, over which they erected a mound of wood, stone, or earth. Nor, indeed, were the ancient Egyptians more considerate of the remains of their fathers.

# MYTHS OF THE AMERICAN INDIANS

## The Hope of Resurrection

American funerary ritual and practice throughout the northern sub-continent plainly indicates a strong and vivid belief in the resurrection of the soul after death. Among many tribes the practice prevailed of interring with the deceased such objects as he might be supposed to require in the other world. These included weapons of war and of the chase for men, and household implements and feminine finery in the case of women.

Among primitive peoples the belief is prevalent that inanimate objects possess doubles, or, as spiritualists would say, 'astral bodies,' or souls, and some Indian tribes supposed that unless such objects were broken or mutilated—that is to say, 'killed'—their doubles would not accompany the spirit of the deceased on its journey.

## Indian Burial Customs

Many methods of disposing of the corpse were, and are, in use among the American Indians. The most common of these were ordinary burial in the earth or under tumuli, burial in caves, tree-burial, raising the dead on platforms, and the disposal of cremated remains in urns. Embalming and mummification were practised to a certain extent by some of the extinct tribes of the east coast, and some of the north-west tribes, notably the Chinooks, buried their dead in canoes, which were raised on poles. The rites which accompanied burial, besides the placing of useful articles and food in the grave, generally consisted in a solemn dance, in which the bereaved relatives cut themselves and blackened their faces, after which they wailed night and morning in solitary places. It was generally regarded as unlucky to mention the name of the deceased, and, indeed, the bereaved family often adopted another name to avoid such a contingency.

### The Soul's Journey

Most of the tribes appear to have believed that the soul had to undertake a long journey before it reached its destination. The belief of the Chinooks in this respect is perhaps a typical one. They imagine that after death the spirit of the deceased drinks at a large hole in the ground, after which it shrinks and passes on to the country of the ghosts, where it is fed with spirit food and drink. After this act of communion with the spirit-world it may not return. They also believe that every one is possessed of two spirits, a greater and a less. During illness the lesser soul is spirited away by the denizens of Ghost-land. The Navahos possess a similar belief, and say that the soul has none of the vital force which animates the body, nor any of the faculties of the mind, but a kind of third quality, or personality, like the *ka* of the ancient Egyptians, which may leave its owner and become lost, much to his danger and discomfort. The Hurons and Iroquois believe that after death the soul must cross a deep and swift stream, by a bridge formed by a single slender tree, upon which it has to combat the attacks of a fierce dog. The Athapascans imagine that the soul must be ferried over a great water in a stone canoe, and the Algonquins and Dakotas believe that departed spirits must cross a stream bridged by an enormous snake.

### Paradise and the Supernatural People

The Red Man appears to have possessed two wholly different conceptions of supernatural life. We find in Indian myth allusions both to a 'Country of the Ghosts' and to a 'Land of the Supernatural People.'

The first appears to be the destination of human beings after death, but the second is apparently the dwelling-place of a spiritual race some degrees higher than mankind. Both these regions are within the reach of mortals, and seem to be mere extensions of the terrestrial sphere. Their inhabitants eat, drink, hunt, and amuse themselves in the same manner as earthly folk, and are by no means invulnerable or immortal. The instinctive dread of the supernatural which primitive man possesses is well exemplified in the myths in which he is brought into contact with the denizens of Ghost-land or the Spirit-world. These myths were undoubtedly framed for the same purpose as the old Welsh poem on the harrying of hell, or the story of the journey of the twin brothers to Xibalba in the Central American *Popol Vuh*. That is to say, the desire was felt for some assurance that man, on entering the spiritual sphere, would only be treading in the footsteps of heroic beings who had preceded him, who had vanquished the forces of death and hell and had stripped them of their terrors.

The mythologies of the North American Indians possess no place of punishment, any more than they possess any deities who are frankly malevolent toward humanity. Should a place of torment be discernible in any Indian mythology at the present day it may unhesitatingly be classed as the product of missionary sophistication. Father Brébeuf, an early French missionary, could only find that the souls of suicides and those killed in war were supposed to dwell apart from the others. "But as to the souls of scoundrels," he adds, "so far from being shut out, they are welcome guests."

# INDIAN TIME AND FESTIVALS

## The Sacred Number Four

Over the length and breadth of the American continent a peculiar sanctity is attached by the aborigines to the four points of the compass. This arises from the circumstance that from these quarters come the winds which carry the fertilizing rains. The Red Man, a dweller in vast undulating plains where landmarks are few, recognized the necessity of such guidance in his wanderings as could alone be received from a strict adherence to the position of the four cardinal points. These he began to regard with veneration as his personal safeguards, and recognized in them the dwelling-places of powerful beings, under whose care he was. Most of his festivals and celebrations had symbolical or direct allusions to the four points of the compass. The ceremony of smoking, without which no treaty could be commenced or ratified, was usually begun by the chief of the tribe exhaling tobacco-smoke toward the four quarters of the earth. Among some tribes other points were also recognized, as, for example, one in the sky and one in the earth. All these points had their symbolical colours, and were presided over by various animal or other divinities. Thus the Apaches took black for the east, white for the south, yellow for the west, and blue for the north, the Cherokees red, white, black, and blue for the same points, and the Navahos white, blue, yellow, and black, with white and black for the lower regions and blue for the upper or ethereal world.

## Indian Time and Festivals

The North American tribes have various ways of computing time. Some of them rely merely upon the changes in season and the growth of crops for guidance

131

as to when their annual festivals and seasonal celebrations should take place. Others fix their system of festivals on the changes of the moon and the habits of animals and birds. It was, however, upon the moon that most of these peoples depended for information regarding the passage of time. Most of them assigned twelve moons to the year, while others considered thirteen a more correct number. The Kiowa reckoned the year to consist of twelve and a half moons, the other half being carried over to the year following.

The Zuñi of New Mexico allude to the year as a 'passage of time,' and call the seasons the 'steps of the year.' The first six months of the Zuñi year possess names which have an agricultural or natural significance, while the last six have ritualistic names. Captain Jonathan Carver, who travelled among the Sioux at the end of the eighteenth century, says that some tribes among them reckoned their years by moons, and made them consist of twelve lunar months, observing when thirty moons had waned to add a supernumerary one, which they termed the 'lost moon.' They gave a name to each month as follows, the year beginning at the first new moon after the spring equinox: March, Worm Moon; April, Moon of Plants; May, Moon of Flowers; June, Hot Moon; July, Buck Moon; August, Sturgeon Moon; September, Corn Moon; October, Travelling Moon; November, Beaver Moon; December, Hunting Moon; January, Cold Moon; February, Snow Moon. These people had no division into weeks, but counted days by 'sleeps,' half-days by pointing to the sun at noon, and quarter-days by the rising and setting of the sun, for all of which they possessed symbolic signs. Many tribes kept records of events by means of such signs, as has already been indicated. The eastern Sioux measure time by knotted leather thongs, similar to the *quipos* of the ancient Peruvians. Other tribes have even more primitive methods. The Hupa of California tell a person's age by examining his teeth. The Maidu divide the seasons into Rain Season, Leaf Season, Dry Season, and Falling-leaf Season. The Pima of Southern Arizona record events by means of notched sticks, which no one but the persons who mark them can understand.

The chief reason for the computation of time among savage peoples is the correct observance of religious festivals. With the rude methods at their command they are not always able to hit upon the exact date on which these should occur. These festivals are often of a highly elaborate nature, and occupy many days in their celebration, the most minute attention being paid to the proper performance of the various rites connected with them. They consist for the most part of a preliminary fast, followed by symbolic dances or magical ceremonies, and concluding with a gluttonous orgy. Most of these observances possess great similarity one to another, and visible differences may be accounted for by circumstances of environment or seasonal variations.

When the white man first came into contact with the Algonquian race it was observed that they held regularly recurring festivals to celebrate the ripening of fruits and grain, and more irregular feasts to mark the return of wild-fowl and the hunting season in general. Dances were engaged in, and heroic songs chanted. Indeed, the entire observance appears to have been identical in its general features with the festival of to-day.

One of the most remarkable of these celebrations is that of the Creeks called the 'Busk,' a contraction for its native name, Pushkita. Commencing with a rigorous fast which lasts three days, the entire tribe assembles on the fourth day to watch the high-priest produce a new fire by means of friction. From this flame the members of the tribe are supplied, and feasting and dancing are then engaged in for three days. Four logs are arranged in the form of a cross pointing to the four quarters of the earth, and burnt as an offering to the four winds.

### The Buffalo Dance

The Mandans, a Dakota tribe, each year celebrate as their principal festival the Buffalo Dance, a feast which marks the return of the buffalo-hunting season. Eight men wearing buffalo-skins on their backs, and painted black, red, or white, imitate the actions of buffaloes. Each of them holds a rattle in his right hand and a slender rod six feet long in his left, and carries a bunch of green willow boughs on his back. The ceremony is held at the season of the year when the willow is in full leaf. The dancers take up their positions at four different points of a canoe to represent the four cardinal points of the compass. Two men dressed as grizzly bears stand beside the canoe, growling and threatening to spring upon any one who interferes with the ceremony. The bystanders throw them pieces of food, which are at once pounced upon by two other men, and carried off by them to the prairie. During the ceremony the old men of the tribe beat upon sacks, chanting prayers for the success of the buffalo-hunt. On the fourth day a man enters the camp in the guise of an evil spirit, and is driven from the vicinity with stones and curses.

The elucidation of this ceremony may perhaps be as

follows : From some one of the four points of the compass the buffalo must come ; therefore all are requested to send goodly supplies. The men dressed as bears symbolize the wild beasts which might deflect the progress of the herds of buffalo toward the territory of the tribe, and therefore must be placated. The demon who visits the camp after the ceremony is, of course, famine.

### Dance-Festivals of the Hopi

The most highly developed North American festival system is that of the Hopi or Moqui of Arizona, the observances of which are almost of a theatrical nature. All the Pueblo Indians, of whom the Hopi are a division, possess similar festivals, which recur at various seasons or under the auspices of different totem clans or secret societies. Most of these 'dances' are arranged by the Katcina clan, and take place in dance-houses known as *kivas*. These ceremonies have their origin in the universal reverence shown to the serpent in America— a reverence based on the idea that the symbol of the serpent, tail in mouth, represented the round, full sun of August. In the summer 'dances' snake-charming feats are performed, but in the Katcina ceremony serpents are never employed.

Devil-dances are by no means uncommon among the Indians. The purpose of these is to drive evil spirits from the vicinity of the tribe.

### Medicine-Men

The native American priesthood, whether known as medicine-men, *shamans*, or wizards, were in most tribes a caste apart, exercising not only the priestly function, but those of physician and prophet as well. The name 'medicine-men,' therefore, is scarcely a misnomer.

135

They were skilled in the handling of occult forces such as hypnotism, and thus exercised unlimited sway over the rank and file of the tribe. But we shall first consider them in their religious aspect. In many of the Indian tribes the priesthood was a hereditary office; in others it was obtained through natural fitness or revelation in dreams. With the Cherokees, for example, the seventh son of a family was usually marked out as a suitable person for the priesthood. As a rule the religious body did not share in the general life of the tribe, from which to a great degree it isolated itself. For example, Bartram in his *Travels in the Carolinas* describes the younger priests of the Creeks as being arrayed in white robes, and carrying on their heads or arms " a great owl-skin stuffed very ingeniously as an insignia of wisdom and divination. These bachelors are also distinguishable from the other people by their taciturnity, grave and solemn counten-ance, dignified step, and singing to themselves songs or hymns in a low, sweet voice as they stroll about the towns." To add to the feeling of awe which they inspired among the laymen of the tribe, the priests conversed with one another in a secret tongue. Thus the magical formulæ of some of the Algonquin priests were not in the ordinary language, but in a dialect of their own invention. The Choctaws, Cherokees, and Zuñi employed similar esoteric dialects, all of which are now known to be merely modifications of their several tribal languages, fortified with obsolete words, or else mere borrowings from the idioms of other tribes.

### Medicine-Men as Healers

It was, however, as healers that the medicine-men were pre-eminent. The Indian assigns all illness or bodily discomfort to supernatural agency. He cannot comprehend that indisposition may arise within his own system, but believes that it must necessarily proceed from some external source. Some supernatural being whom he has offended, the soul of an animal which he has slain, or perhaps a malevolent sorcerer, torments him. If the bodies of mankind were not afflicted in this mysterious manner their owners would endure for ever. When the Indian falls sick he betakes himself to a medicine-man, to whom he relates his symptoms, at the same time acquainting him with any circumstances which he may suspect of having brought about his condition. If he has slain a deer and omitted the usual formula of placation afterward he suspects that the spirit of the beast is actively harming him. Should he have shot a bird and have subsequently observed any of the same species near his dwelling, he will almost invariably conclude that they were bent on a mission of vengeance and have by some means injured him. The medicine-man, in the first instance, may give his patient some simple native remedy. If this treatment does not avail he will arrange to go to the sufferer's lodge for the purpose of making a more thorough examination. Having located the seat of the pain, he will blow upon it several times, and then proceed to massage it vigorously, invoking the while the aid of the natural enemy of the spirit which he suspects is tormenting the sick man. Thus if a deer's spirit be suspected he will call upon the mountain lion or the Great Dog to drive it away, but if a bird of any of the smaller varieties he will invoke the Great Eagle who dwells in the zenith to slay or devour it. Upon the supposed approach of these potent beings he will become more excited, and, vigorously slapping the patient, will chant incantations

137

in a loud and sonorous voice, which are supposed to hasten the advent of the friendly beings whom he has summoned. At last, producing by sleight of hand an image of the disturbing spirit worked in bone, he calls for a vessel of boiling water, into which he promptly plunges the supposed cause of his patient's illness. The bone figure is withdrawn from the boiling water after a space, and on being examined may be found to have one or more scores on its surface. Each of these shows that it has already slain its man, and the patient is assured that had the native Æsculapius not adopted severe measures the malign spirit would have added him to the number of its victims.

Should these methods not result in a cure, others are resorted to. The patient is regaled with the choicest food and drink, while incantations are chanted and music performed to frighten away the malign influences.

### Professional Etiquette

The priestly class is not given to levying exorbitant fees upon its patients. As a rule the Indian medicine-man strongly resents any allusion to a fee. Should the payment be of a perishable nature, such as food, he usually shares it with his relatives, brother-priests, or even his patients, but should it consist of something that may be retained, such as cloth, teeth necklaces, or skins, he will carefully hoard it to afford provision for his old age. The Indian practitioner is strongly of opinion that white doctors are of little service in the cure of native illnesses. White medicine, he says, is good only for white men, and Indian medicine for the red man ; in which conclusion he is probably justified.

### Journeys in Spirit-land

In many Indian myths we read how the *shamans*, singly or in companies, seek the Spirit-land, either to search for the souls of those who are ill, but not yet dead, or to seek advice from supernatural beings. These thaumaturgical practices were usually undertaken by three medicine-men acting in concert. Falling into a trance, in which their souls were supposed to become temporarily disunited from their bodies, they would follow the track of the sick man's spirit into the spirit-world. The order in which they travelled was determined by the relative strength of their guardian spirits, those with the strongest being first and last, and he who had the weakest being placed in the middle. If the sick man's track turned to the left they said he would die, but if to the right, he would recover. From the trail they could also divine whether any supernatural danger was near, and the foremost priest would utter a magic chant to avert such evils if they came from the front, while if the danger came from the rear the incantation was sung by the priest who came last. Generally their sojourn occupied one or two nights, and, having rescued the soul of the patient, they returned to place it in his body.

Not only was the *shaman* endowed with the power of projecting his own 'astral body' into the Land of Spirits. By placing cedar-wood charms in the hands of persons who had not yet received a guardian spirit he could impart to them his clairvoyant gifts, enabling them to visit the Spirit-land and make any observations required by him.

The souls of chiefs, instead of following the usual route, went directly to the sea-shore, where only the most gifted *shamans* could follow their trail. The sea was regarded as the highway to the supernatural regions. A sick man was in the greatest peril at high water, but when the tide was low the danger was less.

The means adopted by the medicine-men to lure ghosts away from their pursuit of a soul was to create an 'astral' deer. The ghosts would turn from hunting the man's soul to follow that of the beast.

## The Savage and Religion

It cannot be said that the religious sense was exceptionally strong in the mind of the North American Indian. But this was due principally to the stage of culture at which he stood, and in some cases still stands. In man in his savage or barbarian condition the sense of reverence as we conceive it is small, and its place is largely filled by fear and superstition. It is only at a later stage, when civilizing influences have to some extent banished the grosser terrors of animism and fetishism, that the gods reveal themselves in a more spiritual aspect.

# CHAPTER III: ALGONQUIAN MYTHS AND LEGENDS

## Glooskap and Malsum

THE Algonquin Indians have perhaps a more extensive mythology than the majority of Indian peoples, and as they have been known to civilization for several centuries their myths have the advantage of having been thoroughly examined.

One of the most interesting figures in their pantheon is Glooskap, which means 'The Liar'; but so far from an affront being intended to the deity by this appellation, it was bestowed as a compliment to his craftiness, cunning being regarded as one of the virtues by all savage peoples.

Glooskap and his brother Malsum, the Wolf, were twins, and from this we may infer that they were the opposites of a dualistic system, Glooskap standing for what seems 'good' to the savage, and Malsum for all that was 'bad.'[1] Their mother died at their birth, and out of her body Glooskap formed the sun and moon, animals, fishes, and the human race, while the malicious Malsum made mountains, valleys, serpents, and every manner of thing which he considered would inconvenience the race of men.

Each of the brothers possessed a secret as to what would kill him, as do many other beings in myth and fairy story, notably Llew Llaw Gyffes in Welsh romance.

Malsum asked Glooskap in what manner he could be killed, and the elder brother, to try his sincerity, replied that the only way in which his life could be taken was by the touch of an owl's feather—or, as

---

[1] This 'goodness' and 'badness,' however, is purely relative and of modern origin, such deities, as already explained, being figures in a light-and-darkness myth.

some variants of the myth say, by that of a flowering rush. Malsum in his turn confided to Glooskap that he could only perish by a blow from a fern-root. The malicious Wolf, taking his bow, brought down an owl, and while Glooskap slept struck him with a feather plucked from its wing. Glooskap immediately expired, but to Malsum's chagrin came to life again. This tale is surprisingly reminiscent of the Scandinavian myth of Balder, who would only die if struck by a sprig of mistletoe by his brother Hodur. Like Balder, Glooskap is a sun-god, as is well proved by the circumstance that when he dies he does not fail to revive.

But Malsum resolved to learn his brother's secret and to destroy him at the first opportunity. Glooskap had told him subsequently to his first attempt that only a pine-root could kill him, and with this Malsum struck him while he slept as before, but Glooskap, rising up and laughing, drove Malsum into the forest, and seated himself by a stream, where he murmured, as if musing to himself: "Only a flowering rush can kill me." Now he said this because he knew that Quah-beet, the Great Beaver, was hidden among the rushes on the bank of the stream and would hear every word he uttered. The Beaver went at once to Malsum and told him what he regarded as his brother's vital secret. The wicked Malsum was so glad that he promised to give the Beaver whatever he might ask for. But when the beast asked for wings like a pigeon Malsum burst into mocking laughter and cried: "Ho, you with the tail like a file, what need have you of wings?" At this the Beaver was wroth, and, going to Glooskap, made a clean breast of what he had done. Glooskap, now thoroughly infuriated, dug up a fern-root, and, rushing into the recesses of the forest, sought out his treacherous brother and with a blow of the fatal plant struck him dead.

## Scandinavian Analogies

But although Malsum was slain he subsequently appears in Algonquian myth as Lox, or Loki, the chief of the wolves, a mischievous and restless spirit. In his account of the Algonquian mythology Charles Godfrey Leland appears to think that the entire system has been sophisticated by Norse mythology filtering through the Eskimo. Although the probabilities are against such a theory, there are many points in common between the two systems, as we shall see later, and among them few are more striking than the fact that the Scandinavian and Algonquian evil influences possess one and the same name.

When Glooskap had completed the world he made man and the smaller supernatural beings, such as fairies and dwarfs. He formed man from the trunk of an ash-tree, and the elves from its bark. Like Odin, he trained two birds to bring him the news of the world, but their absences were so prolonged that he selected a black and a white wolf as his attendants. He waged a strenuous and exterminating warfare on the evil monsters which then infested the world, and on the sorcerers and witches who were harmful to man. He levelled the hills and restrained the forces of nature in his mighty struggles, in which he towered to giant stature, his head and shoulders rising high above the clouds. Yet in his dealings with men he was gentle and quietly humorous, not to say ingenuous.

On one occasion he sought out a giant sorcerer named Win-pe, one of the most powerful of the evil influences then dwelling upon the earth. Win-pe shot upward till his head was above the tallest pine of the forest, but Glooskap, with a god-like laugh, grew till his head reached the stars, and tapped the wizard gently with the butt of his bow, so that he fell dead at his feet.

But although he exterminated many monsters and placed a check upon the advance of the forces of evil, Glooskap did not find that the race of men grew any better or wiser. In fact, the more he accomplished on their behalf the worse they became, until at last they reached such a pitch of evil conduct that the god resolved to quit the world altogether. But, with a feeling of consideration still for the beings he had created, he announced that within the next seven years he would grant to all and sundry any request they might make. A great many people were desirous of profiting by this offer, but it was with the utmost difficulty that they could discover where Glooskap was. Those who did find him and who chose injudiciously were severely punished, while those whose desires were reasonable were substantially rewarded.

### Glooskap's Gifts

Four Indians who won to Glooskap's abode found it a place of magical delights, a land fairer than the mind could conceive. Asked by the god what had brought them thither, one replied that his heart was evil and that anger had made him its slave, but that he wished to be meek and pious. The second, a poor man, desired to be rich, and the third, who was of low estate and despised by the folk of his tribe, wished to be universally honoured and respected. The fourth was a vain man, conscious of his good looks, whose appearance was eloquent of conceit. Although he was tall, he had stuffed fur into his moccasins to make him appear still taller, and his wish was that he might become bigger than any man of his tribe and that he might live for ages.

144

# GLOOSKAP AND THE BABY

Glooskap drew four small boxes from his medicine-bag and gave one to each, desiring that they should not open them until they reached home. When the first three arrived at their respective lodges each opened his box, and found therein an unguent of great fragrance and richness, with which he rubbed himself. The wicked man became meek and patient, the poor man speedily grew wealthy, and the despised man became stately and respected. But the conceited man had stopped on his way home in a clearing in the woods, and, taking out his box, had anointed himself with the ointment it contained. His wish also was granted, but not exactly in the manner he expected, for he was changed into a pine-tree, the first of the species, and the tallest tree of the forest at that.

### Glooskap and the Baby

Glooskap, having conquered the Kewawkqu', a race of giants and magicians, and the Medecolin, who were cunning sorcerers, and Pamola, a wicked spirit of the night, besides hosts of fiends, goblins, cannibals, and witches, felt himself great indeed, and boasted to a certain woman that there was nothing left for him to subdue.

But the woman laughed and said : "Are you quite sure, Master ? There is still one who remains unconquered, and nothing can overcome him."

In some surprise Glooskap inquired the name of this mighty individual.

" He is called Wasis," replied the woman ; " but I strongly advise you to have no dealings with him."

Wasis was only the baby, who sat on the floor sucking a piece of maple-sugar and crooning a little song to himself. Now Glooskap had never married and was quite ignorant of how children are managed,

145

but with perfect confidence he smiled to the baby and asked it to come to him. The baby smiled back to him, but never moved, whereupon Glooskap imitated the beautiful song of a certain bird. Wasis, however, paid no heed to him, but went on sucking his maple-sugar. Glooskap, unaccustomed to such treatment, lashed himself into a furious rage, and in terrible and threatening accents ordered Wasis to come crawling to him at once. But Wasis burst into direful howling, which quite drowned the god's thunderous accents, and for all the threatenings of the deity he would not budge. Glooskap, now thoroughly aroused, brought all his magical resources to his aid. He recited the most terrible spells, the most dreadful incantations. He sang the songs which raise the dead, and which sent the devil scurrying to the nethermost depths of the pit. But Wasis evidently seemed to think this was all some sort of a game, for he merely smiled wearily and looked a trifle bored. At last Glooskap in despair rushed from the hut, while Wasis, sitting on the floor, cried, "Goo, goo," and crowed triumphantly. And to this day the Indians say that when a baby cries "Goo" he remembers the time when he conquered the mighty Glooskap.

### Glooskap's Farewell

At length the day on which Glooskap was to leave the earth arrived, and to celebrate the event he caused a great feast to be made on the shores of Lake Minas. It was attended by all the animals, and when it drew to a close Glooskap entered his great canoe and slowly drifted out of sight. When they could see him no longer they still heard his beautiful singing growing fainter and fainter in the distance, until at last it died away altogether. Then a strange thing happened.

## HOW GLOOSKAP CAUGHT THE SUMMER

The beasts, who up to this time had spoken but one language, could no longer understand each other, and in confusion fled away, never again to meet in friendly converse until Glooskap shall return and revive the halcyon days of the Golden Age.

This tradition of Glooskap strikingly recalls that of the Mexican god Quetzalcoatl, who drifted from the shores of Mexico eastward toward the fabled land of Tlapallan, whence he had originally come. Glooskap, like the Mexican deity alluded to, is, as has already been indicated, a sun-god, or, more properly speaking, a son of the sun, who has come to earth on a mission of enlightenment and civilization, to render the world habitable for mankind and to sow the seeds of the arts, domestic and agricultural. Quetzalcoatl disappeared toward the east because it was the original home of his father, the sun, and not toward the west, which is merely the sun's resting-place for the night. But Glooskap drifted westward, as most sun-children do.

### How Glooskap Caught the Summer

A very beautiful myth tells how Glooskap captured the Summer. The form in which it is preserved is a kind of poetry possessing something in the nature of metre, which until a few generations ago was recited by many Algonquian firesides. A long time ago Glooskap wandered very far north to the Ice-country, and, feeling tired and cold, sought shelter at a wigwam where dwelt a great giant—the giant Winter. Winter received the god hospitably, filled a pipe of tobacco for him, and entertained him with charming stories of the old time as he smoked. All the time Winter was casting his spell over Glooskap, for as he talked drowsily and monotonously he gave forth a freezing atmosphere, so that Glooskap first dozed and then fell into a deep sleep—the heavy slumber of the winter season. For six whole months he slept; then the spell of the frost arose from his brain and he awoke. He took his way homeward and southward, and the farther south he fared the warmer it felt, and the flowers began to spring up around his steps.

At length he came to a vast, trackless forest, where, under primeval trees, many little people were dancing. The queen of these folk was Summer, a most exquisitely beautiful, if very tiny, creature. Glooskap caught the queen up in his great hand, and, cutting a long lasso from the hide of a moose, secured it round her tiny frame. Then he ran away, letting the cord trail loosely behind him.

### The Elves of Light

The tiny people, who were the Elves of Light, came clamouring shrilly after him, pulling frantically at the lasso. But as Glooskap ran the cord ran out, and pull as they might they were left far behind.

Northward he journeyed once more, and came to the wigwam of Winter. The giant again received him hospitably, and began to tell the old stories whose vague charm had exercised such a fascination upon the god. But Glooskap in his turn began to speak. Summer was lying in his bosom, and her strength and heat sent forth such powerful magic that at length Winter began to show signs of distress. The sweat poured profusely down his face, and gradually he commenced to melt, as did his dwelling. Then slowly nature awoke, the song of birds was heard, first faintly, then more clearly and joyously. The thin green shoots of the young grass appeared, and the dead leaves of last autumn were carried down to the river by the melting snow. Lastly the fairies came out, and

Glooskap, leaving Summer with them, once more bent his steps southward.

This is obviously a nature-myth conceived by a people dwelling in a climate where the rigours of winter gave way for a more or less brief space only to the blandishments of summer. To them winter was a giant, and summer an elf of pigmy proportions. The stories told during the winter season are eloquent of the life led by people dwelling in a sub-arctic climate, where the traditional tale, the father of epic poetry, whiles away the long dark hours, while the winter tempest roars furiously without and the heaped-up snow renders the daily occupation of the hunter impossible.

### Glooskap's Wigwam

The Indians say that Glooskap lives far away, no one knows where, in a very great wigwam. His chief occupation is making arrows, and it would appear that each of these stands for a day. One side of his wigwam is covered with arrows, and when his lodge shall be filled with them the last great day will arrive. Then he will call upon his army of good spirits and go forth to attack Malsum in a wonderful canoe, which by magical means can be made to expand so as to hold an army or contract so that it may be carried in the palm of the hand. The war with his evil brother will be one of extermination, and not one single individual on either side will be left. But the good will go to Glooskap's beautiful abode, and all will be well at last.

### The Snow-Lodge

Chill breezes had long forewarned the geese of the coming cold season, and the constant cry from above of "Honk, honk," told the Indians that the birds' migration was in progress.

The buffalo-hunters of the Blackfeet, an Algonquian tribe, were abroad with the object of procuring the thick robes and the rich meat which would keep them warm and provide good fare through the desolate winter moons. Sacred Otter had been lucky. Many buffaloes had fallen to him, and he was busily occupied in skinning them. But while the braves plied the knife quickly and deftly they heeded not the dun, lowering clouds heavy with tempest hanging like a black curtain over the northern horizon. Suddenly the clouds swooped down from their place in the heavens like a flight of black eagles, and with a roar the blizzard was upon them.

Sacred Otter and his son crouched beneath the carcass of a dead buffalo for shelter. But the air was frore as water in which the ice is floating, and he knew that they would quickly perish unless they could find some better protection from the bitter wind. So he made a small *tepee*, or tent, out of the buffalo's hide, and both crawled inside. Against this crazy shelter the snow quickly gathered and drifted, so that soon the inmates of the tiny lodge sank into a comfortable drowse induced by the gentle warmth. As Sacred Otter slept he dreamed. Away in the distance he descried a great *tepee*, crowned with a colour like the gold of sunlight, and painted with a cluster of stars symbolic of the North. The ruddy disc of the sun was pictured at the back, and to this was affixed the tail of the Sacred Buffalo. The skirts of the *tepee* were painted to represent ice, and on its side had been drawn four yellow legs with green claws, typical of the Thunder-bird. A buffalo in glaring red frowned above the door, and bunches of crow-feathers, with small bells attached, swung and tinkled in the breeze.

Sacred Otter, surprised at the unusual nature of the

paintings, stood before the *tepee* lost in admiration of its decorations, when he was startled to hear a voice say:
"Who walks round my *tepee*? Come in—come in!"

### The Lord of Cold Weather

Sacred Otter entered, and beheld a tall, white-haired man, clothed all in white, sitting at the back of the lodge, of which he was the sole occupant. Sacred Otter took a seat, but the owner of the *tepee* never looked his way, smoking on in stolid silence. Before him was an earthen altar, on which was laid juniper, as in the Sun ceremonial. His face was painted yellow, with a red line in the region of the mouth, and another across the eyes to the ears. Across his breast he wore a mink-skin, and round his waist small strips of otter-skin, to all of which bells were attached. For a long time he kept silence, but at length he laid down his black stone pipe and addressed Sacred Otter as follows:

"I am Es-tonea-pesta, the Lord of Cold Weather, and this, my dwelling, is the Snow-tepee, or Yellow Paint Lodge. I control and send the driving snow and biting winds from the Northland. You are here because I have taken pity upon you, and on your son who was caught in the blizzard with you. Take this Snow-tepee with its symbols and medicines. Take also this mink-skin tobacco-pouch, this black stone pipe, and my supernatural power. You must make a *tepee* similar to this on your return to camp."

The Lord of Cold Weather then minutely explained to Sacred Otter the symbols of which he must make use in painting the lodge, and gave him the songs and ceremonial connected with it. At this juncture Sacred Otter awoke. He observed that the storm had abated somewhat, and as soon as it grew fair enough he and his son crawled from their shelter and tramped home waist-high through the soft snow. Sacred Otter spent the long, cold nights in making a model of the Snow-tepee and painting it as he had been directed in his dream. He also collected the 'medicines' necessary for the ceremonial, and in the spring, when new lodges were made, he built and painted the Snow-tepee.

The power of Sacred Otter waxed great because of his possession of the Snow-lodge which the Lord of Cold had vouchsafed to him in dream. Soon was it proved. Once more while hunting buffalo he and several companions were caught in a blizzard when many a weary mile from camp. They appealed to Sacred Otter to utilize the 'medicine' of the Lord of Cold. Directing that several women and children who were with the party should be placed on sledges, and that the men should go in advance and break a passage through the snow for the horses, he took the mink tobacco-pouch and the black stone pipe he had received from the Cold-maker and commenced to smoke. He blew the smoke in the direction whence the storm came and prayed to the Lord of Cold to have pity on the people. Gradually the storm-clouds broke and cleared and on every side the blue sky was seen. The people hastened on, as they knew the blizzard was only being held back for a space. But their camp was at hand, and they soon reached it in safety.

Never again, however, would Sacred Otter use his mystic power. For he dreaded that he might offend the Lord of Cold. And who could afford to do that?

### The Star-Maiden

A pretty legend of the Chippeways, an Algonquian tribe, tells how Algon, a hunter, won for his bride the daughter of a star. While walking over the prairies he discovered a circular pathway, worn as if by the tread

of many feet, though there were no foot-marks visible
outside its bounds. The young hunter, who had never
before encountered one of these 'fairy rings,' was filled
with surprise at the discovery, and hid himself in the
long grass to see whether an explanation might not be
forthcoming. He had not long to wait. In a little
while he heard the sound of music, so faint and
sweet that it surpassed anything he had ever dreamed
of. The strains grew fuller and richer, and as they
seemed to come from above he turned his eyes
toward the sky. Far in the blue he could see a tiny
white speck like a floating cloud. Nearer and nearer it
came, and the astonished hunter saw that it was no
cloud, but a dainty osier car, in which were seated
twelve beautiful maidens. The music he had heard
was the sound of their voices as they sang strange and
magical songs. Descending into the charmed ring,
they danced round and round with such exquisite grace
and abandon that it was a sheer delight to watch them.
But after the first moments of dazzled surprise Algon
had eyes only for the youngest of the group, a slight,
vivacious creature, so fragile and delicate that it seemed
to the stalwart hunter that a breath would blow her
away.

He was, indeed, seized with a fierce passion for the
dainty sprite, and he speedily decided to spring from
the grass and carry her off. But the pretty creatures
were too quick for him. The fairy of his choice skilfully eluded his grasp and rushed to the car. The
others followed, and in a moment they were soaring
up in the air, singing a sweet, unearthly song. The
disconsolate hunter returned to his lodge, but try as
he might he could not get the thought of the Star-
maiden out of his head, and next day, long before the
hour of the fairies' arrival, he lay in the grass awaiting

the sweet sounds that would herald their approach. At
length the car appeared. The twelve ethereal beings
danced as before. Again Algon made a desperate
attempt to seize the youngest, and again he was unsuccessful.

"Let us stay," said one of the Star-maidens.
"Perhaps the mortal wishes to teach us his earthly
dances." But the youngest sister would not hear of
it, and they all rose out of sight in their osier basket.

### Algon's Strategy

Poor Algon returned home more unhappy than ever.
All night he lay awake dreaming of the pretty, elusive
creature who had wound a chain of gossamer round his
heart and brain, and early in the morning he repaired
to the enchanted spot. Casting about for some means
of gaining his end, he came upon the hollow trunk of
a tree in which a number of mice gambolled. With
the aid of the charms in his 'medicine'-bag he turned
himself into one of these little animals, thinking the
fair sisters would never pierce his disguise.

That day when the osier car descended its occupants
alighted and danced merrily as they were wont in the
magic circle, till the youngest saw the hollow tree-
trunk (which had not been there on the previous day)
and turned to fly. Her sisters laughed at her fears,
and tried to reassure her by overturning the tree-trunk.
The mice scampered in all directions, and were quickly
pursued by the Star-maidens, who killed them all
except Algon. The latter regained his own shape just
as the youngest fairy raised her hand to strike him.
Clasping her in his arms, he bore her to his village,
while her frightened sisters ascended to their Star-
country.

Arrived at his home, Algon married the maiden, and

by his kindness and gentleness soon won her affection.
However, her thoughts still dwelt on her own people,
and though she indulged her sorrow only in secret,
lest it should trouble her husband, she never ceased to
lament her lost home.

### The Star-Maiden's Escape

One day while she was out with her little son she
made a basket of osiers, like the one in which she had
first came to earth. Gathering together some flowers
and gifts for the Star-people, she took the child with
her into the basket, sang the magical songs she still
remembered, and soon floated up to her own country,
where she was welcomed by the king, her father.

Algon's grief was bitter indeed when he found that
his wife and child had left him. But he had no means
of following them. Every day he would go to the
magic circle on the prairie and give vent to his sorrow,
but the years went past and there was no sign of his
dear ones returning.

Meanwhile the woman and her son had almost
forgotten Algon and the earth-country. However,
when the boy grew old enough to hear the story he
wished to go and see his father. His mother consented, and arranged to go with him. While they
were preparing to descend the Star-people said :

" Bring Algon with you when you return, and ask
him to bring some feature from every beast and bird
he has killed in the chase."

Algon, who had latterly spent almost all his time at
the charmed circle, was overjoyed to see his wife and
son come back to him, and willingly agreed to go with
them to the Star-country. He worked very hard to
obtain a specimen of all the rare and curious birds and
beasts in his land, and when at last he had gathered

the relics—a claw of one, a feather of another, and so on—he piled them in the osier car, climbed in himself with his wife and boy, and set off to the Star-country.

The people there were delighted with the curious gifts Algon had brought them, and, being permitted by their king to take one apiece, they did so. Those who took a tail or a claw of any beast at once became the quadruped represented by the fragment, and those who took the wings of birds became birds themselves. Algon and his wife and son took the feathers of a white falcon and flew down to the prairies, where their descendants may still be seen.

### Cloud-Carrier and the Star-Folk

A handsome youth once dwelt with his parents on the banks of Lake Huron. The old people were very proud of their boy, and intended that he should become a great warrior. When he grew old enough to prepare his 'medicine'-bag he set off into the forest for that purpose. As he journeyed he grew weary, and lay down to sleep, and while he slept he heard a gentle voice whisper :

"Cloud-carrier, I have come to fetch you. Follow me."

The young man started to his feet.

"I am dreaming. It is but an illusion," he muttered to himself, as he gazed at the owner of the soft voice, who was a damsel of such marvellous beauty that the sleepy eyes of Cloud-carrier were quite dazzled.

"Follow me," she said again, and rose softly from the ground like thistledown. To his surprise the youth rose along with her, as lightly and as easily. Higher they went, and still higher, far above the tree-tops, and into the sky, till they passed at length through an opening in the spreading vault, and Cloud-carrier saw that he was in the country of the Star-people, and that his beautiful guide was no mortal maiden, but a supernatural being. So fascinated was he by her sweetness and gentleness that he followed her without question till they came to a large lodge. Entering it at the invitation of the Star-maiden, Cloud-carrier found it filled with weapons and ornaments of silver, worked in strange and grotesque designs. For a time he wandered through the lodge admiring and praising all he saw, his warrior-blood stirring at the sight of the rare weapons. Suddenly the lady cried :

" Hush ! My brother approaches ! Let me hide you. Quick ! "

The young man crouched in a corner, and the damsel threw a richly coloured scarf over him. Scarcely had she done so when a grave and dignified warrior stalked into the lodge.

" Nemissa, my dear sister," he said, after a moment's pause, " have you not been forbidden to speak to the Earth-people ? Perhaps you imagine you have hidden the young man, but you have not." Then, turning from the blushing Nemissa to Cloud-carrier, he added, good-naturedly :

" If you stay long there you will be very hungry. Come out and let us have a talk."

The youth did as he was bid, and the brother of Nemissa gave him a pipe and a bow and arrows. He gave him also Nemissa for his wife, and for a long time they lived together very happily.

### The Star-Country

Now the young man observed that his brother-in-law was in the habit of going away every day by himself, and feeling curious to know what his business might be, he asked one morning whether he might accompany him.

The brother-in-law consented readily, and the two

set off. Travelling in the Star-country was very pleasant. The foliage was richer than that of the earth, the flowers more delicately coloured, the air softer and more fragrant, and the birds and beasts more graceful and harmless. As the day wore on to noon Cloud-carrier became very hungry.

"When can we get something to eat?" he asked his brother-in-law.

"Very soon," was the reassuring reply. "We are just going to make a repast." As he spoke they came to a large opening, through which they could see the lodges and lakes and forests of the earth. At one place some hunters were preparing for the chase. By the banks of a river some women were gathering reeds, and down in a village a number of children were playing happily.

"Do you see that boy down there in the centre of the group?" said the brother of Nemissa, and as he spoke he threw something at the child. The poor boy fell down instantly, and was carried, more dead than alive, to the nearest hut.

### The Sacrifice

Cloud-carrier was much perplexed at the act of his supernatural relative. He saw the medicine-men gather round the child and chant prayers for his recovery.

"It is the will of Manitou," said one priest, "that we offer a white dog as a sacrifice."

So they procured a white dog, skinned and roasted it, and put it on a plate. It flew up in the air and provided a meal for the hungry Cloud-carrier and his companion. The child recovered and returned to his play.

"Your medicine-men," said Nemissa's brother, "get

a great reputation for wisdom simply because they direct the people to me. You think they are very clever, but all they do is to advise you to sacrifice to me. It is I who recover the sick."

Cloud-carrier found in this spot a new source of interest, but at length the delights of the celestial regions began to pall. He longed for the companionship of his own kin, for the old commonplace pastimes of the Earth-country. He became, in short, very homesick, and begged his wife's permission to return to earth. Very reluctantly she consented.

"Remember," she said, "that I shall have the power to recall you when I please, for you will still be my husband. And above all do not marry an Earth-woman, or you will taste of my vengeance."

The young man readily promised to respect her injunctions. So he went to sleep, and awoke a little later to find himself lying on the grass close by his father's lodge. His parents greeted him joyfully. He had been absent, they told him, for more than a year, and they had not hoped to see him again.

The remembrance of his sojourn among the Star-people faded gradually to a dim recollection. By and by, forgetting the wife he had left there, he married a young and handsome woman belonging to his own village. Four days after the wedding she died, but Cloud-carrier failed to draw a lesson from this unfortunate occurrence. He married a third wife. But one day he was missing, and was never again heard of. His Star-wife had recalled him to the sky.

### The Snow-Man Husband

In a northern village of the Algonquins dwelt a young girl so exquisitely beautiful that she attracted hosts of admirers. The fame of her beauty spread far and wide, and warriors and hunters thronged to her father's lodge in order to behold her. By universal consent she received the name of 'Handsome.' One of the braves who was most assiduous in paying her his addresses was surnamed 'Elegant,' because of the richness of his costume and the nobility of his features. Desiring to know his fate, the young man confided the secret of his love for Handsome to another of his suitors, and proposed that they two should that day approach her and ask her hand in marriage. But the coquettish maiden dismissed the young braves disdainfully, and, to add to the indignity of her refusal, repeated it in public outside her father's lodge. Elegant, who was extremely sensitive, was so humiliated and mortified that he fell into ill-health. A deep melancholy settled on his mind. He refused all nourishment, and for hours he would sit with his eyes fixed on the ground in moody contemplation. A profound sense of disgrace seized upon him, and notwithstanding the arguments of his relations and comrades he sank deeper into lethargy. Finally he took to his bed, and even when his family were preparing for the annual migration customary with the tribe he refused to rise from it, although they removed the tent from above his head and packed it up for transport.

### The Lover's Revenge

After his family had gone Elegant appealed to his guardian spirit or totem to revenge him on the maiden who had thus cast him into despondency. Going from lodge to lodge, he collected all the rags that he could find, and, kneading snow over a framework of animals' bones, he moulded it into the shape of a man, which he attired in the tatters he had gathered, finally covering the whole with brilliant beads and gaudy feathers so

that it presented a very imposing appearance. By
magic art he animated this singular figure, placed a bow
and arrows into its hands, and bestowed on it the name
of Moowis.

Together the pair set out for the new encampment
of the tribe. The brilliant appearance of Moowis
caused him to be received by all with the most marked
distinction. The chieftain of the tribe begged him to
enter his lodge, and entertained him as an honoured
guest. But none was so struck by the bearing of the
noble-looking stranger as Handsome. Her mother
requested him to accept the hospitality of her lodge,
which he duly graced with his presence, but being unable to approach too closely to the hearth, on which a
great fire was burning, he placed a boy between him
and the blaze, in order that he should run no risk of
melting. Soon the news that Moowis was to wed
Handsome ran through the encampment, and the
nuptials were celebrated. On the following day Moowis
announced his intention of undertaking a long journey.
Handsome pleaded for leave to accompany him, but he
refused on the ground that the distance was too great
and that the fatigues and dangers of the route would
prove too much for her strength. Finally, however,
she overcame his resistance, and the two set out.

### A Strange Transformation

A rough and rugged road had to be traversed by the
newly wedded pair. On every hand they encountered
obstacles, and the unfortunate Handsome, whose feet
were cut and bleeding, found the greatest difficulty in
keeping up with her more active husband. At first it
was bitterly cold, but at length the sun came out and
shone in all his strength, so that the girl forgot her
woes and began to sing gaily. But on the appearance

of the luminary a strange transformation had slowly overtaken her spouse. At first he attempted to keep in the shade, to avoid the golden beams that he knew meant death to him, but all to no purpose. The air became gradually warmer, and slowly he dissolved and fell to pieces, so that his frenzied wife now only beheld his garments, the bones that had composed his framework, and the gaudy plumes and beads with which he had been bedecked. Long she sought his real self, thinking that some trick had been played upon her ; but at length, exhausted with fatigue and sorrow, she cast herself on the ground, and with his name on her lips breathed her last. So was Elegant avenged.

### The Spirit-Bride

A story is told of a young Algonquin brave whose bride died on the day fixed for their wedding. Before this sad event he had been the most courageous and high-spirited of warriors and the most skilful of hunters, but afterward his pride and his bravery seemed to desert him. In vain his friends urged him to seek the chase and begged him to take a greater interest in life. The more they pressed him the more melancholy he became, till at length he passed most of his time by the grave of his bride.

He was roused from his state of apathy one day, however, by hearing some old men discussing the existence of a path to the Spirit-world, which they supposed lay to the south. A gleam of hope shone in the young brave's breast, and, worn with sorrow as he was, he armed himself and set off southward. For a long time he saw no appreciable change in his surroundings—rivers, mountains, lakes, and forests similar to those of his own country environed him. But after a weary journey of many days he fancied he saw a difference. The sky was more blue, the prairie more fertile, the scenery more gloriously beautiful. From the conversation he had overheard before he set out, the young brave judged that he was nearing the Spirit-world. Just as he emerged from a spreading forest he saw before him a little lodge set high on a hill. Thinking its occupants might be able to direct him to his destination, he climbed to the lodge and accosted an aged man who stood in the doorway.

"Can you tell me the way to the Spirit-world?" he inquired.

## The Island of the Blessed

"Yes," said the old man gravely, throwing aside his cloak of swan's skin. "Only a few days ago she whom you seek rested in my lodge. If you will leave your body here you may follow her. To reach the Island of the Blessed you must cross yonder gulf you see in the distance. But I warn you the crossing will be no easy matter. Do you still wish to go?"

"Oh, yes, yes," cried the warrior eagerly, and as the words were uttered he felt himself grow suddenly lighter. The whole aspect, too, of the scene was changed. Everything looked brighter and more ethereal. He found himself in a moment walking through thickets which offered no resistance to his passage, and he knew that he was a spirit, travelling in the Spirit-world. When he reached the gulf which the old man had indicated he found to his delight a wonderful canoe ready on the shore. It was cut from a single white stone, and shone and sparkled in the sun like a jewel. The warrior lost no time in embarking, and as he put off from the shore he saw his pretty bride enter just such another canoe as his and imitate all his movements. Side by side they made for the Island of the Blessed, a

163

charming woody islet set in the middle of the water, like an emerald in silver. When they were about half-way across a sudden storm arose, and the huge waves threatened to engulf them. Many other people had embarked on the perilous waters by this time, some of whom perished in the furious tempest. But the youth and maiden still battled on bravely, never losing sight of one another. Because they were good and innocent, the Master of Life had decreed that they should arrive safely at the fair island, and after a weary struggle they felt their canoes grate on the shore.

Hand in hand the lovers walked among the beautiful sights and sounds that greeted their eyes and ears from every quarter. There was no trace of the recent storm. The sea was as smooth as glass and the sky as clear as crystal. The youth and his bride felt that they could wander on thus for ever. But at length a faint, sweet voice bade the former return to his home in the Earth-country.

### The Master of Life

"You must finish your mortal course," it whispered softly. "You will become a great chief among your own people. Rule wisely and well, and when your earthly career is over you shall return to your bride, who will retain her youth and beauty for ever."

The young man recognized the voice as that of the Master of Life, and sadly bade farewell to the woman. He was not without hope now, however, but looked forward to another and more lasting reunion.

Returning to the old man's lodge, he regained his body, went home as the gentle voice on the island had commanded him, and became a father to his people for many years. By his just and kindly rule he won the hearts of all who knew him, and ensured for himself a safe passage to the Island of the Blessed, where he arrived at last to partake of everlasting happiness with his beautiful bride.

## Otter-Heart

In the heart of a great forest lay a nameless little lake, and by its side dwelt two children. Wicked magicians had slain their parents while they were yet of tender years, and the little orphans were obliged to fend for themselves. The younger of the two, a boy, learned to shoot with bow and arrow, and he soon acquired such skill that he rarely returned from a hunting expedition without a specimen of his prowess in the shape of a bird or a hare, which his elder sister would dress and cook.

When the boy grew older he naturally felt the need of some companionship other than that of his sister. During his long, solitary journeys in search of food he thought a good deal about the great world outside the barrier of the still, silent forest. He longed for the sound of human voices to replace the murmuring of the trees and the cries of the birds.

"Are there no Indians but ourselves in the whole world?" he would ask wistfully.

"I do not know," his sister invariably replied. Busying herself cheerfully about her household tasks, she knew nothing of the strange thoughts that were stirring in the mind of her brother.

But one day he returned from the chase in so discontented a mood that his unrest could no longer pass unnoticed. In response to solicitous inquiries from his sister, he said abruptly:

"Make me ten pairs of moccasins. To-morrow I am going to travel into the great world."

The girl was much disturbed by this communication,

but like a good Indian maiden she did as he requested her and kept a respectful silence.

Early on the following morning the youth, whose name was Otter-heart, set out on his quest. He soon came to a clearing in the forest, but to his disappointment he found that the tree-stumps were old and rotten.

"It is a long, long time," he said mournfully, "since there were Indians here."

In order that he might find his way back, he suspended a pair of moccasins from the branch of a tree, and continued his journey. Other clearings he reached in due time, each showing traces of a more recent occupation than the last, but still it seemed to him that a long time must have elapsed since the trees were cut down, so he hung up a pair of moccasins at each stage of his journey, and pursued his course in search of human beings.

At last he saw before him an Indian village, which he approached with mingled feelings of pleasure and trepidation, natural enough when it is remembered that since his early childhood he had spoken to no one but his sister.

### The Ball-Players

On the outskirts of the village some youths of about his own age were engaged in a game of ball, in which they courteously invited the stranger to join. Very soon he had forgotten his natural shyness so far as to enter into the sport with whole-hearted zest and enjoyment. His new companions, for their part, were filled with astonishment at his skill and agility, and, wishing to do him honour, led him to the great lodge and introduced him to their chief.

Now the chief had two daughters, one of whom was

surnamed 'The Good' and the other 'The Wicked.'
To the guest the names sounded rather suggestive,
and he was not a little embarrassed when the chief
begged him to marry the maidens.

"I will marry 'The Good,'" he declared.

But the chief would not agree to that.

"You must marry both," he said firmly.

Here was a dilemma for our hero, who had no wish
to wed the cross, ugly sister. He tried hard to think
of a way of escape.

"I am going to visit So-and-so," he said at last,
mentioning the name of one of his companions at ball,
and he dressed himself carefully as though he were about
to pay a ceremonious visit.

Directly he was out of sight of the chief's lodge,
however, he took to his heels and ran into the forest
as hard as he could. Meanwhile the maidens sat
waiting their intended bridegroom. When some hours
passed without there being any signs of his coming
they became alarmed, and set off to look for him.

Toward nightfall the young Otter-heart relaxed his
speed. "I am quite safe now," he thought. He did
not know that the sisters had the resources of magic
at their command. Suddenly he heard wild laughter
behind him. Recognizing the shrill voice of The
Wicked, he knew that he was discovered, and cast
about for a refuge. The only likely place was in
the branches of a dense fir-tree, and almost as soon
as the thought entered his mind he was at the top.
His satisfaction was short-lived. In a moment the
laughter of the women broke out anew, and they
commenced to hew down the tree. But Otter-heart
himself was not without some acquaintance with magic
art. Plucking a small fir-cone from the tree-top, he
threw it into the air, jumped astride it, and rode down

the wind for half a mile or more. The sisters, absorbed in their task of cutting down the tree, did not notice that their bird was flown. When at last the great fir crashed to the ground and the youth was nowhere to be seen the pursuers tore their hair in rage and disappointment.

### Otter-Heart's Stratagem

Only on the following evening did they overtake Otter-heart again. This time he had entered a hollow cedar-tree, the hard wood of which he thought would defy their axes. But he had under-estimated the energy of the sisters. In a short time the tree showed the effect of their blows, and Otter-heart called on his guardian spirit to break one of the axes.

His wish was promptly gratified, but the other sister continued her labours with increased energy. Otter-heart now wished that the other axe might break, and again his desire was fulfilled. The sisters were at a loss to know what to do.

"We cannot take him by force," said one ; "we must take him by subtlety. Let each do her best, and the one who gets him can keep him."

So they departed, and Otter-heart was free to emerge from his prison. He travelled another day's journey from the spot, and at last, reaching a place where he thought he would be safe, he laid down his blanket and went in search of food. Fortune favoured the hunter, and he shortly returned with a fine beaver. What was his amazement when he beheld a handsome lodge where he had left his blanket !

"It must be those women again," he muttered, preparing to fly. But the light shone so warmly from the lodge, and he was so tired and hungry, that he conquered his fears and entered. Within he found a

168

tall, thin woman, pale and hungry-eyed, but rather
pretty. Taking the beaver, she proceeded to cook it.
As she did so Otter-heart noticed that she ate all the
best parts herself, and when the meal was set out only
the poorest pieces remained for him. This was so
unlike an Indian housewife that he cast reproaches at
her and accused her of greediness. As he spoke a
curious change came over her. Her features grew
longer and thinner. In a moment she had turned
into a wolf and slunk into the forest. It was The
Wicked, who had made herself pretty by means of
magic, but could not conceal her voracious nature.

Otter-heart was glad to have found her out. He
journeyed on still farther, laid down his blanket, and
went to look for game. This time several beavers
rewarded his skill, and he carried them to the place
where he had left his blanket. Another handsome
lodge had been erected there! More than ever he
wanted to run away, but once more his hunger and
fatigue detained him.

"Perhaps it is The Good," he said. "I shall go
inside, and if she has laid my blanket near her couch
I shall take it for a sign and she shall become my wife."

### The Beaver-Woman

He entered the lodge, and found a small, pretty
woman busily engaged in household duties. Sure
enough she had laid his blanket near her couch. When
she had dressed and cooked the beavers she gave the
finest morsels to her husband, who was thoroughly
pleased with his wife.

Hearing a sound in the night, Otter-heart awoke,
and fancied he saw his wife chewing birch-bark. When
he told her of the dream in the morning she did not
laugh, but looked very serious.

" Tell me," asked Otter-heart, "why did you examine the beavers so closely yesterday ? "

" They were my relatives," she replied ; " my cousin, my aunt, and my great-uncle."

Otter-heart was more than ever delighted, for the otters, his totem-kin, and the beavers had always been on very good terms. He promised never to kill any more beavers, but only deer and birds, and he and his wife, The Good, lived together very happily for a long time.

### The Fairy Wives

Once upon a time there dwelt in the forest two braves, one of whom was called the Moose and the other the Marten. Moose was a great hunter, and never returned from the chase without a fine deer or buffalo, which he would give to his old grandmother to prepare for cooking. Marten, on the other hand, was an idler, and never hunted at all if he could obtain food by any other means. When Moose brought home a trophy of his skill in the hunt Marten would repair to his friend's lodge and beg for a portion of the meat. Being a good-natured fellow, Moose generally gave him what he asked for, to the indignation of the old grandmother, who declared that the lazy creature had much better learn to work for himself.

" Do not encourage his idle habits," said she to her grandson. " If you stop giving him food he will go and hunt for himself."

Moose agreed with the old woman, and having on his next expedition killed a bear, he told the grandmother to hide it, so that Marten might know nothing of it.

When the time came to cook the bear-meat, however, the grandmother found that her kettle would not hold water, and remembering that Marten had just got a nice new kettle, she went to borrow his.

"I will clean it well before I return it," she thought. "He will never know what I want it for."

But Marten made a very good guess, so he laid a spell on the kettle before lending it, and afterward set out for Moose's lodge. Looking in, he beheld a great quantity of bear-meat.

"I shall have a fine feast to-morrow," said he, laughing, as he stole quietly away without being seen.

On the following day the old grandmother of Moose took the borrowed kettle, cleaned it carefully, and carried it to its owner. She never dreamed that he would suspect anything.

"Oh," said Marten, "what a fine kettleful of bear-meat you have brought me !"

"I have brought you nothing," the old woman began in astonishment, but a glance at her kettle showed her that it was full of steaming bear-meat. She was much confused, and knew that Marten had discovered her plot by magic art.

### Moose Demands a Wife

Though Marten was by no means so brave or so industrious as Moose, he nevertheless had two very beautiful wives, while his companion had not even one. Moose thought this rather unfair, so he ventured to ask Marten for one of his wives. To this Marten would not agree, nor would either of the women consent to be handed over to Moose, so there was nothing for it but that the braves should fight for the wives, who, all unknown to their husband, were fairies. And fight they did, that day and the next and the next, till it grew to be a habit with them, and they fought as regularly as they slept.

In the morning Moose would say : "Give me one of your wives." "Paddle your own canoe," Marten would retort, and the fight would begin. Next morning Moose would say again : "Give me one of your wives." "Fish for your own minnows," the reply would come, and the quarrel would be continued with tomahawks for arguments.

"Give me one of your wives," Moose persisted.

"Skin your own rabbits !"

Meanwhile the wives of Marten had grown tired of the perpetual skirmishing. So they made up their minds to run away. Moose and Marten never missed them : they were too busy fighting.

All day the fairy wives, whose name was Weasel, travelled as fast as they could, for they did not want to be caught. But when night came they lay down on the banks of a stream and watched the stars shining through the pine-branches.

"If you were a Star-maiden," said one, "and wished to marry a star, which one would you choose ?"

"I would marry that bright little red one," said the other. "I am sure he must be a merry little fellow."

"I," said her companion, "should like to marry that big yellow one. I think he must be a great warrior." And so saying she fell asleep.

### The Red Star and the Yellow Star

When they awoke in the morning the fairies found that their wishes were fulfilled. One was the wife of the great yellow star, and the other the wife of the little red one.

This was the work of an Indian spirit, whose duty it is to punish unfaithful wives, and who had overheard their remarks on the previous night. Knowing that the fulfilment of their wishes would be the best

172

punishment, he transported them to the Star-country, where they were wedded to the stars of their choice. And punishment it was, for the Yellow Star was a fierce warrior who frightened his wife nearly out of her wits, and the Red Star was an irritable old man, and his wife was obliged to wait on him hand and foot. Before very long the fairies found their life in the Star-country exceedingly irksome, and they wished they had never quitted their home.

Not far from their lodges was a large white stone, which their husbands had forbidden them to touch, but which their curiosity one day tempted them to remove. Far below they saw the Earth-country, and they became sadder and more home-sick than ever. The Star-husbands, whose magic powers told them that their wives had been disobedient, were not really cruel or unkind at heart, so they decided to let the fairies return to earth.

"We do not want wives who will not obey," they said, "so you may go to your own country if you will be obedient once."

The fairies joyfully promised to do whatever was required of them if they might return home.

"Very well," the stars replied. "You must sleep to-night, and in the morning you will wake and hear the song of the chickadee, but do not open your eyes. Then you will hear the voice of the ground-squirrel; still you must not rise. The red squirrel also you shall hear, but the success of our scheme depends on your remaining quiet. Only when you hear the striped squirrel you may get up."

### The Return to Earth

The fairies went to their couch and slept, but their sleep was broken by impatience. In the morning the chickadee woke them with its song. The younger fairy eagerly started up, but the other drew her back.

" Let us wait till we hear the striped squirrel," said she.

When the red squirrel's note was heard the younger fairy could no longer curb her impatience. She sprang to her feet, dragging her companion with her. They had indeed reached the Earth-country, but in a way that helped them but little, for they found themselves in the topmost branches of the highest tree in the forest, with no prospect of getting down. In vain they called to the birds and animals to help them; all the creatures were too busy to pay any attention to their plight. At last Lox, the wolverine, passed under the tree, and though he was the wickedest of the animals the Weasels cried to him for help.

"If you will promise to come to my lodge," said Lox, "I will help you."

"We will build lodges for you," cried the elder fairy, who had been thinking of a way of escape.

"That is well," said Lox; "I will take you down."

While he was descending the tree with the younger of the fairies the elder one wound her magic hair-string in the branches, knotting it skilfully, so that the task of undoing it would be no light one. When she in her turn had been carried to the ground she begged Lox to return for her hair-string, which, she said, had become entangled among the branches.

"Pray do not break it," she added, "for if you do I shall have no good fortune."

### The Escape from Lox

Once more Lox ascended the tall pine, and strove with the knots which the cunning fairy had tied. Meanwhile the Weasels built him a wigwam. They

174

filled it with thorns and briers and all sorts of prickly things, and induced their friends the ants and hornets to make their nests inside. So long did Lox take to untie the knotted hair-string that when he came down it was quite dark. He was in a very bad temper, and pushed his way angrily into the new lodge. All the little creatures attacked him instantly, the ants bit him, the thorns pricked him, so that he cried out with anger and pain.

The fairies ran away as fast as they could, and by and by found themselves on the brink of a wide river. The younger sat down and began to weep, thinking that Lox would certainly overtake them. But the elder was more resourceful. She saw the Crane, who was ferryman, standing close by, and sang a very sweet song in praise of his long legs and soft feathers.

"Will you carry us over the river?" she asked at length.

"Willingly," replied the Crane, who was very susceptible to flattery, and he ferried them across the river.

They were just in time. Scarcely had they reached the opposite bank when Lox appeared on the scene, very angry and out of breath.

"Ferry me across, Old Crooked-legs," said he, and added other still more uncomplimentary remarks.

The Crane was furious, but he said nothing, and bore Lox out on the river.

"I see you," cried Lox to the trembling fairies. "I shall have you soon!"

"You shall not, wicked one," said the Crane, and he threw Lox into the deepest part of the stream.

The fairies turned their faces homeward and saw him no more.

### The Malicious Mother-in-Law

An Ojibway or Chippeway legend tells of a
hunter who was greatly devoted to his wife. As a
proof of his affection he presented her with the most
delicate morsels from the game he killed. This aroused
the jealousy and envy of his mother, who lived with
them, and who imagined that these little attentions
should be paid to her, and not to the younger woman.
The latter, quite unaware of her mother-in-law's attitude, cooked and ate the gifts her husband brought
her. Being a woman of a gentle and agreeable disposition, who spent most of her time attending to her
household duties and watching over her child and a
little orphan boy whom she had adopted, she tried to
make friends with the old dame, and was grieved and
disappointed when the latter would not respond to her
advances.

The mother-in-law nursed her grievance until it
seemed of gigantic proportions. Her heart grew
blacker and blacker against her son's wife, and at last
she determined to kill her. For a time she could think
of no way to put her evil intent into action, but finally
she hit upon a plan.

One day she disappeared from the lodge, and returned
after a space looking very happy and good-tempered.
The younger woman was surprised and delighted at
the alteration. This was an agreeably different person
from the nagging, cross-grained old creature who had
made her life a burden! The old woman repeatedly
absented herself from her home after this, returning
on each occasion with a pleased and contented smile
on her wrinkled face. By and by the wife allowed her
curiosity to get the better of her, and she asked the
meaning of her mother-in-law's happiness.

176

The Death-Swing

"If you must know," replied the old woman, "I have made a beautiful swing down by the lake, and always when I swing on it I feel so well and happy that I cannot help smiling."

The young woman begged that she too might be allowed to enjoy the swing.

"To-morrow you may accompany me," was the reply. But next day the old woman had some excuse, and so on, day after day, till the curiosity of her son's wife was very keen. Thus when the elder woman said one day, "Come with me, and I will take you to the swing. Tie up your baby and leave him in charge of the orphan," the other complied eagerly, and was ready in a moment to go with her mother-in-law.

When they reached the shores of the lake they found a lithe sapling which hung over the water.

"Here is my swing," said the old creature, and she cast aside her robe, fastened a thong to her waist and to the sapling, and swung far over the lake. She laughed so much and seemed to find the pastime so pleasant that her daughter-in-law was more anxious than ever to try it for herself.

"Let me tie the thong for you," said the old woman, when she had tired of swinging. Her companion threw off her robe and allowed the leather thong to be fastened round her waist. When all was ready she was commanded to swing. Out over the water she went fearlessly, but as she did so the jealous old mother-in-law cut the thong, and she fell into the lake.

The old creature, exulting over the success of her cruel scheme, dressed herself in her victim's clothes and returned to the lodge. But the baby cried and refused to be fed by her, and the orphan boy cried too, for the young woman had been almost a mother to him since his parents had died.

"Where is the baby's mother?" he asked, when some hours had passed and she did not return.

"At the swing," replied the old woman roughly.

When the hunter returned from the chase he brought with him, as usual, some morsels of game for his wife, and, never dreaming that the woman bending over the child might not be she, he gave them to her. The lodge was dark, for it was evening, and his mother wore the clothes of his wife and imitated her voice and movements, so that his error was not surprising. Greedily she seized the tender pieces of meat, and cooked and ate them.

The heart of the little orphan was so sore that he could not sleep. In the middle of the night he rose and went to look for his foster-mother. Down by the lake he found the swing with the thong cut, and he knew that she had been killed. Crying bitterly, he crept home to his couch, and in the morning told the hunter all that he had seen.

"Say nothing," said the chief, "but come with me to hunt, and in the evening return to the shores of the lake with the child, while I pray to Manitou that he may send me back my wife."

### The Silver Girdle

So they went off in search of game without a word to the old woman ; nor did they stay to eat, but set out directly it was light. At sunset they made their way to the lake-side, the little orphan carrying the baby. Here the hunter blackened his face and prayed earnestly that the Great Manitou might send back his wife. While he prayed the orphan amused the child by singing quaint little songs ; but at last the baby grew weary and hungry and began to cry.

Far in the lake his mother heard the sound, and skimmed over the water in the shape of a great white gull. When she touched the shore she became a woman again, and hugged the child to her heart's content. The orphan boy besought her to return to them.

"Alas!" said she, "I have fallen into the hands of the Water Manitou, and he has wound his silver tail about me, so that I never can escape."

As she spoke the little lad saw that her waist was encircled by a band of gleaming silver, one end of which was in the water. At length she declared that it was time for her to return to the home of the water-god, and after having exacted a promise from the boy that he would bring her baby there every day, she became a gull again and flew away. The hunter was informed of all that had passed, and straightway determined that he would be present on the following evening. All next day he fasted and besought the good-will of Manitou, and when the night began to fall he hid himself on the shore till his wife appeared. Hastily emerging from his concealment, the hunter poised his spear and struck the girdle with all his force. The silver band parted, and the woman was free to return home with her husband.

Overjoyed at her restoration, he led her gently to the lodge, where his mother was sitting by the fire. At the sight of her daughter-in-law, whom she thought she had drowned in the lake, she started up in such fear and astonishment that she tripped, overbalanced, and fell into the fire. Before they could pull her out the flames had risen to the smoke-hole, and when the fire died down no woman was there, but a great black bird, which rose slowly from the smoking embers, flew out of the lodge, and was never seen again.

As for the others, they lived long and happily, undisturbed by the jealousy and hatred of the malicious crone.

### The Maize Spirit

The Chippeways tell a charming story concerning the origin of the zea maize, which runs as follows :

A lad of fourteen or fifteen dwelt with his parents, brothers, and sisters in a beautifully situated little lodge. The family, though poor, were very happy and contented. The father was a hunter who was not lacking in courage and skill, but there were times when he could scarcely supply the wants of his family, and as none of his children was old enough to help him things went hardly with them then. The lad was of a cheerful and contented disposition, like his father, and his great desire was to benefit his people. The time had come for him to observe the initial fast prescribed for all Indian boys of his age, and his mother made him a little fasting-lodge in a remote spot where he might not suffer interruption during his ordeal.

Thither the boy repaired, meditating on the goodness of the Great Spirit, who had made all things beautiful in the fields and forests for the enjoyment of man. The desire to help his fellows was strong upon him, and he prayed that some means to that end might be revealed to him in a dream.

On the third day of his fast he was too weak to ramble through the forest, and as he lay in a state between sleeping and waking there came toward him a beautiful youth, richly dressed in green robes, and wearing on his head wonderful green plumes.

" The Great Spirit has heard your prayers," said the youth, and his voice was like the sound of the wind sighing through the grass. " Hearken to me and you

shall have your desire fulfilled. Arise and wrestle
with me."

## The Struggle

The lad obeyed. Though his limbs were weak his
brain was clear and active, and he felt he could not
but obey the soft-voiced stranger. After a long, silent
struggle the latter said :

" That will do for to-day. To-morrow I shall come
again."

The lad lay back exhausted, but on the morrow the
green-clad stranger reappeared, and the conflict was
renewed. As the struggle went on the youth felt
himself grow stronger and more confident, and before
leaving him for the second time the supernatural visitor
offered him some words of praise and encourage-
ment.

On the third day the youth, pale and feeble, was
again summoned to the contest. As he grasped his
opponent the very contact seemed to give him new
strength, and he fought more and more bravely, till his
lithe companion was forced to cry out that he had had
enough. Ere he took his departure the visitor told
the lad that the following day would put an end to his
trials.

" To-morrow," said he, " your father will bring you
food, and that will help you. In the evening I shall
come and wrestle with you. I know that you are
destined to succeed and to obtain your heart's desire.
When you have thrown me, strip off my garments and
plumes, bury me where I fall, and keep the earth above
me moist and clean. Once a month let my remains be
covered with fresh earth, and you shall see me again,
clothed in my green garments and plumes." So saying,
he vanished.

### The Final Contest

Next day the lad's father brought him food; the youth, however, begged that it might be set aside till evening. Once again the stranger appeared. Though he had eaten nothing, the hero's strength, as before, seemed to increase as he struggled, and at length he threw his opponent. Then he stripped off his garments and plumes, and buried him in the earth, not without sorrow in his heart for the slaying of such a beautiful youth.

His task done, he returned to his parents, and soon recovered his full strength. But he never forgot the grave of his friend. Not a weed was allowed to grow on it, and finally he was rewarded by seeing the green plumes rise above the earth and broaden out into graceful leaves. When the autumn came he requested his father to accompany him to the place. By this time the plant was at its full height, tall and beautiful, with waving leaves and golden tassels. The elder man was filled with surprise and admiration.

"It is my friend," murmured the youth, "the friend of my dreams."

"It is Mon-da-min," said his father, "the spirit's grain, the gift of the Great Spirit."

And in this manner was maize given to the Indians.

### The Seven Brothers

The Blackfeet have a curious legend in explanation of the constellation known as the Plough or Great Bear. Once there dwelt together nine children, seven boys and two girls. While the six older brothers were away on the war-path the elder daughter, whose name was Bearskin-woman, married a grizzly bear. Her father was so enraged that he collected his friends and

ordered them to surround the grizzly's cave and slay
him. When the girl heard that her spouse had been
killed she took a piece of his skin and wore it as an
amulet. Through the agency of her husband's supernatural power, one dark night she was changed into a
grizzly bear, and rushed through the camp, killing and
rending the people, even her own father and mother,
sparing only her youngest brother and her sister, Okinai
and Sinopa. She then took her former shape, and
returned to the lodge occupied by the two orphans, who
were greatly terrified when they heard her muttering
to herself, planning their deaths.

Sinopa had gone to the river one day, when she met
her six brothers returning from the war-path. She
told them what had happened in their absence. They
reassured her, and bade her gather a large number of
prickly pears. These she was to strew in front of the
lodge, leaving only a small path uncovered by them.
In the dead of night Okinai and Sinopa crept out of the
lodge, picking their way down the little path that was
free from the prickly pears, and meeting their six
brothers, who were awaiting them. The Bearskin-
woman heard them leaving the lodge, and rushed out
into the open, only to tread on the prickly pears.
Roaring with pain and anger, she immediately assumed
her bear shape and rushed furiously at her brothers. But
Okinai rose to the occasion. He shot an arrow into
the air, and so far as it flew the brothers and sister
found themselves just that distance in front of the
savage animal behind them.

### The Chase

The beast gained on them, however; but Okinai
waved a magic feather, and thick underbrush rose
in its path. Again Bearskin-woman made headway.

Okinai caused a lake to spring up before her. Yet again she neared the brothers and sister, and this time Okinai raised a great tree, into which the refugees climbed. The Grizzly-woman, however, succeeded in dragging four of the brothers from the tree, when Okinai shot an arrow into the air. Immediately his little sister sailed into the sky. Six times more he shot an arrow, and each time a brother went up, Okinai himself following them as the last arrow soared into the blue. Thus the orphans became stars; and one can see that they took the same position in the sky as they had occupied in the tree, for the small star at one side of the bunch is Sinopa, while the four who huddle together at the bottom are those who had been dragged from the branches by Bearskin-woman.

### The Beaver Medicine Legend [1]

Two brothers dwelt together in the old time. The elder, who was named Nopatsis, was married to a woman who was wholly evil, and who hated his younger brother, Akaiyan. Daily the wife pestered her husband to be rid of Akaiyan, but he would not agree to part with his only brother, for they had been together through long years of privation—indeed, since their parents had left them together as little helpless orphans —and they were all in all to each other. So the wife of Nopatsis had resort to a ruse well known to women whose hearts are evil. One day when her husband returned from the chase he found her lamenting with torn clothes and disordered appearance. She told him that Akaiyan had treated her brutally. The lie entered into the heart of Nopatsis and made it heavy, so that in time he conceived a hatred of his innocent brother, and

[1] The first portion of this legend has its exact counterpart in Egyptian story. See Wiedemann, *Popular Literature of Ancient Egypt*, p. 45.

debated with himself how he should rid himself of
Akaiyan.

Summer arrived, and with it the moulting season
when the wild water-fowl shed their feathers, with
which the Indians fledge their arrows. Near Nopatsis's
lodge there was a great lake, to which these birds
resorted in large numbers, and to this place the brothers
went to collect feathers with which to plume their darts.
They built a raft to enable them to reach an island in
the middle of the lake, making it of logs bound securely
with buffalo-hide. Embarking, they sailed to the little
island, along the shores of which they walked, looking
for suitable feathers. They parted in the quest, and
after some time Akaiyan, who had wandered far along
the strand, suddenly looked up to see his brother on
the raft sailing toward the mainland. He called loudly
to him to return, but Nopatsis replied that he deserved
to perish there because of the brutal manner in which
he had treated his sister-in-law. Akaiyan solemnly
swore that he had not injured her in any way, but
Nopatsis only jeered at him, and rowed away. Soon
he was lost to sight, and Akaiyan sat down and wept
bitterly. He prayed earnestly to the nature spirits and
to the sun and moon, after which he felt greatly up-
lifted. Then he improvised a shelter of branches, and
made a bed of feathers of the most comfortable description. He lived well on the ducks and geese which
frequented the island, and made a warm robe against
the winter season from their skins. He was careful also
to preserve many of the tame birds for his winter food.

One day he encountered the lodge of a beaver, and
while he looked at it curiously he became aware of the
presence of a little beaver.

" My father desires that you will enter his dwelling,"
said the animal. So Akaiyan accepted the invitation

185

and entered the lodge, where the Great Beaver, attended by his wife and family, received him. He was, indeed, the chief of all the beavers, and white with the snows of countless winters. Akaiyan told the Beaver how cruelly he had been treated, and the wise animal condoled with him, and invited him to spend the winter in his lodge, when he would learn many wonderful and useful things. Akaiyan gratefully accepted the invitation, and when the beavers closed up their lodge for the winter he remained with them. They kept him warm by placing their thick, soft tails on his body, and taught him the secret of the healing art, the use of tobacco, and various ceremonial dances, songs, and prayers belonging to the great mystery of 'medicine.'

The summer returned, and on parting the Beaver asked Akaiyan to choose a gift. He chose the Beaver's youngest child, with whom he had contracted a strong friendship ; but the father prized his little one greatly, and would not at first permit him to go. At length, however, Great Beaver gave way to Akaiyan's entreaties and allowed him to take Little Beaver with him, counselling him to construct a sacred Beaver Bundle when he arrived at his native village.

In due time Nopatsis came to the island on his raft, and, making sure that his brother was dead, began to search for his remains. But while he searched, Akaiyan caught up Little Beaver in his arms and, embarking on the raft, made for the mainland, espied by Nopatsis. When Akaiyan arrived at his native village he told his story to the chief, gathered a Beaver Bundle, and commenced to teach the people the mystery of 'medicine,' with its accompanying songs and dances. Then he invited the chiefs of the animal tribes to contribute their knowledge to the Beaver Medicine, which many of them did.

# THE SACRED BEAR-SPEAR

Having accomplished his task of instruction, which occupied him all the winter, Akaiyan returned to the island with Little Beaver, who had been of immense service to him in teaching the Indians the 'medicine' songs and dances. He returned Little Beaver to his parents, and received in exchange for him a sacred pipe, being also instructed in its accompanying songs and ceremonial dances. On the island he found the bones of his credulous and vengeful brother, who had met with the fate he had purposed for the innocent Akaiyan. Every spring Akaiyan visited the beavers, and as regularly he received something to add to the Beaver Medicine Bundle, until it reached the great size it now has. And he married and founded a race of medicine-men who have handed down the traditions and ceremonials of the Beaver Medicine to the present day.

## The Sacred Bear-Spear

An interesting Blackfoot myth relates how that tribe obtained its sacred Bear-spear. Many generations ago, even before the Blackfeet used horses as beasts of burden, the tribe was undertaking its autumn migration, when one evening before striking camp for the night it was reported that a dog-sledge or cart belonging to the chief was missing. To make matters worse, the chief's ermine robe and his wife's buckskin dress, with her sacred elk-skin robe, had been packed in the little cart. Strangely enough, no one could recollect having noticed the dog during the march. Messengers were dispatched to the camping-site of the night before, but to no avail. At last the chief's son, Sokumapi, a boy about twelve years of age, begged to be allowed to search for the missing dog, a proposal to which his father, after some demur, consented. Sokumapi set out alone for the last camping-ground, which was under

187

the shadows of the Rocky Mountains, and carefully examined the site. Soon he found a single dog-sledge track leading into a deep gulch, near the entrance to which he discovered a large cave. A heap of freshly turned earth stood in front of the cave, beside which was the missing cart. As he stood looking at it, wondering what had become of the dog which had drawn it, an immense grizzly-bear suddenly dashed out. So rapid was its attack that Sokumapi had no chance either to defend himself or to take refuge in flight. The bear, giving vent to the most terrific roars, dragged him into the cave, hugging him with such force that he fainted. When he regained consciousness it was to find the bear's great head within a foot of his own, and he thought that he saw a kindly and almost human expression in its big brown eyes. For a long time he lay still, until at last, to his intense surprise, the Bear broke the silence by addressing him in human speech.

"Have no fear," said the grizzly. "I am the Great Bear, and my power is extensive. I know the circumstances of your search, and I have drawn you to this cavern because I desired to assist you. Winter is upon us, and you had better remain with me during the cold season, in the course of which I will reveal to you the secret of my supernatural power."

### Bear Magic

It will be observed that the circumstances of this tale are almost identical with those which relate to the manner in which the Beaver Medicine was revealed to mankind. The hero of both stories remains during the winter with the animal, the chief of its species, who in the period of hibernation instructs him in certain potent mysteries.

# HOW THE MAGIC WORKED

The Bear, having reassured Sokumapi, showed him how to transform various substances into food. His strange host slept during most of the winter; but when the warm winds of spring returned and the snows melted from the hills the grizzly became restless, and told Sokumapi that it was time to leave the cave. Before they quitted it, however, he taught the lad the secret of his supernatural power. Among other things, he showed him how to make a Bear-spear. He instructed him to take a long stick, to one end of which he must secure a sharp point, to symbolize the bear's tusks. To the staff must be attached a bear's nose and teeth, while the rest of the spear was to be covered with bear's skin, painted the sacred colour, red. The Bear also told him to decorate the handle with eagle's feathers and grizzly claws, and in war-time to wear a grizzly claw in his hair, so that the strength of the Great Bear might go with him in battle, and to imitate the noise a grizzly makes when it charges. The Bear furthermore instructed him what songs should be used in order to heal the sick, and how to paint his face and body so that he would be invulnerable in battle, and, lastly, told him of the sacred nature of the spear, which was only to be employed in warfare and for curing disease. Thus if a person was sick unto death, and a relative purchased the Bear-spear, its supernatural power would restore the ailing man to health. Equipped with this knowledge, Sokumapi returned to his people, who had long mourned him as dead. After a feast had been given to celebrate his home-coming he began to manufacture the Bear-spear as directed by his friend.

## How the Magic Worked

Shortly after his return the Crows made war upon the Blackfeet, and on the meeting of the two tribes in battle Sokumapi appeared in front of his people carrying the Bear-spear on his back. His face and body were painted as the Great Bear had instructed him, and he sang the battle-songs that the grizzly had taught him. After these ceremonies he impetuously charged the enemy, followed by all his braves in a solid phalanx, and such was the efficacy of the Bear magic that the Crows immediately took to flight. The victorious Blackfeet brought back Sokumapi to their camp in triumph, to the accompaniment of the Bear songs. He was made a war-chief, and ever afterward the spear which he had used was regarded as the palladium of the Blackfoot Indians. In the spring the Bear-spear is unrolled from its covering and produced when the first thunder is heard, and when the Bear begins to quit his winter quarters; but when the Bear returns to his den to hibernate the spear is once more rolled up and put away. The greatest care is taken to protect it against injury. It has a special guardian, and no woman is permitted to touch it.

## The Young Dog Dance

A dance resembling the Sun Dance was formerly known to the Pawnee Indians, who called it the Young Dog Dance. It was, they said, borrowed from the Crees, who produced the following myth to account for it.

One day a young brave of the Cree tribe had gone out from his village to catch eagles, in order to provide himself with feathers for a war-bonnet, or to tie in his hair. Now the Crees caught eagles in this fashion. On the top of a hill frequented by these birds they would dig a pit and cover it over with a roof of poles, cunningly concealing the structure with grass. A piece of meat was fastened to the poles, so that the eagles

190

could not carry it off. Then the Indian, taking off his clothes, would descend into the pit, and remain there for hours, or days, as the case might be, until an eagle was attracted by the bait, when he would put his hand between the poles, seize the bird by the feet, and quickly dispatch it.

The young brave whose fortune it was to discover the Young Dog Dance had prepared the trap in this wise, and was lying in the pit praying that an eagle might come and bring his uncomfortable vigil to an end. Suddenly he heard a sound of drumming, distant but quite distinct, though he could not tell from what direction it proceeded. All night the mysterious noise continued. Next night as he lay in the same position he heard it again, and resolved to find out its origin, so he clambered out of his pit and went off in the direction from which the drum-beating seemed to proceed. At last, when dawn was near, he reached the shores of a great lake. Here he stopped, for the sounds quite evidently came from the lake. All that day he sat by the water bemoaning his ill-luck and praying for better fortune. When night fell the drumming began anew, and the young man saw countless animals and birds swimming in the lake. Four days he remained on the lake-shore, till at length, worn out by fatigue and hunger (for many days had elapsed since he had eaten), he fell asleep.

### The Lodge of Animals

When he awoke he found himself in a large lodge, surrounded by many people, some of whom were dancing, while others sat round the walls. All these people wore robes made from the skins of various animals or birds. They were, in fact, the animals the young Indian had seen swimming in the water, who had changed themselves into human shape. A chief at the back of the lodge stood up and addressed him thus :

"My friend, we have heard your prayers, and our desire is to help you. You see these people? They represent the animals. I am the Dog. The Great Spirit is very fond of dogs. I have much power, and my power I shall give to you, so that you may be like me, and my spirit will always protect you. Take this dance home to your people, and it will make them lucky in war." And he imparted the nature of the rite to the Indian by action.

The Dog turned from the Cree brave and his eye swept the company.

### The Gift

"Brothers," he said, "I have given him my power. Will you not pity him and give him the power you have?"

For a time there was silence. No one seemed disposed to respond to the chief's appeal. At last the Owl rose.

"I will help you," he said to the young man. "I have power to see in the dark wherever I may go. When you go out at night I will be near you, and you shall see as well as I do. Take these feathers and tie them in your hair." And, giving him a bunch of feathers, the Owl sat down.

There was a pause, and the next to rise was the Buffalo Bull, who gave to the young Indian his strength and endurance and the power to trample his enemies underfoot. As a token he gave him a shoulder-belt of tanned buffalo-hide, bidding him wear it when he went on the war-path.

By and by the Porcupine stood up and addressed

the guest. Giving him some of his quills with which to ornament the leather belt, he said :

"I also will help you. I can make my enemies as weak as women, so that they fly before me. When you fight your foes shall flee and you shall overcome them."

Another long silence ensued, and when at last the Eagle rose every one listened to hear what he had to say.

"I also," he said majestically, "will be with you wherever you go, and will give you my prowess in war, so that you may kill your foes as I do." As he spoke he handed to the brave some eagle feathers to tie in his hair.

The Whooping Crane followed, and gave him a bone from its wing for a war-whistle to frighten his enemies away.

The Deer and the Bear came next, the one giving him swiftness, with a rattle as token, and the other hardiness, and a strip of fur for his belt.

After he had received these gifts from the animals the brave lay down and fell asleep again. When he awoke he found himself on the shores of the lake once more.

Returning home, he taught the Crees the Young Dog Dance, which was to make them skilful in war, and showed them the articles he had received. So the young men formed a Society of Young Dogs, which practised the dance and obtained the benefits.

### The Medicine Wolf

A quaint story of a 'medicine' wolf is told among the Blackfoot Indians. On one occasion when the Blackfeet were moving camp they were attacked by a number of Crow Indians who had been lying in wait for them. The Blackfeet were travelling slowly in a

193

long, straggling line, with the old men and the women and children in the middle, and a band of warriors in front and in the rear. The Crows, as has been said, made an ambush for their enemies, and rushed out on the middle portion of the line. Before either party of the Blackfoot warriors could reach the scene of the struggle many of the women and children had perished, and others were taken captive by the attacking force. Among the prisoners was a young woman called Sits-by-the-door. Many weary miles lay between them and the Crow camp on the Yellowstone River, but at length the tired captives, mounted with their captors on jaded horses, arrived at their destination. The warrior who had taken Sits-by-the-door prisoner now presented her to a friend of his, who in turn gave her into the keeping of his wife, who was somewhat older than her charge. The young Blackfoot woman was cruelly treated by the Crow into whose possession she had passed. Every night he tied her feet together so that she might not escape, and also tied a rope round her waist, the other end of which he fastened to his wife. The Crow woman, however, was not unmoved by the wretchedness of her prisoner. While her husband was out she managed to converse with her and to show her that she pitied her misfortunes. One day she informed Sits-by-the-door that she had over-heard her husband and his companions plotting to kill her, but she added that when darkness fell she would help her to escape. When night came the Crow woman waited until the deep breathing of her husband told her that he was sound asleep ; then, rising cautiously, she loosened the ropes that bound her captive, and, giving her a pair of moccasins, a flint, and a small sack of pemmican, bade her make haste and escape from the fate that would surely befall her

194

if she remained where she was. The trembling woman obeyed, and travelled at a good pace all night. At dawn she hid in the dense undergrowth, hoping to escape observation should her captors pursue her. They, meanwhile, had discovered her absence, and were searching high and low, but no tracks were visible, and at last, wearied with their unprofitable search, they gave up the chase and returned to their homes.

### The Friendly Wolf

When the woman had journeyed on for four nights she stopped concealing herself in the daytime and travelled straight on. She was not yet out of danger, however, for her supply of pemmican was soon exhausted, and she found herself face to face with the miseries of starvation. Her moccasins, besides, were worn to holes and her feet were cut and bleeding, while, to add to her misfortunes, a huge wolf dogged her every movement. In vain she tried to run away ; her strength was exhausted and she sank to the ground. Nearer and nearer came the great wolf, and at last he lay down at her feet. Whenever the woman walked on her way the wolf followed, and when she lay down to rest he lay down also.

At length she begged her strange companion to help her, for she knew that unless she obtained food very soon she must die. The animal trotted away, and returned shortly with a buffalo calf which it had killed, and laid it at the woman's feet. With the aid of the flint—one of the gifts with which the Crow woman had sped her unhappy guest—she built a fire and cooked some of the buffalo meat. Thus refreshed, she proceeded on her way. Again and again the wolf provided food in a similar manner, until at length they reached the Blackfoot camp. The woman led the animal into her lodge, and related to her friends all that had befallen her in the Crow camp, and the manner of her escape. She also told them how the wolf had befriended her, and begged them to treat it kindly. But soon afterward she fell ill, and the poor wolf was driven out of the village by the Indian dogs. Every evening he would come to the top of a hill overlooking the camp and watch the lodge where Sits-by-the-door dwelt. Though he was still fed by her friends, after a time he disappeared and was seen no more.[1]

## The Story of Scar-face

Scar-face was brave but poor. His parents had died while he was yet a boy, and he had no near relations. But his heart was high, and he was a mighty hunter. The old men said that Scar-face had a future before him, but the young braves twitted him because of a mark across his face, left by the rending claw of a great grizzly which he had slain in close fight.

The chief of his tribe possessed a beautiful daughter, whom all the young men desired in marriage. Scar-face also had fallen in love with her, but he felt ashamed to declare his passion because of his poverty. The maiden had already repulsed half the braves of his tribe. Why, he argued, should she accept him, poor and disfigured as he was?

One day he passed her as she sat outside her lodge. He cast a penetrating glance at her—a glance which was observed by one of her unsuccessful suitors, who sneeringly remarked:

" Scar-face would marry our chief's daughter ! She does not desire a man without a blemish. Ha, Scar-face, now is your chance ! "

[1] The reader cannot fail to discern the striking resemblance between this episode and that of Una and the lion in Spenser's *Faerie Queene*.

Scar-face turned upon the jeerer, and in his quiet yet dignified manner remarked that it was his intention to ask the chief's daughter to be his wife. His announcement met with ridicule, but he took no notice of it and sought the girl.

He found her by the river, pulling rushes to make baskets. Approaching, he respectfully addressed her.

"I am poor," he said, "but my heart is rich in love for you. I have no wealth of furs or pemmican. I live by my bow and spear. I love you. Will you dwell with me in my lodge and be my wife?"

### The Sun-God's Decree

The girl regarded him with bright, shy eyes peering up through lashes as the morning sun peers through the branches.

"My husband would not be poor," she faltered, "for my father, the chief, is wealthy and has abundance in his lodge. But it has been laid upon me by the Sun-god that I may not marry."

"These are heavy words," said Scar-face sadly. "May they not be recalled?"

"On one condition only," replied the girl. "Seek the Sun-god and ask him to release me from my promise. If he consents to do so, request him to remove the scar from your face as a sign that I may know that he gives me to you."

Scar-face was sad at heart, for he could not believe that the Sun-god, having chosen such a beautiful maiden for himself, would renounce her. But he gave the chief's daughter his promise that he would seek out the god in his own bright country and ask him to grant his request.

For many moons Scar-face sought the home of the Sun-god. He traversed wide plains and dense forests, crossed rivers and lofty mountains, yet never a trace of the golden gates of the dwelling of the God of Light could he see.

Many inquiries did he make from the wild denizens of the forest—the wolf, the bear, the badger. But none was aware of the way to the home of the Sun-god. He asked the birds, but though they flew far they were likewise in ignorance of the road thither. At last he met a wolverine who told him that he had been there himself, and promised to set him on the way. For a long and weary season they marched onward, until at length they came to a great water, too broad and too deep to cross.

As Scar-face sat despondent on the bank bemoaning his case two beautiful swans advanced from the water, and, requesting him to sit on their backs, bore him across in safety. Landing him on the other side, they showed him which way to take and left him. He had not walked far when he saw a bow and arrows lying before him. But Scar-face was punctilious and would not pick them up because they did not belong to him. Not long afterward he encountered a beautiful youth of handsome form and smiling aspect.

"I have lost a bow and arrows," he said to Scar-face. "Have you seen them?"

Scar-face told him that he had seen them a little way back, and the handsome youth praised him for his honesty in not appropriating them. He further asked him where he was bound for.

"I am seeking the Sun in his home," replied the Indian, "and I believe that I am not far from my destination."

"You are right," replied the youth. "I am the son of the Sun, Apisirahts, the Morning Star, and I will lead you to the presence of my august father."

They walked onward for a little space, and then
Apisirahts pointed out a great lodge, glorious with
golden light and decorated with an art more curious
than any that Scar-face had ever beheld. At the
entrance stood a beautiful woman, the mother of
Morning Star, Kokomikis, the Moon-goddess, who
welcomed the footsore Indian kindly and joyously.

### The Chase of the Savage Birds

Then the great Sun-god appeared, wondrous in his
strength and beauty as the mighty planet over which
he ruled. He too greeted Scar-face kindly, and requested him to be his guest and to hunt with his son.
Scar-face and the youth gladly set out for the chase.
But on departing the Sun-god warned them not to
venture near the Great Water, as there dwelt savage
birds which might slay Morning Star.

Scar-face tarried with the Sun, his wife and child,
fearful of asking his boon too speedily, and desiring to
make as sure as possible of its being granted.

One day he and Morning Star hunted as usual, and
the youth stole away, for he wished to slay the savage
birds of which his father had spoken. But Scar-face
followed, rescued the lad in imminent peril, and killed
the monsters. The Sun was grateful to him for
having saved his son from a terrible death, and asked
him for what reason he had sought his lodge. Scar-
face acquainted him with the circumstances of his love
for the chief's daughter and of his quest. At once the
Sun-god granted his desire.

" Return to the woman you love so much," he said,
"return and make her yours. And as a sign that it
is my will that she should be your wife, I make you
whole."

With a motion of his bright hand the deity removed

the unsightly scar. On quitting the Sun-country the god, his wife and son presented Scar-face with many good gifts, and showed him a short route by which to return to Earth-land once more.

Scar-face soon reached his home. When he sought his chief's daughter she did not know him at first, so rich was the gleaming attire he had obtained in the Sun-country. But when she at last recognized him she fell upon his breast with a glad cry. That same day she was made his wife. The happy pair raised a 'medicine' lodge to the Sun-god, and henceforth Scar-face was called Smooth-face.

### The Legend of Poïa

A variant of this beautiful story is as follows :

One summer morning a beautiful girl called Feather-woman, who had been sleeping outside her lodge among the long prairie grass, awoke just as the Morning Star was rising above the horizon. She gazed intently at it, and so beautiful did it seem that she fell deeply in love with it. She awakened her sister, who was lying beside her, and declared to her that she would marry nobody but the Morning Star. The people of her tribe ridiculed her because of what they considered her absurd preference; so she avoided them as much as possible, and wandered alone, eating her heart out in secret for love of the Morning Star, who seemed to her unapproachable.

One day she went alone to the river for water, and as she returned she beheld a young man standing before her. At first she took him for one of the young men of the tribe, and would have avoided him, but he said :

" I am the Morning Star. I beheld you gazing upward at me, and knew that you loved me. I returned

200

your love, and have descended to ask you to go with me to my dwelling in the sky."

Feather-woman trembled violently, for she knew that he who spoke to her was a god, and replied hesitatingly that she must bid farewell to her father and mother. But this Morning Star would not permit. He took a rich yellow plume from his hair and directed her to hold this in one hand, while she held a juniper branch in the other. Then he commanded her to close her eyes, and when she opened them again she was in the Sky-country, standing before a great and shining lodge. Morning Star told her that this was the home of his parents, the Sun and Moon, and requested her to enter. It was daytime, so that the Sun was away on his diurnal round, but the Moon was at home. She welcomed Feather-woman as the wife of her son, as did the Sun himself when he returned. The Moon clothed her in a soft robe of buckskin, trimmed with elks' teeth. Feather-woman was very happy, and dwelt contentedly in the lodge of Morning Star. They had a little son, whom they called Star-boy. The Moon gave Feather-woman a root-digger, and told her that she could dig up all kinds of roots, but warned her on no account to dig up the large turnip which grew near the home of the Spider Man, telling her that it would bring unhappiness to all of them if she did so.

### The Great Turnip

Feather-woman often saw the large turnip, but always avoided touching it. One day, however, her curiosity got the better of her, and she was tempted to see what might be underneath it. She laid her little son on the ground and dug until her root-digger stuck fast. Two large cranes came flying overhead.

She begged these to help her. They did so, and sang a magic song which enabled them to uproot the turnip.

Now, although she was unaware of it, this very turnip filled up the hole through which Morning Star had brought her into the Sky-country. Gazing downward, she saw the camp of the Blackfeet where she had lived. The smoke was ascending from the lodges, she could hear the song of the women as they went about their work. The sight made her homesick and lonely, and as she went back to her lodge she cried softly to herself. When she arrived Morning Star gazed earnestly at her, and said with a sorrowful expression of countenance : "You have dug up the sacred turnip."

The Moon and Sun were also troubled, and asked her the meaning of her sadness, and when she had told them they said that as she had disobeyed their injunction she must return to earth. Morning Star took her to the Spider Man, who let her down to earth by a web, and the people beheld her coming to earth like a falling star.

### The Return to Earth

She was welcomed by her parents, and returned with her child, whom she had brought with her from the Sky-country, to the home of her youth. But happiness never came back to her. She mourned ceaselessly for her husband, and one morning, climbing to the summit of a high mound, she watched the beautiful Morning Star rise above the horizon, just as on the day when she had first loved him. Stretching out her arms to the eastern sky, she besought him passionately to take her back. At length he spoke to her.

"It is because of your own sin," he said, "that you are for ever shut out from the Sky-country. Your

202

disobedience has brought sorrow upon yourself and upon all your people."

Her pleadings were in vain, and in despair she returned to her lodge, where her unhappy life soon came to a close. Her little son, Star-boy, was now an orphan, and the death of his grandparents deprived him of all his earthly kindred. He was a shy, retiring, timid boy, living in the deepest poverty, notwithstanding his exalted station as grandchild of the Sun. But the most noticeable thing about him was a scar which disfigured his face, because of which he was given the name of Poïa (Scar-face) by the wits of the tribe. As he grew older the scar became more pronounced, and ridicule and abuse were heaped upon him. When he became a man he fell in love with a maiden of surpassing beauty, the daughter of a great chief of his tribe. She, however, laughed him to scorn, and told him that she would marry him when he removed the scar from his face. Poïa, greatly saddened by her unkindness, consulted an old medicine-woman, to see whether the scar might not be removed. She could only tell him that the mark had been placed on his face by the Sun, and that the Sun alone could remove it. This was melancholy news for Poïa. How could he reach the abode of the Sun? Nevertheless, encouraged by the old woman, he resolved to make the attempt. Gratefully accepting her parting gift of pemmican and moccasins, he set off on a journey that was to last for many days.

### The Big Water

After climbing mountains and traversing forests and wandering over trackless prairies he arrived at the Big Water (that is to say, the Pacific Ocean), on the shores of which he sat down, praying and fasting for three

days. On the third day, when the Sun was sinking
behind the rim of the ocean, he saw a bright pathway
leading straight to the abode of the Sun. He resolved
to follow the shining trail, though he knew not what
might lie before him in the great Sky-country. He
arrived quite safely, however, at the wonderful lodge
of the Sun. All night he hid himself outside the lodge,
and in the morning the Sun, who was about to begin
his daily journey, saw a ragged wayfarer lying by his
door. He did not know that the intruder was his
grandson, but, seeing that he had come from the Earth-
country, he determined to kill him, and said so to his
wife, the Moon. But she begged that the stranger's
life should be spared, and Morning Star, who at that
moment issued from the lodge, also gave Poïa his
protection. Poïa lived very happily in the lodge of the
Sun, and having on one occasion killed seven birds
who were about to destroy Morning Star, he earned
the gratitude of his grandparents. At the request of
Morning Star the Sun removed the scar on Poïa's face,
and bade him return with a message to the Blackfeet.
If they would honour him once a year in a Sun Dance
he would consent to heal their sick. The secrets of
the Sun Dance were taught to Poïa, two raven's feathers
were placed in his hair, and he was given a robe of
elk-skin. The latter, he was told, must only be worn
by a virtuous woman, who should then dance the Sun
Dance, so that the sick might be restored to health.
From his father Poïa received an enchanted flute and a
magic song, which would win the heart of the maid he
loved.

Poïa came to earth by the Milky Way, or, as the
Indians call it, the Wolf-trail, and communicated to the
Blackfeet all that he had learned in the Sky-country.
When they were thoroughly conversant with the Sun

Dance he returned to the Sky-country, the home of his father, accompanied by his beautiful bride. Here they dwelt together happily, and Poïa and the Morning Star travelled together through the sky.

## A Blackfoot Day-and-Night Myth

Many stories are told by the Blackfoot Indians of their creator, Nápi, and these chiefly relate to the manner in which he made the world and its inhabitants.

One myth connected with this deity tells how a poor Indian who had a wife and two children lived in the greatest indigence on roots and berries. This man had a dream in which he heard a voice command him to procure a large spider-web, which he was to hang on the trail of the animals where they passed through the forest, by which means he would obtain plenty of food. This he did, and on returning to the place in which he had hung the web he found deer and rabbits entangled in its magical meshes. These he killed for food, for which he was now never at a loss.

Returning with his game on his shoulders one morning, he discovered his wife perfuming herself with sweet pine, which she burned over the fire. He suspected that she was thus making herself attractive for the benefit of some one else, but, preserving silence, he told her that on the following day he would set his spider-web at a greater distance, as the game in the neighbouring forest was beginning to know the trap too well. Accordingly he went farther afield, and caught a deer, which he cut up, carrying part of its meat back with him to his lodge. He told his wife where the remainder of the carcass was to be found, and asked her to go and fetch it.

His wife, however, was not without her own suspicions, and, concluding that she was being watched by her husband, she halted at the top of the nearest hill and looked back to see if he was following her. But he was sitting where she had left him, so she proceeded on her way. When she was quite out of sight the Indian himself climbed the hill, and, seeing that she was not in the vicinity, returned to the camp. He inquired of his children where their mother went to gather firewood, and they pointed to a large patch of dead timber. Proceeding to the clump of leafless trees, the man instituted a thorough search, and after a while discovered a den of rattlesnakes. Now it was one of these reptiles with which his wife was in love, so the Indian in his wrath gathered fragments of dry wood and set the whole plantation in a blaze. Then he returned to his lodge and told his children what he had done, at the same time warning them that their mother would be very wrathful, and would probably attempt to kill them all. He further said that he would wait for her return, but that they had better run away, and that he would provide them with three things which they would find of use. He then handed to the children a stick, a stone, and a bunch of moss, which they were to throw behind them should their mother pursue them. The children at once ran away, and their father hung the spider-web over the door of the lodge. Meanwhile the woman had seen the blaze made by the dry timber-patch from a considerable distance, and in great anger turned and ran back to the lodge. Attempting to enter it, she was at once entangled in the meshes of the spider-web.

### The Pursuing Head

She struggled violently, however, and succeeded in getting her head through the opening, whereupon her husband severed it from her shoulders with his stone axe. He then ran out of the lodge and down the valley, hotly pursued by the woman's body, while her head rolled along the ground in chase of the children. The latter soon descried the grisly object rolling along in their tracks at a great speed, and one of them quickly threw the stick behind him as he had been told to do. Instantly a dense forest sprang up in their rear, which for a space retarded their horrible pursuer. The children made considerable headway, but once more the severed head made its appearance, gnashing its teeth in a frenzy of rage and rolling its eyes horribly, while it shrieked out threats which caused the children's blood to turn to water.

Then another of the boys threw the stone which he had been given behind him, and instantly a great mountain sprang up which occupied the land from sea to sea, so that the progress of the head was quite barred. It could perceive no means of overcoming this immense barrier, until it encountered two rams feeding, which it asked to make a way for it through the mountain, telling them that if they would do so it would marry the chief of the sheep. The rams made a valiant effort to meet this request, and again and again fiercely rushed at the mountain, till their horns were split and broken and they could butt no longer. The head, growing impatient, called upon a colony of ants which dwelt in the neighbourhood to tunnel a passage through the obstacle, and offered, if they were successful, to marry the chief ant as a recompense for their labours. The insects at once took up the task, and toiled incessantly until they had made a tunnel through which the head could roll.

### The Fate of the Head

The children were still running, but felt that the head had not abandoned pursuit. At last, after a long interval, they observed it rolling after them, evidently as fresh as ever. The child who had the bunch of moss now wet it and wrung out the water over their trail, and immediately an immense strait separated them from the land where they had been but a moment before. The head, unable to stop, fell into this great water and was drowned.

The children, seeing that their danger was past, made a raft and sailed back to the land from which they had come. Arrived there, they journeyed eastward through many countries, peopled by many different tribes of Indians, in order to reach their own territory. When they arrived there they found it occupied by tribes unknown to them, so they resolved to separate, one going north and the other south. One of them was shrewd and clever, and the other simple and ingenious. The shrewd boy is he who made the white people and instructed them in their arts. The other, the simple boy, made the Blackfeet, but, being very stupid, was unable to teach them anything. He it was who was called Nápi. As for the mother's body, it continued to chase her husband, and is still following him, for she is the Moon and he is the Sun. If she succeeds in catching him she will slay him, and night will reign for evermore, but as long as he is able to evade her day and night will continue to follow one another.

### Nápi and the Buffalo-Stealer

There was once a great famine among the Blackfeet. For months no buffaloes were killed, and the weaker members of the tribe dropped off one by one, while even the strong braves and hunters began to sink under the privation. The chief in despair prayed that the creator, Nápi, would send them food. Nápi, meanwhile, was far away in the south, painting the plumage of the birds in gorgeous tints. Nevertheless he heard the voice of the chief over all the distance, and hastened northward.

"Who has summoned me?" he demanded.

"It was I," said the chief humbly. "My people are starving, and unless relief comes soon I fear we must all perish."

"You shall have food," answered Nápi. "I will provide game for you."

Taking with him the chief's son, Nápi travelled toward the west. As they went the youth prayed earnestly to the Sun, the Moon, and the Morning Star, but his companion rebuked his impatience and bade him hold his peace. They crossed the Sweet Grass Hills, which Nápi had made from huge handfuls of herbage, and where he loved to rest. Still there was no sign of game. At length they reached a little lodge by the side of a river, and Nápi called a halt.

"There dwells the cause of your misfortunes," said he. "He who lives in that lodge is the Buffalo-stealer. He it is who has taken all the herds from the prairies, so that there is none left."

To further his design, Nápi took the shape of a dog, and turned the youth into a stick. Not long afterward the little son of Buffalo-stealer was passing that way, and immediately desired to take the little dog home with him.

"Very well," said his mother; "take that stick and drive it to the lodge."

But the boy's father frowned angrily.

"I do not like the look of the beast," he said. "Send it away."

The boy refused to part with the dog, and his mother wanted the stick to gather roots with, so the father was obliged to give way. Still he did not show any good-will to the dog. The following day he went out of the lodge, and in a short time returned with a buffalo, which he skinned and prepared for cooking. His wife, who was in the woods gathering berries, came home toward evening, and at her husband's bidding cooked part of the buffalo-meat. The little boy incurred his father's anger again by giving a piece of meat to the dog.

"Have I not told you," cried Buffalo-stealer irately, "that he is an evil thing ? Do not touch him."

That night when all was silent Nápi and the chief's son resumed their human form and supped off the buffalo-meat.

"It is Buffalo-stealer who keeps the herds from coming near the Blackfoot camp," said Nápi. "Wait till morning and see."

### The Herds of Buffalo-Stealer

In the morning they were once more dog and stick. When the woman and her child awoke they set off for the woods again, the former taking the stick to dig for roots, the latter calling for his little dog to accompany him. Alas! when they reached the spot they had fixed upon for root-gathering operations both dog and stick had vanished! And this was the reason for their disappearance. As the dog was trotting through the wood he had observed an opening like the mouth of a cavern, all but concealed by the thick undergrowth, and in the aperture he perceived a buffalo. His short, sharp barking attracted the attention of the stick, which promptly wriggled snake-wise after him. Within the cavern were great herds of deer and buffalo, enough to provide the Blackfeet with food for years and years. Nápi ran among them, barking, and they were driven out to the prairie.

# THE HERDS OF BUFFALO-STEALER

When Buffalo-stealer returned and discovered his loss his wrath knew no bounds. He questioned his wife and son, but they denied all knowledge of the affair.

"Then," said he, "it is that wretched little dog of yours. Where is he now?"

But the child could not tell him.

"We lost him in the woods," said he.

"I shall kill him," shouted the man, "and I shall break the stick as well!"

Nápi overheard the threat, and clung to the long hair of an old buffalo. He advised the stick to conceal itself in the buffalo's hair also, and so the twain escaped unnoticed from the cave, much as did Ulysses from the Cyclops' cavern. Once again they took the form of men, and drove a herd of buffalo to the Blackfoot camp, while Buffalo-stealer and his family sought them in vain.

The people met them with delighted acclamations, and the famine was at an end. Yet there were still some difficulties in the way, for when they tried to get the herd into the enclosure a large grey bird so frightened the animals with its dismal note that they refused to enter. This occurred so often that Nápi suspected that the grey bird was no other than Buffalo-stealer. Changing himself into an otter, he lay by the side of a river and pretended to be dead. The greedy bird saw what he thought to be a dead otter, and pounced upon it, whereupon Nápi seized him by the leg and bore him off to the camp. By way of punishment he was tied over the smoke-hole of the wigwam, where his grey feathers soon became black and his life a burden to him.

"Spare me!" he cried. "Let me return to my wife and child. They will surely starve."

His piteous appeals moved the heart of Nápi, and he let him go, but not without an admonition.

"Go," said he, "and hunt for food, that you may support your wife and child. But do not take more than you need, or you shall die."

The bird did as he was bidden. But to this day the feathers of the raven are black, and not grey.

### The Story of Kutoyis

There once lived on the banks of the Missouri an old couple who had one daughter, their only child. When she grew to be a woman she had a suitor who was cruel and overbearing, but as she loved him her parents offered no opposition to their marriage. Indeed, they gave the bride the best part of their possessions for a dowry, so that she and her husband were rich, while her father and mother lived in a poor lodge and had very little to eat. The wicked son-in-law took advantage of their kindness in every way. He forced the old man to accompany him on his hunting expeditions, and then refused to share the game with him. Sometimes one would kill a buffalo and sometimes the other, but always it was the younger man who got the best of the meat and who made himself robes and moccasins from the hide.

Thus the aged couple were nearly perishing from cold and hunger. Only when her husband was out hunting would the daughter venture to carry a morsel of meat to her parents.

On one occasion the younger man called in his overbearing way to his father-in-law, bidding him help in a buffalo-hunt. The old man, reduced by want almost to a skeleton, was too much afraid of the tyrant to venture to disobey him, so he accompanied him in the chase. Ere long they encountered a fine buffalo, whereupon both drew their bows and fired. But it was the arrow of the elder man which pierced the animal and brought it to the ground. The old man set himself to skin the buffalo, for his son-in-law never shared in these tasks, but left them to his companion. While he was thus engaged the latter observed a drop of blood on one of his arrows which had fallen to the ground.

Thinking that even a drop of blood was better than nothing, he replaced the arrow in its quiver and set off home. As it happened, no more of the buffalo than that fell to his share, the rest being appropriated by his son-in-law.

On his return the old man called to his wife to heap fuel on the fire and put on the kettle. She, thinking he had brought home some buffalo-meat, hastened to do his bidding. She waited curiously till the water in the kettle had boiled; then to her surprise she saw him place in it an arrow with a drop of blood on it.

### How Kutoyis was Born

" Why do you do that ? " she asked.

" Something will come of it," he replied. " My spirit tells me so."

They waited in silence.

Then a strange sound was heard in their lonely little lodge—the crying of a child. Half fearfully, half curiously, the old couple lifted the lid of the kettle, and there within was a little baby boy.

" He shall bring us good luck," said the old Indian.

They called the child Kutoyis—that is, 'Drop of Blood '—and wrapped him up as is customary with Indian babies.

" Let us tell our son-in-law," said the old man, " that it is a little girl, and he will let it live. If we say it is a boy he will surely kill it."

Kutoyis became a great favourite in the little lodge to which he had come. He was always laughing, and his merriment won the hearts of the old people. One day, while they thought him much too young to speak, they were astonished to hear his voice.

"Lash me up and hang me from the lodge pole," said he, "and I shall become a man."

When they had recovered from their astonishment they lashed him to the lodge pole. In a moment he had burst the lashings and grown before their eyes into a tall, strong man. Looking round the lodge, which seemed scarcely large enough to hold him, Kutoyis perceived that there was no food about.

"Give me some arrows," said he, "and I will bring you food."

"We have no arrows," replied the old man, "only four arrow-heads."

Kutoyis fetched some wood, from which he cut a fine bow, and shafts to fit the flint arrow-heads. He begged the old Indian to lead him to a good hunting-ground, and when he had done so they quickly killed a magnificent buffalo.

Meanwhile the old Indian had told Kutoyis how badly his son-in-law had treated him, and as they were skinning the buffalo who should pass by but the subject of their conversation. Kutoyis hid behind the dead animal to see what would happen, and a moment later the angry voice of the son-in-law was heard.

Getting no reply, the cowardly hunter fitted an arrow to his bow and shot it at his father-in-law. Enraged at the cruel act, Kutoyis rose from his hiding-place behind the dead buffalo and fired all his arrows at the young man, whom he slew. He afterward gave food in plenty to the old man and his wife, and bade them return to their home. They were delighted to find

214

themselves once more free from persecution, but their daughter wept so much that finally Kutoyis asked her whether she would have another husband or whether she wished to follow her first spouse to the Land of Shadows, as she must do if she persisted in lamenting him.

The lady chose the former alternative as the lesser evil, and Kutoyis found her an excellent husband, with whom she lived happily for a long time.

### Kutoyis on his Travels

At length Kutoyis tired of his monotonous life, and desired to see more of the world. So his host directed him to a distant village, where he was welcomed by two old women. They set before their handsome guest the best fare at their disposal, which was buffalo-meat of a rather unattractive appearance.

" Is there no good meat ? " queried Kutoyis.

The old women explained that one of the lodges was occupied by a fierce bear, who seized upon all the good meat and left only the dry, poor sort for his neighbours. Without hesitation Kutoyis went out and killed a buffalo calf, which he presented to the women, desiring them to place the best parts of the meat in a prominent position outside the lodge, where the big bear could not fail to see it.

This they did, and sure enough one of the bear-cubs shortly passed by and seized the meat. Kutoyis, who had been lying in wait, rushed out and hit the animal as hard as he could. The cub carried his tale of woe to his father, and the big bear, growling threats of vengeance, gathered his whole family round him and rushed to the lodge of the old women, intending to kill the bold hunter.

However, Kutoyis was more than a match for all of

them, and very soon the bears were slain. Still he was unsatisfied, and longed for further adventures.

"Tell me," said he, "where shall I find another village?"

### The Wrestling Woman

"There is a village by the Big River," said the old women, "but you must not go there, for a wicked woman dwells in it who wrestles with and slays all who approach."

No sooner did Kutoyis hear this than he determined to seek the village, for his mission was to destroy evil beings who were a danger to his fellow-men. So in spite of the dissuasions of the old women he departed.

As he had been warned, the woman came out of her lodge on the approach of the stranger and invited him to wrestle with her.

"I cannot," said he, pretending to be frightened.

The woman mocked and jeered at him, while he made various excuses, but all the time he was observing how the land lay. When he drew nearer he saw that she had covered the ground with sharp flints, over which she had strewn grass. At last he said: "Very well, I will wrestle with you."

It was no wonder that she had killed many braves, for she was very strong. But Kutoyis was still stronger. With all her skill she could not throw him, and at last she grew tired, and was herself thrown on the sharp flints, on which she bled to death. The people rejoiced greatly when they heard of her death, and Kutoyis was universally acclaimed as a hero.

Kutoyis did many other high deeds before he departed to the Shadowland, and when he went he left sorrow in many lodges.

# CHAPTER IV : IROQUOIS MYTHS AND LEGENDS

## Iroquois Gods and Heroes

THE myths of the Iroquois are of exceptional interest because of the portraits they present of several semi-historical heroes. The earliest substratum of the myths of this people deals with the adventures of their principal deity, Hi'nun, the Thunder-god, who, with his brother, the West Wind, finally overcame and exterminated the powerful race of Stone Giants. Coming to a later period, we find that a number of legends cluster round the names of the chiefs Atotarho and Hiawatha, who in all probability at one time really existed. These present a good instance of the rapidity with which myth gathers round a famous name. Atotarho, the mighty warrior, is now regarded as the wizard *par excellence* of the Iroquois, but probably this does not result from the fact that he was cunning and cruel, as some writers on the tribe appear to think, but from the circumstance that as a great warrior he was clothed in a garment of serpents, and these reptiles, besides being looked upon as powerful war-physic, also possessed a deep magical significance. The original Hiawatha (He who seeks the Wampum-belt) is pictured as the father of a long line of persons of the same name, who appear to have been important functionaries in the tribal government. To him was ascribed the honour of having established the great confederacy of the Iroquois, which so long rendered them formidable opponents to the tribes which surrounded them. Like many other heroes in myth—the Celtic Mananan, for example—Hiawatha possessed a magic canoe which would obey his slightest behest, and in which he finally quitted the terrestrial sphere for that shadowy region to which all heroes finally take their departure.

## Hi'nun

Many interesting myths are related of the manner in which Hi'nun destroyed the monsters and giants which infested the early world. A hunter, caught in a heavy thunder-shower, took refuge in the woods. Crouching under the shelter of a great tree, he became aware of a mysterious voice which urged him to follow it. He was conscious of a sensation of slowly rising from the earth, and he soon found himself gazing downward from a point near the clouds, the height of many trees from the ground. He was surrounded by beings who had all the appearance of men, with one among them who seemed to be their chief. They asked him to cast his eyes toward the earth and tell them whether he could see a huge water-serpent. Unable to descry such a monster, the chief anointed his eyes with a sacred ointment, which gave him supernatural sight and permitted him to behold a dragon-like shape in the watery depths far below him. The chief commanded one of his warriors to dispatch the monster, but arrow after arrow failed to transfix it, whereupon the hunter was requested to display his skill as an archer. Drawing his bow, he took careful aim. The arrow whizzed down the depths and was speedily lost to sight, but a terrible commotion arose in the lake below, the body of the great serpent leaping from the blood-stained water with dreadful writhings and contortions. So appalling was the din that rose up to them that even the heavenly beings by whom the hunter was surrounded fell into a great trembling; but gradually the tempest of sound subsided, and the huge bulk of the mortally wounded serpent sank back into the lake, the surface of which became gradually more still, until finally all was peace once more. The chief thanked the hunter for the service he had rendered, and he was conducted back to earth. Thus was man first brought into contact with the beneficent Hi'nun, and thus did he learn the existence of a power which would protect him from forces unfriendly to humanity.

## The Thunderers

Once in early Iroquois days three braves set out upon an expedition. After they had journeyed for some time a misfortune occurred, one of their number breaking his leg. The others fashioned a litter with the object of carrying him back to his home, as Indian custom exacted. Retracing their steps, they came to a range of high mountains, the steep slopes of which taxed their strength to the utmost. To rest themselves they placed the disabled man on the ground and withdrew to a little distance.

" Why should we be thus burdened with a wounded man ?" said one to the other.

" You speak truly," was the rejoinder. " Why should we, indeed, since his hurt has come upon him by reason of his own carelessness ?"

As they spoke their eyes met in a meaning glance, and one of them pointed to a deep hole or pit opening in the side of the mountain at a little distance from the place where they were sitting. Returning to the injured man, they raised him as if about to proceed on the journey, and when passing the brink of the pit suddenly hurled him into it with great force. Then without loss of time they set their faces homeward. When they arrived in camp they reported that their comrade had died of wounds received in fight, but that he had not fallen into the enemy's hands, having received careful attention from them in his dying moments and honourable burial. The unfortunate man's aged mother was prostrate with grief at the sad news, but was somewhat relieved to think that her son had been kindly ministered to at the end.

When the brave who had been thrown into the pit regained his senses after the severe fall he had sustained he perceived a man of venerable aspect bending over him solicitously. When this person saw that the young man had regained consciousness he asked him what had been the intention of his comrades in so cruelly casting him into that abyss. The young man replied that his fellows had become tired of carrying him and had thus rid themselves of him. The old hermit—for so he seemed to be—made a hasty examination of the Indian's injuries, and announced that he would speedily cure him, on one condition. The other pledged his word to accept this, whatever it might be, whereupon the recluse told him that all he required was that he should hunt for him and bring home to him such game as he should slay. To this the brave gave a ready assent. The old man lost no time in performing his part of the bargain. He applied herbs to his injuries and assiduously tended his guest, who made a speedy and satisfactory recovery. The grateful warrior, once more enabled to follow the chase, brought home many trophies of his skill as a hunter to the cave on the mountain-side, and soon the pair had formed a strong attachment. One day, when in the forest, the warrior encountered an enormous bear, which he succeeded in slaying after a desperate struggle. As he was pondering how best he could remove it to the cave he became aware of a murmur of voices behind him, and glancing round he saw three men, or beings in the shape of men, clad in strange diaphanous garments, standing near. In reply to his question as to what brought them there, they told him that they were the Thunderers, or people of Hi'nun, whose mission it was to keep the earth in good order for the benefit of humanity, and to slay or destroy every agency inimical to mankind. They told him that the old man with whom he had been residing was by no means the sort of person he seemed to think, and that they had come to earth with the express intention of compassing his destruction. In this they requested his assistance, and promised him that if he would vouchsafe it he would speedily be transported back to his mother's lodge. Overjoyed at this proposal, the hunter did not scruple to return to the cave and tell the hermit that he had killed the bear, which he wished his help in bringing home. The old man seemed very uneasy, and begged him to examine the sky and tell him whether he perceived the least sign of clouds. The young brave reassured him and told him that not a cloud was to be seen, whereupon, emerging from his shelter, he made for the spot where the bear was lying. Hastily picking up the carcass, he requested his companion to place it all on his shoulders, which the young man did, expressing surprise at his great strength. He had proceeded with his burden for some distance when a terrific clap of thunder burst from the menacing black clouds which had speedily gathered overhead. In great terror the old man threw down his load and commenced to run with an agility which belied his years, but when a second peal broke forth he suddenly assumed the shape of a gigantic porcupine, which dashed through the undergrowth, discharging its quills like arrows as it ran. A veritable hail of thunderbolts now crashed down upon the creature's spiny back. As it reached the entrance to the cave one larger than the rest struck it with such tremendous force that it rolled dead into its den.

Then the Thunderers swooped down from the sky in triumph, mightily pleased at the death of their victim. The young hunter now requested them to discharge the promise they had made him to transport him back to his mother's lodge ; so, having fastened cloud-wings on his shoulders, they speedily brought him thither, carrying him carefully through the air and depositing him just outside the hut. The widow was delighted to see her son, whom she had believed to be long dead, and the Thunderers were so pleased with the assistance he had lent them that they asked him to accompany them in their monster-destroying mission every spring. He assented, and on one of these expeditions flew earthward to drink from a certain pool. When he rejoined his companions they observed that the water with which his lips were moist had caused them to shine as if smeared with oil. At their request he indicated the pool from which he had drunk, and they informed him that in its depths there dwelt a monster for which they had searched for years. With that they hurled a great thunderbolt into the pool, which immediately dried up, revealing an immense grub of the species which destroys the standing crops. The monster was, indeed, the King of Grubs, and his death set back the conspiracies of his kind for many generations. The youth subsequently returned to earth, and having narrated to the members of his tribe the services which Hi'nun had performed on their behalf, they considered it fitting to institute a special worship of the deity, and, in fact, to make him supreme god of their nation. Even to-day many Iroquois allude to Hi'nun as their grandfather, and evince extraordinary veneration at the mention of his name.

**Hiawatha**

Much confusion exists with regard to the true status of the reputed Iroquois hero Hiawatha. We find him variously represented as a historical personage and a mythical demi-god, and as belonging to both the Iroquois and the Algonquins. In solid history and in the wildest myth he is a figure of equal importance. This confusion is largely due to the popularity of Longfellow's poem *Hiawatha*, which by its very excellence has given the greater prominence to the fallacies it contains. The fact is that Longfellow, following in the path of Schoolcraft, has really confused *two* personages in the character of Hiawatha, one the entirely mythical Manabozho, or Michabo—which name he at first intended to bestow on his poem— and the other the almost wholly historical Hiawatha. Manabozho, according to tradition, was a demi-god of the Ojibways, and to him, and not to Hiawatha, must be credited the exploits described in the poem. There is no doubt that myths have grown up round the name of the Iroquois hero, for myth is the ivy that binds all historical ruins and makes them picturesque to the eye ; but it has been proved that there is a solid structure of fact behind the legendary stories of Hiawatha, and even the period of his activity has been fixed with tolerable accuracy by modern American historians.

Hiawatha, or Hai-en-Wat-ha, was a chief of Iroquois stock, belonging either to the Onondaga or the Mohawk tribe. His most important feat was the union of the Five Nations of the Iroquois into a Grand League, an event which was of more than national significance, since it so largely affected the fortunes of European peoples when they afterward fought for American supremacy. As the Five Nations are known to have come together in the sixteenth century, it follows that Hiawatha must have lived and worked about that time. In later days the League was called the Six Nations, and still more recently the Seven Nations.

When the Iroquois, or 'Long House People,' were found by the French and Dutch they occupied the western part of what is now New York State, and were at a much more advanced stage of culture than most of the Indian tribes. They tilled the ground, cultivating maize and tobacco, and were skilled in the arts of war and diplomacy. They were greatly strengthened by the Grand League, or 'Kayanerenh Kowa,' which, as has been said, was founded by the chief Hiawatha, and were much the most important of the North American tribes.

If we look to tradition for an account of the origin of the Grand League, we learn that the union was effected by Hiawatha in the fourteenth century. The Hurons and Iroquois, we are told, were at one time one people, but later they separated, the Hurons going to the lake which is named after them, and the Iroquois to New York, where their five tribes were united under a General Council. But tradition is quite evidently wrong in assigning so early a date to this important event, for one of the two branches of the Iroquois family (that which comprises the Mohawks and the Oneidas) has left but few traces of an early occupation, and these, in the shape of some old town-sites, are judged to belong to the latter part of the sixteenth century.

The early connexion between the Iroquois and the Hurons, and their subsequent separation, remains undisputed. The Iroquois family was divided into two branches, the Sinnekes (Onondagas, Cayugas, and

224

Senecas) and the Caniengas (Mohawks and Oneidas),
of which the subdivisions composed the Five Nations.
The Sinnekes had established themselves in the western
portion of New York, and the Caniengas at Hochelaga
(Montreal) and elsewhere on the St. Lawrence, where
they lived amicably enough with their Algonquin neighbours. But in 1560 a quarrel arose between the
Caniengas and the Algonquins, in which the latter
called in the aid of the Hurons. This was the beginning of a long war, in which the Caniengas had the
worst of it. Gradually the Caniengas were driven
along the shores of Lake Champlain and Lake George
till they reached the valley of the Mohawk River, where
they established themselves in a country bordering on
that of the Onondagas.

Now the Onondagas were a formidable tribe, fierce
and warlike, and the Caniengas, being long accustomed
to war, were not the most peaceable of nations, and
ere long there was trouble between them, while both
were at war with the Hurons. At the head of the
Onondagas was the great chief Atotarho, whose sanguinary exploits and crafty stratagems had become
the dread of the neighbouring peoples, and among his
warriors was the generous Hiawatha. Hiawatha was filled
with horror at the sight of the suffering caused by
Atotarho's expeditions, and already his statesman's
mind was forming projects of peace. He saw that in
confederation lay the means not only of preserving
peace among his people, but of withstanding alien
foes as well. In two consecutive years he called an
assembly to consider his plan, but on each occasion the
grim presence of Atotarho made discussion impossible. Hiawatha in despair fled from the land of the
Onondagas, journeyed eastward through the country
of the Oneidas, and at last took up his residence

among the Mohawks, into which tribe he was adopted. It has been said by some authorities, and the idea does not lack probability, that Hiawatha was originally a Mohawk, and that he spent some time among the Onondagas, afterward returning to his own people. At all events, the Mohawks proved more amenable to reason than the Onondagas had done. Among the chiefs of his adopted tribe Hiawatha found one—Dekanewidah—who fell in with his confederation plans, and agreed to work along with him. Messengers were dispatched to the Oneidas, who bade them return in a year, at the end of which period negotiations were renewed. The result was that the Oneida chiefs signed a treaty inaugurating the Kayanerenh Kowa. An embassy to the Onondagas was fruitless, as Atotarho persistently obstructed the new scheme ; but later, when the Kayanerenh Kowa embraced the Cayugas, messages were once more sent to the powerful Onondagas, diplomatically suggesting that Atotarho should take the lead in the Grand Council. The grim warrior was mollified by this sop to his vanity, and condescended to accept the proposal. Not only that, but he soon became an enthusiastic worker in the cause of confederation, and secured the inclusion of the Senecas in the League.

The confederacy of the Five Nations was now complete, and the ' Silver Chain,' as their Grand Council was called, met together on the shores of the Salt Lake. The number of chiefs chosen from each tribe bore some relation to its numerical status, the largest number, fourteen, being supplied by the Onondagas. The office of representative in the Council was to be an hereditary one, descending in the female line, as with the Picts of Scotland and other primitive peoples, and never from father to son.

# HIAWATHA

So powerful did the League become that the name of 'Long House People' was held in the greatest awe. They annihilated their ancient enemies, the Hurons, and they attacked and subdued the Micmacs, Mohicans, Pawnees, Algonquins, Cherokees, and many other tribes. The effect of the League on British history is incalculable. When the Frenchman Champlain arrived in 1611 he interfered on behalf of the Hurons, an action whose far-reaching consequences he could not foresee, but from that period dated the hatred of the Iroquois for the French which ensured Britain's success in the long struggle between the European nations in America. Without the assistance of the native factor, who shall say how the struggle might have ended ?

But the Iroquois were not altogether a bloodthirsty people. A strong bond of brotherhood existed between the Five Nations, among themselves they were kind and gentle, and in part at least Hiawatha's dream of peace was realized. It is not, of course, very easy to say how far Hiawatha intended the scheme of universal brotherhood with which he is credited. Whether he conceived a Grand League embracing all the nations of the earth or whether his full ambition was realized in the union of the Five Nations is a point which history does not make clear. But even in the more limited sense his work was a great one, and the lofty and noble character which Longfellow has given to his hero seems not unsuited to the actual Hiawatha, who realizes the ideal of the 'noble savage' more fully, perhaps, than any one else in the annals of primitive peoples.

As in the case of King Arthur and Dietrich of Berne, many myths soon gathered round the popular and revered name of Hiawatha. Among barbarians three, or even two, generations usually suffice to render a great and outstanding figure mythical. But one prefers to think of this Iroquois statesman as a real man, a bright particular star in a dark sky of savagery and ignorance.

### The Stone Giants

The Iroquois believed that in early days there existed a malignant race of giants whose bodies were fashioned out of stone. It is difficult to say how the idea of such beings arose, but it is possible that the generally distributed conception of a gigantic race springing from Mother Earth was in this instance fused with another belief that stones and rocks composed the earth's bony framework. We find an example of this belief in the beautiful old Greek myth of Deucalion and Pyrrha, which much resembles that of Noah. When after the great flood which submerged Hellas the survivors' ship grounded upon Mount Parnassus they inquired of the oracle of Themis in what manner the human race might be restored. They were bidden by the oracle to veil themselves and to throw the bones of their mother behind them. These they interpreted to mean the stones of the earth. Picking up loose pieces of stone, they cast them over their shoulders, and from those thrown by Deucalion there sprang men, while those cast by Pyrrha became women.

These Stone Giants of the Iroquois, dwelling in the far west, took counsel with one another and resolved to invade the Indian territory and exterminate the race of men. A party of Indians just starting on the war-path were apprised of the invasion, and were bidden by the gods to challenge the giants to combat. This they did, and the opposing bands faced each other at a spot near a great gulf. But as the monsters advanced upon their human enemies the god of the west wind, who was

228

lying in wait for them, swooped down upon the Titans, so that they were hurled over the edge of the gulf, far down into the dark abyss below, where they perished miserably.

## The Pigmies

In contradistinction to their belief in giants, the Iroquois imagined the existence of a race of pigmies, who had many of the attributes of the Teutonic gnomes. They were responsible for the beauty of terrestrial scenery, which they carved and sculptured in cliff, scar, and rock, and, like the thunder-gods, they protected the human race against the many monsters which infested the world in early times.

## Witches and Witchcraft

The Iroquois belief in witchcraft was very strong, and the following tale is supposed to account for the origin of witches and sorcery. A boy who was out hunting found a snake the colours of whose skin were so intensely beautiful that he resolved to capture it. He caught it and tended it carefully, feeding it on birds and small game, and housing it in a little bowl made of bark, which he filled with water. In the bottom of the bowl he placed down, small feathers, and wood fibre, and on going to feed the snake he discovered that these things had become living beings. From this he gathered that the reptile was endowed with supernatural powers, and he found that other articles placed in the water along with it soon showed signs of life. He procured more snakes and placed them in the bowl. Observing some men of the tribe rubbing ointment on their eyes to enable them to see more clearly, he used some of the water from the bowl in which the snakes were immersed upon his own, and

229

lo ! he found on climbing a tall tree that nothing was hidden from his sight, which pierced all intervening obstacles. He could see far into the earth, where lay hidden precious stones and rich minerals. His sight pierced the trunks of trees ; he could see through mountains, and could discern objects lying deep down in the bed of a river.

He concluded that the greater the number of reptiles the snake-liquid contained the more potent would it become. Accordingly he captured several snakes, and suspended them over his bowl in such a manner that the essential oil they contained dropped into the water, with the result that the activity of the beings which had been so strangely bred in it was increased. In course of time he found that by merely placing one of his fingers in the liquid and pointing it at any person he could instantly bewitch him. He added some roots to the water in the bowl, some of which he then drank. By blowing this from his mouth a great light was produced, by rubbing his eyes with it he could see in the dark, and by other applications of it he could render himself invisible, or take the shape of a snake. If he dipped an arrow into the liquid and discharged it at any living being it would kill it although it might not strike it. Not content with discovering this magic fluid, the youth resolved to search for antidotes to it, and these he collected.

### A 'Medicine' Legend

A similar legend is told by the Senecas to account for the origin of their 'medicine.' Nearly two hundred years ago—in the Indian estimation this is a very great period of time—an Indian went into the woods on a hunting expedition. One night while asleep in his solitary camp he was awakened by a great noise of

singing and drum-beating, such as is heard at festivals.
Starting up, he made his way to the place whence the
sounds came, and although he could not see any one
there he observed a heap of corn and a large squash
vine with three squashes on it, and three ears of corn
which lay apart from the rest. Feeling very uneasy,
he once more pursued his hunting operations, and when
night came again laid himself down to rest. But his
sleep was destined to be broken yet a second time, and
awaking he perceived a man bending over him, who
said in menacing tones :

" Beware : what you saw was sacred. You deserve to
die."

A rustling among the branches denoted the presence
of a number of people, who, after some hesitation,
gathered round the hunter, and informed him that
they would pardon his curiosity and would tell him
their secret. " The great medicine for wounds," said
the man who had first awakened him, " is squash and
corn. Come with me and I will teach you how to
make and apply it."

With these words he led the hunter to the spot at
which he had surprised the 'medicine'-making operations on the previous night, where he beheld a great fire
and a strange-looking laurel-bush, which seemed as if
made of iron. Chanting a weird song, the people circled
slowly round the bush to the accompaniment of a
rattling of gourd-shells. On the hunter's asking them
to explain this procedure, one of them heated a stick
and thrust it right through his cheek. He immediately
applied some of the 'medicine' to the wound, so that
it healed instantly. Having thus demonstrated the
power of the drug, they sang a tune which they called
the 'medicine-song,' which their pupil learnt by heart.

The hunter then turned to depart, and all at once he

saw that the beings who surrounded him were not human, as he had thought, but animals—foxes, bears, and beavers—who fled as he looked at them. Surprised and even terrified at the turn matters had taken, he made his way homeward with all speed, conning over the prescription which the strange beings had given him the while. They had told him to take one stalk of corn, to dry the cob and pound it very fine, then to take one squash, cut it up and pound it, and to mix the whole with water from a running stream, near its source. This prescription he used with very great success among his people, and it proved the origin of the great 'medicine' of the Senecas. Once a year at the season when the deer changes his coat they prepare it as the forest folk did, singing the weird song and dancing round it to the rhythmic accompaniment of the gourd-shell rattles, while they burn tobacco to the gods.

### Great Head and the Ten Brothers

It was commonly believed among the Iroquois Indians that there existed a curious and malevolent being whom they called Great Head. This odd creature was merely an enormous head poised on slender legs. He made his dwelling on a rugged rock, and directly he saw any living person approach he would growl fiercely in true ogre fashion : " I see thee, I see thee ! Thou shalt die."

Far away in a remote spot an orphaned family of ten boys lived with their uncle. The older brothers went out every day to hunt, but the younger ones, not yet fitted for so rigorous a life, remained at home with their uncle, or at least did not venture much beyond the immediate vicinity of their lodge. One day the hunters did not return at their usual hour. As the evening passed without bringing any sign of the missing

232

youths the little band at home became alarmed. At length the eldest of the boys left in the lodge volunteered to go in search of his brothers. His uncle consented, and he set off, but he did not return.

In the morning another brother said: "I will go to seek my brothers." Having obtained permission, he went, but he also did not come back. Another and another took upon himself the task of finding the lost hunters, but of the searchers as well as of those sought for there was no news forthcoming. At length only the youngest of the lads remained at home, and to his entreaties to be allowed to seek for his brothers the uncle turned a deaf ear, for he feared to lose the last of his young nephews.

One day when uncle and nephew were out in the forest the latter fancied he heard a deep groan, which seemed to proceed from the earth exactly under his feet. They stopped to listen. The sound was repeated—unmistakably a human groan. Hastily they began digging in the earth, and in a moment or two came upon a man covered with mould and apparently unconscious.

The pair carried the unfortunate one to their lodge, where they rubbed him with bear's oil till he recovered consciousness. When he was able to speak he could give no explanation of how he came to be buried alive. He had been out hunting, he said, when suddenly his mind became a blank, and he remembered nothing more till he found himself in the lodge with the old man and the boy. His hosts begged the stranger to stay with them, and they soon discovered that he was no ordinary mortal, but a powerful magician. At times he behaved very strangely. One night, while a great storm raged without, he tossed restlessly on his couch instead of going to sleep. At last he sought the old uncle.

233

"Do you hear that noise?" he said. "That is my brother, Great Head, who is riding on the wind. Do you not hear him howling?"

The old man considered this astounding speech for a moment; then he asked: "Would he come here if you sent for him?"

"No," said the other, thoughtfully, "but we might bring him here by magic. Should he come you must have food ready for him, in the shape of huge blocks of maple-wood, for that is what he lives on."

The stranger departed in search of his brother Great Head, taking with him his bow, and on the way he came across a hickory-tree, whose roots provided him with arrows. About midday he drew near to the dwelling of his brother, Great Head. In order to see without being seen, he changed himself into a mole, and crept through the grass till he saw Great Head perched on a rock, frowning fiercely. "I see thee!" he growled, with his wild eyes fixed on an owl. The man-mole drew his bow and shot an arrow at Great Head. The arrow became larger and larger as it flew toward the monster, but it returned to him who had fired it, and as it did so it regained its natural size. The man seized it and rushed back the way he had come. Very soon he heard Great Head in pursuit, puffing and snorting along on the wings of a hurricane. When the creature had almost overtaken him he turned and discharged another arrow. Again and again he repulsed his pursuer in this fashion, till he lured him to the lodge where his benefactors lived. When Great Head burst into the house the uncle and nephew began to hammer him vigorously with mallets. To their surprise the monster broke into laughter, for he had recognized his brother and was very pleased to see him. He ate the maple-blocks they brought him with a hearty appetite, whereupon they told him the story of the missing hunters.

"I know what has become of them," said Great Head. "They have fallen into the hands of a witch. If this young man," indicating the nephew, "will accompany me, I will show him her dwelling, and the bones of his brothers."

The youth, who loved adventure, and was besides very anxious to learn the fate of his brothers, at once consented to seek the home of the witch. So he and Great Head started off, and lost no time in getting to the place. They found the space in front of the lodge strewn with dry bones, and the witch sitting in the doorway singing. When she saw them she muttered the magic word which turned living people into dry bones, but on Great Head and his companion it had no effect whatever. Acting on a prearranged signal, Great Head and the youth attacked the witch and killed her. No sooner had she expired than her flesh turned into birds and beasts and fishes. What was left of her they burned to ashes.

Their next act was to select the bones of the nine brothers from among the heap, and this they found no easy task. But at last it was accomplished, and Great Head said to his companion : "I am going home to my rock. When I pass overhead in a great storm I will bid these bones arise, and they will get up and return with you."

The youth stood alone for a little while till he heard the sound of a fierce tempest. Out of the hurricane Great Head called to the brothers to arise. In a moment they were all on their feet, receiving the congratulations of their younger brother and each other, and filled with joy at their reunion.

## The Seneca's Revenge

A striking story is told of a Seneca youth who for many years and through a wearisome captivity nourished the hope of vengeance so dear to a prisoner. A certain tribe of the Senecas had settled on the shores of Lake Erie, when they were surprised by their ancient enemies the Illinois, and in spite of a stout resistance many of them were slain, and a woman and a boy taken prisoner. When the victors halted for the night they built a great fire, and proceeded to celebrate their success by singing triumphant songs, in which they commanded the boy to join them. The lad pretended that he did not know their language, but said that he would sing their song in his own tongue, to which they assented; but instead of a pæan in their praise he sang a song of vengeance, in which he vowed that if he were spared all of them would lose their scalps. A few days afterward the woman became so exhausted that she could walk no farther, so the Illinois slew her. But before she died she extracted a promise from the boy that he would avenge her, and would never cease to be a Seneca.

In a few days they arrived at the Illinois camp, where a council was held to consider the fate of the captive lad. Some were for instantly putting him to death, but their chief ruled that should he be able to live through their tortures he would be worthy of becoming an Illinois. They seized the wretched lad and held his bare feet to the glowing council-fire, then after piercing them they told him to run a race. He bounded forward, and ran so swiftly that he soon gained the Great House of the tribe, where he seated himself upon a wild-cat skin.

Another council was held, and the Illinois braves

236

agreed that the lad possessed high courage and would make a great warrior ; but others argued that he knew their war-path and might betray them, and it was finally decided that he should be burnt at the stake. As he was about to perish in this manner an aged warrior suggested that if he were able to withstand their last torture he should be permitted to live. Accordingly he held the unfortunate lad under water in a pool until only a spark of life remained in him, but he survived, and became an Illinois warrior.

Years passed, and the boy reached manhood and married a chief's daughter. His strength and endurance became proverbial, but the warriors of the tribe of his adoption would never permit him to take part in their warlike expeditions. At length a raid against the Senecas was mooted, and he begged so hard to be allowed to accompany the braves that at last they consented. Indeed, so great was their admiration of the skill with which he outlined a plan of campaign that they made him chief of the expedition. For many days the party marched toward the Seneca country ; but when at last they neared it their scouts reported that there were no signs of the tribe, and that the Senecas must have quitted their territory. Their leader, however, proposed to go in search of the enemy himself, along with another warrior of the tribe, and this was agreed to.

When the pair had gone five or six miles the leader said to his companion that it would be better if they separated, as they would then be able to cover more ground. Passing on to where he knew he would find the Senecas, he warned them of their danger, and arranged that an ambush of his kinsfolk should lie in wait for the Illinois.

Returning to the Illinois camp, he reported that he had seen nothing, but that he well remembered the

Seneca hiding-place. He asked to be given the bravest warriors, and assured the council that he would soon bring them the scalps of their foes. Suspecting nothing, they assented to his proposal, and he was followed by the flower of the Illinois tribe, all unaware that five hundred Senecas awaited them in the valley. The youth led his men right into the heart of the ambush ; then, pretending to miss his footing, he fell. This was the signal for the Senecas to rise on every side. Yelling their war-cry, they rushed from their shelter and fell on the dismayed Illinois, who gave way on every side. The slaughter was immense. Vengeance nerved the arms of the Seneca braves, and of three hundred Illinois but two escaped. The leader of the expedition was borne in triumph to the Seneca village, where to listening hundreds he told the story of his capture and long-meditated revenge. He became a great chief among his people, and even to this day his name is uttered by them with honour and reverence.

### The Boy Magician

In the heart of the wilderness there lived an old woman and her little grandson. The two found no lack of occupation from day to day, the woman busying herself with cooking and cleaning and the boy with shooting and hunting. The grandmother frequently spoke of the time when the child would grow up and go out into the world.

"Always go to the east," she would say. "Never go to the west, for there lies danger."

But what the danger was she would not tell him, in spite of his importunate questioning. Other boys went west, he thought to himself, and why should not he ? Nevertheless his grandmother made him promise that he would not go west.

238

Years passed by, and the child grew to be a man, though he still retained the curiosity and high spirits of his boyhood. His persistent inquiries drew from the old grandmother a reluctant explanation of her warning.

"In the west," said she, "there dwells a being who is anxious to do us harm. If he sees you it will mean death for both of us."

This statement, instead of frightening the young Indian, only strengthened in him a secret resolution he had formed to go west on the first opportunity. Not that he wished to bring any misfortune on his poor old grandmother, any more than on himself, but he trusted to his strong arm and clear head to deliver them from their enemy. So with a laugh on his lips he set off to the west.

Toward evening he came to a lake, where he rested. He had not been there long when he heard a voice saying : "Aha, my fine fellow, I see you !"

The youth looked all round him, and up into the sky above, but he saw no one.

"I am going to send a hurricane," the mysterious voice continued, "to break your grandmother's hut to pieces. How will you like that ?"

"Oh, very well," answered the young man gaily. "We are always in need of firewood, and now we shall have plenty."

"Go home and see," the voice said mockingly. "I daresay you will not like it so well."

Nothing daunted, the young adventurer retraced his steps. As he neared home a great wind sprang up, seeming to tear the very trees out by the roots.

"Make haste !" cried the grandmother from the doorway. "We shall both be killed !"

When she had drawn him inside and shut the door

she scolded him heartily for his disobedience, and bewailed the fate before them. The young man soothed her fears, saying : "Don't cry, grandmother. We shall turn the lodge into a rock, and so we shall be saved."

Having some skill in magic, he did as he had said, and the hurricane passed harmlessly over their heads. When it had ceased they emerged from their retreat, and found an abundance of firewood all round them.

## The Hailstorm

Next day the youth was on the point of setting off toward the west once more, but the urgent entreaties of his grandmother moved him to proceed eastward— for a time. Directly he was out of sight of the lodge he turned his face once more to the west. Arrived at the lake, he heard the voice once more, though its owner was still invisible.

"I am going to send a great hailstorm on your grandmother's hut," it said. "What do you think of that ? "

"Oh," was the response, "I think I should like it. I have always wanted a bundle of spears."

"Go home and see," said the voice.

Away the youth went through the woods. The sky became darker and darker as he neared his home, and just as he was within a bowshot of the little hut a fierce hailstorm broke, and he thought he would be killed before he reached shelter.

"Alas ! " cried the old woman when he was safely indoors, "we shall be destroyed this time. How can we save ourselves ? "

Again the young man exercised his magic powers, and transformed the frail hut into a hollow rock, upon which the shafts of the hailstorm spent themselves in vain. At last the sky cleared, the lodge resumed its former shape, and the young man saw a multitude of sharp, beautiful spear-heads on the ground.

"I will get poles," said he, "to fit to them for fishing."

When he returned in a few minutes with the poles he found that the spears had vanished.

"Where are my beautiful spears?" he asked his grandmother.

"They were only ice-spears," she replied. "They have all melted away."

The young Indian was greatly disappointed, and wondered how he could avenge himself on the being who had played him this malicious trick.

"Be warned in time," said the aged grandmother, shaking her head at him. "Take my advice and leave him alone."

### The Charmed Stone

But the youth's adventurous spirit impelled him to see the end of the matter, so he took a stone and tied it round his neck for a charm, and sought the lake once again. Carefully observing the direction from which the voice proceeded, he saw in the middle of the lake a huge head with a face on every side of it.

"Aha! uncle," he exclaimed, "I see you! How would you like it if the lake dried up?"

"Nonsense!" said the voice angrily, "that will never happen."

"Go home and see," shouted the youth, mimicking the mocking tone the other had adopted on the previous occasions. As he spoke he swung his charmed stone round his head and threw it into the air. As it descended it grew larger and larger, and the moment it entered the lake the water began to boil.

The lad returned home and told his grandmother what he had done.

" It is of no use," said she. " Many have tried to slay him, but all have perished in the attempt."

Next morning our hero went westward again, and found the lake quite dry, and the animals in it dead, with the exception of a large green frog, who was in reality the malicious being who had tormented the Indian and his grandmother. A quick blow with a stick put an end to the creature, and the triumphant youth bore the good news to his old grandmother, who from that time was left in peace and quietness.

### The Friendly Skeleton

A little boy living in the woods with his old uncle was warned by him not to go eastward, but to play close to the lodge or walk toward the west. The child felt a natural curiosity to know what lay in the forbidden direction, and one day took advantage of his uncle's absence on a hunting expedition to wander away to the east. At length he came to a large lake, on the shores of which he stopped to rest. Here he was accosted by a man, who asked him his name and where he lived.

"Come," said the stranger, when he had finished questioning the boy, "let us see who can shoot an arrow the highest."

This they did, and the boy's arrow went much higher than that of his companion.

The stranger then suggested a swimming match.

" Let us see," he said, "who can swim farthest under water without taking a breath."

Again the boy beat his rival, who next proposed that they should sail out to an island in the middle of the lake, to see the beautiful birds that were to be found there. The child consented readily, and they embarked in a curious canoe, which was propelled by three swans harnessed to either side of it. Directly they had taken their seats the man began to sing, and the canoe moved off. In a very short time they had reached the island. Here the little Indian realized that his confidence in his new-found friend was misplaced. The stranger took all his clothes from him, put them in the canoe, and jumped in himself, saying :

" Come, swans, let us go home."

The obedient swans set off at a good pace, and soon left the island far behind. The boy was very angry at having been so badly used, but when it grew dark his resentment changed to fear, and he sat down and cried with cold and misery. Suddenly he heard a husky voice close at hand, and, looking round, he saw a skeleton on the ground.

" I am very sorry for you," said the skeleton in hoarse tones. " I will do what I can to help you. But first you must do something for me. Go and dig by that tree, and you shall find a tobacco-pouch with some tobacco in it, a pipe, and a flint."

The boy did as he was asked, and when he had filled the pipe he lit it and placed it in the mouth of the skeleton. He saw that the latter's body was full of mice, and that the smoke frightened them away.

" There is a man coming to-night with three dogs," said the skeleton. " He is coming to look for you. You must make tracks all over the island, so that they may not find you, and then hide in a hollow tree."

Again the boy obeyed his gaunt instructor, and when he was safely hidden he saw a man come ashore with three dogs. All night they hunted him, but he had made so many tracks that the dogs were confused, and at last the man departed in anger. Next day the trembling boy emerged and went to the skeleton.

"To-night," said the latter, "the man who brought you here is coming to drink your blood. You must dig a hole in the sand and hide. When he comes out of the canoe you must enter it. Say, 'Come, swans, let us go home,' and if the man calls you do not look back."

### The Lost Sister

Everything fell out as the skeleton had foretold. The boy hid in the sand, and directly he saw his tormentor step ashore he jumped into the canoe, saying hastily, "Come, swans, let us go home." Then he began to sing as he had heard the man do when they first embarked. In vain the man called him back; he refused to look round. The swans carried the canoe to a cave in a high rock, where the boy found his clothes, as well as a fire and food. When he had donned his garments and satisfied his hunger he lay down and slept. In the morning he returned to the island, where he found the tyrant quite dead. The skeleton now commanded him to sail eastward to seek for his sister, whom a fierce man had carried away. He set out eagerly on his new quest, and a three days' journey brought him to the place where his sister was. He lost no time in finding her.

"Come, my sister," said he, "let us flee away together."

"Alas! I cannot," answered the young woman. "A wicked man keeps me here. It is time for him to return home, and he would be sure to catch us. But let me hide you now, and in the morning we shall go away."

So she dug a pit and hid her brother, though not a moment too soon, for the footsteps of her husband were heard approaching the hut. The woman had cooked a child, and this she placed before the man.

244

"You have had visitors," he said, seeing his dogs snuffing around uneasily.

"No," was the reply, "I have seen no one but you."

"I shall wait till to-morrow," said the man to himself. "Then I shall kill and eat him." He had already guessed that his wife had not spoken the truth. However, he said nothing more, but waited till morning, when, instead of going to a distant swamp to seek for food, as he pretended to do, he concealed himself at a short distance from the hut, and at length saw the brother and sister making for a canoe. They were hardly seated when they saw him running toward them. In his hand he bore a large hook, with which he caught the frail vessel; but the lad broke the hook with a stone, and the canoe darted out on to the lake. The man was at a loss for a moment, and could only shout incoherent threats after the pair. Then an idea occurred to him, and, lying down on the shore, he began to drink the water. This caused the canoe to rush back again, but once more the boy was equal to the occasion. Seizing the large stone with which he had broken the hook, he threw it at the man and slew him, the water at the same time rushing back into the lake. Thus the brother and sister escaped, and in three days they had arrived at the island, where they heartily thanked their benefactor, the skeleton. He, however, had still another task for the young Indian to perform.

"Take your sister home to your uncle's lodge," said he; "then return here yourself, and say to the many bones which you will find on the island, 'Arise,' and they shall come to life again."

When the brother and sister reached their home they found that their old uncle had been grievously lamenting the loss of his nephew, and he was quite overjoyed at seeing them. On his recommendation they built a large lodge to accommodate the people they were to bring back with them. When it was completed, the youth revisited the island, bade the bones arise, and was delighted to see them obey his bidding and become men and women. He led them to the lodge he had built, where they all dwelt happily for a long time.

### The Pigmies

When the Cherokees were dwelling in the swamps of Florida the Iroquois made a practice of swooping down on them and raiding their camps. On one occasion the raiding party was absent from home for close on two years. On the eve of their return one of their number, a chieftain, fell ill, and the rest of the party were at a loss to know what to do with him. Obviously, if they carried him home with them he would considerably impede their progress. Besides, there was the possibility that he might not recover, and all their labour would be to no purpose. Thus they debated far into the night, and finally decided to abandon him to his fate and return by themselves. The sick man, unable to stir hand or foot, overheard their decision, but he bore it stoically, like an Indian warrior. Nevertheless, when he heard the last swish of their paddles as they crossed the river he could not help thinking of the friends and kindred he would probably never see again.

When the raiders reached home they were closely questioned as to the whereabouts of the missing chief, and the inquiries were all the more anxious because the sick man had been a great favourite among his people. The guilty warriors answered evasively. They did not know what had become of their comrade, they said. Possibly he had been lost or killed in Florida.

Meanwhile the sick man lay dying on the banks of the river. Suddenly he heard, quite close at hand, the gentle sound of a canoe. The vessel drew in close to the bank, and, full in view of the warrior, three pigmy men disembarked. They regarded the stranger with some surprise. At length one who seemed to be the leader advanced and spoke to him, bidding him await their return, and promising to look after him. They were going, he said, to a certain 'salt-lick,' where many curious animals watered, in order to kill some for food.

### The Salt-Lick

When the pigmies arrived at the place they found that no animals were as yet to be seen, but very soon a large buffalo bull came to drink. Immediately a buffalo cow arose from the lick, and when they had satisfied their thirst the two animals lay down on the bank. The pigmies concluded that the time was ripe for killing them, and, drawing their bows, they succeeded in dispatching the buffaloes. Returning to the sick man, they amply fulfilled their promise to take care of him, skilfully tending him until he had made a complete recovery. They then conveyed him to his friends, who now learnt that the story told them by the raiders was false. Bitterly indignant at the deception and heartless cruelty of these men, they fell upon them and punished them according to their deserts.

Later the chief headed a band of people who were curious to see the lick, which they found surrounded by the bones of numberless large animals which had been killed by the pigmies.

This story is interesting as a record of what were perhaps the last vestiges of a pigmy folk who at one time inhabited the eastern portion of North America, before the coming of the Red Man. We have already alluded to this people, in the pages dealing with the discoveries of the Norsemen in the continent.

## The Magical Serpent

In the seventeenth century a strange legend concerning a huge serpent was found among the Hurons, who probably got it from the neighbouring Algonquins. This monster had on its head a horn which would pierce anything, even the hardest rock. Any one possessing a piece of it was supposed to have very good fortune. The Hurons did not know where the creature was to be found, but said that the Algonquins were in the habit of selling them small pieces of the magic horn.

It is possible that the mercenary Shawnees had borrowed this myth from the Cherokees for their own purposes. At all events a similar legend existed among both tribes which told of a monster snake, the King of Rattlesnakes, who dwelt up among the mountain-passes, attended by a retinue of his kind. Instead of a crown, he wore on his head a beautiful jewel which possessed magic properties. Many a brave tried to obtain possession of this desirable gem, but all fell victims to the venomous reptiles. At length a more ingenious warrior clothed himself entirely in leather, and so rendered himself impervious to their attack. Making his way to the haunt of the serpents, he slew their monster chief. Then, triumphantly taking possession of the wonderful jewel, he bore it to his tribe, by whom it was regarded with profound veneration and jealously preserved.

## The Origin of Medicine

An interesting Cherokee myth is that which recounts the origin of disease, and the consequent institution of curative medicine. In the old days, we are told, the members of the brute creation were gifted with speech and dwelt in amity with the human race, but mankind multiplied so quickly that the animals were crowded into the forests and desert places of the earth, so that the old friendship between them was soon forgotten. The breach was farther widened by the invention of lethal weapons, by the aid of which man commenced the wholesale slaughter of the beasts for the sake of their flesh and skins. The animals, at first surprised, soon grew angry, and resolved upon measures of retaliation. The bear tribe met in council, presided over by the Old White Bear, their chief. After several speakers had denounced mankind for their bloodthirsty tendencies, war was unanimously decided upon, but the lack of weapons was regarded as a serious drawback. However, it was suggested that man's instruments should be turned against himself, and as the bow and arrow were considered to be the principal human agency of destruction, it was resolved to fashion a specimen. A suitable piece of wood was procured, and one of the bears sacrificed himself to provide gut for a bowstring. When the weapon was completed it was discovered that the claws of the bears spoiled their shooting. One of the bears, however, cut his claws, and succeeded in hitting the mark, but the Old White Bear very wisely remarked that without claws they could not climb trees or bring down game, and that were they to cut them off they must all starve.

The deer also met in council, under their chief, the Little Deer, when it was decided that those hunters who

249

slew one of their number without asking pardon in a suitable manner should be afflicted with rheumatism. They gave notice of this decision to the nearest settlement of Indians, and instructed them how to make propitiation when forced by necessity to kill one of the deer-folk. So when a deer is slain by the hunter the Little Deer runs to the spot, and, bending over the blood-stains, asks the spirit of the deer if it has heard the prayer of the hunter for pardon. If the reply be ' Yes,' all is well, and the Little Deer departs ; but if the answer be in the negative, he tracks the hunter to his cabin, and strikes him with rheumatism, so that he becomes a helpless cripple. Sometimes hunters who have not learned the proper formula for pardon attempt to turn aside the Little Deer from his pursuit by building a fire behind them in the trail.

## The Council of the Fishes

The fishes and reptiles then held a joint council, and arranged to haunt those human beings who tormented them with hideous dreams of serpents twining round them and of eating fish which had become decayed. These snake and fish dreams seem to be of common occurrence among the Cherokees, and the services of the *shamans* to banish them are in constant demand.

Lastly, the birds and the insects, with the smaller animals, gathered together for a similar purpose, the grub-worm presiding over the meeting. Each in turn expressed an opinion, and the consensus was against mankind. They devised and named various diseases.

When the plants, which were friendly to man, heard what had been arranged by the animals, they determined to frustrate their evil designs. Each tree, shrub, and herb, down even to the grasses and mosses, agreed to furnish a remedy for some one of the diseases named.

Thus did medicine come into being. When the *shaman* is in doubt as to what treatment to apply for the relief of a patient the spirit of the plant suggests a fitting remedy.

### The Wonderful Kettle

A story is told among the Iroquois of two brothers who lived in the wilderness far from all human habitation. The elder brother went into the forest to hunt game, while the younger stayed at home and tended the hut, cooked the food, and gathered firewood.

One evening the tired hunter returned from the chase, and the younger brother took the game from him as usual and dressed it for supper. "I will smoke awhile before I eat," said the hunter, and he smoked in silence for a time. When he was tired of smoking he lay down and went to sleep.

"Strange," said the boy; "I should have thought he would want to eat first."

When the hunter awoke he found that his brother had prepared the supper and was waiting for him.

"Go to bed," said he; "I wish to be alone."

Wondering much, the boy did as he was bidden, but he could not help asking himself how his brother could possibly live if he did not eat. In the morning he observed that the hunter went away without tasting any food, and on many succeeding mornings and evenings the same thing happened.

"I must watch him at night," said the boy to himself, "for he must eat at night, since he eats at no other time."

That same evening, when the lad was told as usual to go to bed, he lay down and pretended to be sound asleep, but all the time one of his eyes was open. In this cautious fashion he watched his brother, and saw

him rise from his couch and pass through a trap-door
in the floor, from which he shortly emerged bearing
a rusty kettle, the bottom of which he scraped in-
dustriously. Filling it with water, he set it on the
blazing fire. As he did so he struck it with a whip,
saying at every blow : "Grow larger, my kettle ! "

The obedient kettle became of gigantic proportions,
and after setting it aside to cool the man ate its contents
with evident relish.

His watchful younger brother, well content with
the result of his observation, turned over and went to
sleep.

When the elder had set off next morning, the boy,
filled with curiosity, opened the trap-door and discovered the kettle. "I wonder what he eats," he said,
and there within the vessel was half a chestnut ! He
was rather surprised at this discovery, but he thought
to himself how pleased his brother would be if on his
return he found a meal to his taste awaiting him.
When evening drew near he put the kettle on the
fire, took a whip, and, hitting it repeatedly, exclaimed :
"Grow larger, my kettle ! "

The kettle grew larger, but to the boy's alarm it
kept on growing until it filled the room, and he was
obliged to get on the roof and stir it through the
chimney.

"What are you doing up there ?" shouted the hunter,
when he came within hail.

"I took your kettle to get your supper ready,"
answered the boy.

"Alas !" cried the other, "now I must die ! "

He quickly reduced the kettle to its original proportions and put it in its place. But he still wore such
a sad and serious air that his brother was filled with
dismay, and prayed that he might be permitted to

undo the mischief he had wrought. When the days went past and he found that his brother no longer went out to hunt or displayed any interest in life, but grew gradually thinner and more melancholy, his distress knew no bounds.

"Let me fetch you some chestnuts," he begged earnestly. "Tell me where they may be found."

### The White Heron

"You must travel a full day's journey," said the hunter in response to his entreaties. "You will then reach a river which is most difficult to ford. On the opposite bank there stands a lodge, and near by a chestnut-tree. Even then your difficulties will only be begun. The tree is guarded by a white heron, which never loses sight of it for a moment. He is employed for that purpose by the six women who live in the lodge, and with their war-clubs they slay any one who has the temerity to approach. I beg of you, do not think of going on such a hopeless errand."

But the boy felt that were the chance of success even more slender he must make the attempt for the sake of his brother, whom his thoughtlessness had brought low.

He made a little canoe about three inches long, and set off on his journey, in the direction indicated by his brother. At the end of a day he came to the river, whose size had not been underestimated. Taking his little canoe from his pocket, he drew it out till it was of a suitable length, and launched it in the great stream. A few minutes sufficed to carry him to the opposite bank, and there he beheld the lodge and the chestnut-tree. On his way he had managed to procure some seeds of a sort greatly liked by herons, and these he scattered before the beautiful white bird strutting round the tree. While the heron was busily engaged in

253

picking them up the young man seized his opportunity and gathered quantities of the chestnuts, which were lying thickly on the ground. Ere his task was finished, however, the heron perceived the intruder, and called a loud warning to the women in the lodge, who were not slow to respond. They rushed out with their fishing-lines in their hands, and gave chase to the thief. But fear, for his brother as well as for himself, lent the youth wings, and he was well out on the river in his canoe when the shrieking women reached the bank. The eldest threw her line and caught him, but with a sharp pull he broke it. Another line met with the same fate, and so on, until all the women had thrown their lines. They could do nothing further, and were obliged to watch the retreating canoe in impotent rage.

At length the youth, having come safely through the perils of the journey, arrived home with his precious burden of chestnuts. He found his brother still alive, but so weak that he could hardly speak. A meal of the chestnuts, however, helped to revive him, and he quickly recovered.

### The Stone Giantess

In bygone times it was customary for a hunter's wife to accompany her husband when he sought the chase. A dutiful wife on these occasions would carry home the game killed by the hunter and dress and cook it for him.

There was once a chief among the Iroquois who was a very skilful hunter. In all his expeditions his wife was his companion and helper. On one excursion he found such large quantities of game that he built a wigwam at the place, and settled there for a time with his wife and child. One day he struck out on a new track, while his wife followed the path they had taken on the previous day, in order to gather the game killed then. As the woman turned her steps homeward after a hard day's work she heard the sound of another woman's voice inside the hut. Filled with surprise, she entered, but found to her consternation that her visitor was no other than a Stone Giantess. To add to her alarm, she saw that the creature had in her arms the chief's baby. While the mother stood in the doorway, wondering how she could rescue her child from the clutches of the giantess, the latter said in a gentle and soothing voice : "Do not be afraid : come inside."

The hunter's wife hesitated no longer, but boldly entered the wigwam. Once inside, her fear changed to pity, for the giantess was evidently much worn with trouble and fatigue. She told the hunter's wife, who was kindly and sympathetic, how she had travelled from the land of the Stone Giants, fleeing from her cruel husband, who had sought to kill her, and how she had finally taken shelter in the solitary wigwam. She besought the young woman to let her remain for a while, promising to assist her in her daily tasks. She also said she was very hungry, but warned her hostess that she must be exceedingly careful about the food she gave her. It must not be raw or at all underdone, for if once she tasted blood she might wish to kill the hunter and his wife and child.

So the wife prepared some food for her, taking care that it was thoroughly cooked, and the two sat down to dine together. The Stone Giantess knew that the woman was in the habit of carrying home the game, and she now declared that she would do it in her stead. Moreover, she said she already knew where it was to be found, and insisted on setting out for it at once. She very shortly returned, bearing in one hand a load of game which four men could scarcely have carried, and the woman recognized in her a very valuable assistant.

The time of the hunter's return drew near, and the Stone Giantess bade the wife go out and meet her husband and tell him of her visitor. The man was very well pleased to learn how the new-comer had helped his wife, and he gave her a hearty welcome. In the morning he went out hunting as usual. When he had disappeared from sight in the forest the giantess turned quickly to the woman and said :

"I have a secret to tell you. My cruel husband is after me, and in three days he will arrive here. On the third day your husband must remain at home and help me to slay him."

When the third day came round the hunter remained at home, obedient to the instructions of his guest.

"Now," said the giantess at last, "I hear him coming. You must both help me to hold him. Strike him where I bid you, and we shall certainly kill him."

The hunter and his wife were seized with terror when a great commotion outside announced the arrival of the Stone Giant, but the firmness and courage of the giantess reassured them, and with something like calmness they awaited the monster's approach. Directly he came in sight the giantess rushed forward, grappled with him and threw him to the ground.

"Strike him on the arms!" she cried to the others. "Now on the nape of the neck!"

The trembling couple obeyed, and very shortly they had succeeded in killing the huge creature.

"I will go and bury him," said the giantess. And that was the end of the Stone Giant.

The strange guest stayed on in the wigwam till the time came for the hunter and his family to go back to

256

the settlement, when she announced her intention of returning to her own people.

"My husband is dead," said she ; "I have no longer anything to fear." Thus, having bade them farewell, she departed.

### The Healing Waters

The Iroquois have a touching story of how a brave of their race once saved his wife and his people from extinction.

It was winter, the snow lay thickly on the ground, and there was sorrow in the encampment, for with the cold weather a dreadful plague had visited the people. There was not one but had lost some relative, and in some cases whole families had been swept away. Among those who had been most sorely bereaved was Nekumonta, a handsome young brave, whose parents, brothers, sisters, and children had died one by one before his eyes, the while he was powerless to help them. And now his wife, the beautiful Shanewis, was weak and ill. The dreaded disease had laid its awful finger on her brow, and she knew that she must shortly bid her husband farewell and take her departure for the place of the dead. Already she saw her dead friends beckoning to her and inviting her to join them, but it grieved her terribly to think that she must leave her young husband in sorrow and loneliness. His despair was piteous to behold when she broke the sad news to him, but after the first outburst of grief he bore up bravely, and determined to fight the plague with all his strength.

"I must find the healing herbs which the Great Manitou has planted," said he. "Wherever they may be, I must find them."

So he made his wife comfortable on her couch,

covering her with warm furs, and then, embracing her gently, he set out on his difficult mission.

All day he sought eagerly in the forest for the healing herbs, but everywhere the snow lay deep, and not so much as a blade of grass was visible. When night came he crept along the frozen ground, thinking that his sense of smell might aid him in his search. Thus for three days and nights he wandered through the forest, over hills and across rivers, in a vain attempt to discover the means of curing the malady of Shanewis.

When he met a little scurrying rabbit in the path he cried eagerly : " Tell me, where shall I find the herbs which Manitou has planted ? "

But the rabbit hurried away without reply, for he knew that the herbs had not yet risen above the ground, and he was very sorry for the brave.

Nekumonta came by and by to the den of a big bear, and of this animal also he asked the same question. But the bear could give him no reply, and he was obliged to resume his weary journey. He consulted all the beasts of the forest in turn, but from none could he get any help. How could they tell him, indeed, that his search was hopeless ?

### The Pity of the Trees

On the third night he was very weak and ill, for he had tasted no food since he had first set out, and he was numbed with cold and despair. He stumbled over a withered branch hidden under the snow, and so tired was he that he lay where he fell, and immediately went to sleep. All the birds and the beasts, all the multitude of creatures that inhabit the forest, came to watch over his slumbers. They remembered his kindness to them in former days, how he had never slain an animal unless he really needed it for food or clothing, how he had loved and protected the trees and the flowers. Their hearts were touched by his courageous fight for Shanewis, and they pitied his misfortunes. All that they could do to aid him they did. They cried to the Great Manitou to save his wife from the plague which held her, and the Great Spirit heard the manifold whispering and responded to their prayers.

While Nekumonta lay asleep there came to him the messenger of Manitou, and he dreamed. In his dream he saw his beautiful Shanewis, pale and thin, but as lovely as ever, and as he looked she smiled at him, and sang a strange, sweet song, like the murmuring of a distant waterfall. Then the scene changed, and it really was a waterfall he heard. In musical language it called him by name, saying: " Seek us, O Nekumonta, and when you find us Shanewis shall live. We are the Healing Waters of the Great Manitou."

Nekumonta awoke with the words of the song still ringing in his ears. Starting to his feet, he looked in every direction ; but there was no water to be seen, though the murmuring sound of a waterfall was distinctly audible. He fancied he could even distinguish words in it.

### The Finding of the Waters

" Release us ! " it seemed to say. " Set us free, and Shanewis shall be saved ! "

Nekumonta searched in vain for the waters. Then it suddenly occurred to him that they must be underground, directly under his feet. Seizing branches, stones, flints, he dug feverishly into the earth. So arduous was the task that before it was finished he was completely exhausted. But at last the hidden spring was disclosed, and the waters were rippling merrily down the vale, carrying life and happiness wherever they went. The young man bathed his aching limbs in the healing stream, and in a moment he was well and strong.

Raising his hands, he gave thanks to Manitou. With eager fingers he made a jar of clay, and baked it in the fire, so that he might carry life to Shanewis. As he pursued his way homeward with his treasure his despair was changed to rejoicing and he sped like the wind.

When he reached his village his companions ran to greet him. Their faces were sad and hopeless, for the plague still raged. However, Nekumonta directed them to the Healing Waters and inspired them with new hope. Shanewis he found on the verge of the Shadow-land, and scarcely able to murmur a farewell to her husband. But Nekumonta did not listen to her broken adieux. He forced some of the Healing Water between her parched lips, and bathed her hands and her brow till she fell into a gentle slumber. When she awoke the fever had left her, she was serene and smiling, and Nekumonta's heart was filled with a great happiness.

The tribe was for ever rid of the dreaded plague, and the people gave to Nekumonta the title of ' Chief of the Healing Waters,' so that all might know that it was he who had brought them the gift of Manitou.

## Sayadio in Spirit-land

A legend of the Wyandot tribe of the Iroquois relates how Sayadio, a young Indian, mourned greatly for a beautiful sister who had died young. So deeply did he grieve for her that at length he resolved to seek her in the Land of Spirits. Long he sought the maiden, and many adventures did he meet with. Years passed in the search, which he was about to abandon as wholly

in vain, when he encountered an old man, who gave
him some good advice. This venerable person also
bestowed upon him a magic calabash in which he
might catch and retain the spirit of his sister should
he succeed in finding her. He afterward discovered
that this old man was the keeper of that part of the
Spirit-land which he sought.

Delighted to have achieved so much, Sayadio pursued his way, and in due time reached the Land of
Souls. But to his dismay he perceived that the spirits,
instead of advancing to meet him as he had expected,
fled from him in terror. Greatly dejected, he approached Tarenyawago, the spirit master of ceremonies,
who took compassion upon him and informed him that
the dead had gathered together for a great dance festival, just such as the Indians themselves celebrate at
certain seasons of the year. Soon the dancing commenced, and Sayadio saw the spirits floating round in
a mazy measure like wreaths of mist. Among them
he perceived his sister, and sprang forward to embrace
her, but she eluded his grasp and dissolved into air.

Much cast down, the youth once more appealed to
the sympathetic master of ceremonies, who gave him a
magic rattle of great power, by the sound of which he
might bring her back. Again the spirit-music sounded
for the dance, and the dead folk thronged into the circle.
Once more Sayadio saw his sister, and observed that she
was so wholly entranced with the music that she took
no heed of his presence. Quick as thought the young
Indian dipped up the ghost with his calabash as one
nets a fish, and secured the cover, in spite of all the
efforts of the captured soul to regain its liberty.

Retracing his steps earthward, he had no difficulty
in making his way back to his native village, where he
summoned his friends to come and behold his sister's

resuscitation. The girl's corpse was brought from its resting-place to be reanimated with its spirit, and all was prepared for the ceremony, when a witless Indian maiden must needs peep into the calabash in her curiosity to see how a disembodied spirit looked. Instantly, as a bird rises when its cage bars are opened and flies forth to freedom, the spirit of Sayadio's sister flew from the calabash before the startled youth could dash forward and shut down the cover. For a while Sayadio could not realize his loss, but at length his straining eyes revealed to him that the spirit of his sister was not within sight. In a flash he saw the ruin of his hopes, and with a broken heart he sank senseless to the earth.

### The Peace Queen

A brave of the Oneida tribe of the Iroquois hunted in the forest. The red buck flashed past him, but not swifter than his arrow, for as the deer leaped he loosed his shaft and it pierced the dappled hide.

The young man strode toward the carcass, knife in hand, but as he seized the horns the branches parted, and the angry face of an Onondaga warrior lowered between them.

"Leave the buck, Oneida," he commanded fiercely. "It is the spoil of my bow. I wounded the beast ere you saw it."

The Oneida laughed. "My brother may have shot at the buck," he said, "but what avails that if he did not slay it?"

"The carcass is mine by right of forest law," cried the other in a rage. "Will you quit it or will you fight?"

The Oneida drew himself up and regarded the Onondaga scornfully.

"As my brother pleases," he replied. Next moment the two were locked in a life-and-death struggle.

Tall was the Onondaga and strong as a great tree of the forest. The Oneida, lithe as a panther, fought with all the courage of youth. To and fro they swayed, till their breathing came thick and fast and the falling sweat blinded their eyes. At length they could struggle no longer, and by a mutual impulse they sprang apart.

## The Quarrel

"Ho! Onondaga," cried the younger man, "what profits it thus to strive for a buck? Is there no meat in the lodges of your people that they must fight for it like the mountain lion?"

"Peace, young man!" retorted the grave Onondaga. "I had not fought for the buck had not your evil tongue roused me. But I am older than you, and, I trust, wiser. Let us seek the lodge of the Peace Queen hard by, and she will award the buck to him who has the best right to it."

"It is well," said the Oneida, and side by side they sought the lodge of the Peace Queen.

Now the Five Nations in their wisdom had set apart a Seneca maiden dwelling alone in the forest as arbiter of quarrels between braves. This maiden the men of all tribes regarded as sacred and as apart from other women. Like the ancient Vestals, she could not become the bride of any man.

As the Peace Queen heard the wrathful clamour of the braves outside her lodge she stepped forth, little pleased that they should thus profane the vicinity of her dwelling.

"Peace!" she cried. "If you have a grievance enter and state it. It is not fitting that braves should quarrel where the Peace Queen dwells."

At her words the men stood abashed. They entered the lodge and told the story of their meeting and the circumstances of their quarrel.

When they had finished the Peace Queen smiled scornfully. " So two such braves as you can quarrel about a buck ? " she said. " Go, Onondaga, as the elder, and take one half of the spoil, and bear it back to your wife and children."

But the Onondaga stood his ground.

### The Offers

"O Queen," he said, "my wife is in the Land of Spirits, snatched from me by the Plague Demon. But my lodge does not lack food. I would wive again, and thine eyes have looked into my heart as the sun pierces the darkness of the forest. Will you come to my lodge and cook my venison ?"

But the Peace Queen shook her head.

"You know that the Five Nations have placed Genetaska apart to be Peace Queen," she replied firmly, "and that her vows may not be broken. Go in peace."

The Onondaga was silent.

Then spoke the Oneida. "O Peace Queen," he said, gazing steadfastly at Genetaska, whose eyes dropped before his glance, "I know that you are set apart by the Five Nations. But it is in my mind to ask you to go with me to my lodge, for I love you. What says Genetaska ?"

The Peace Queen blushed and answered : " To you also I say, go in peace," but her voice was a whisper which ended in a stifled sob.

The two warriors departed, good friends now that they possessed a common sorrow. But the Peace Maiden had for ever lost her peace. For she could

264

not forget the young Oneida brave, so tall, so strong, and so gentle.

Summer darkened into autumn, and autumn whitened into winter. Warriors innumerable came to the Peace Lodge for the settlement of disputes. Outwardly Genetaska was calm and untroubled, but though she gave solace to others her own breast could find none.

One day she sat by the lodge fire, which had burned down to a heap of cinders. She was thinking, dreaming of the young Oneida. Her thoughts went out to him as birds fly southward to seek the sun. Suddenly a crackling of twigs under a firm step roused her from her reverie. Quickly she glanced upward. Before her stood the youth of her dreams, pale and worn.

" Peace Queen," he said sadly, "you have brought darkness to the soul of the Oneida. No longer may he follow the hunt. The deer may sport in quiet for him. No longer may he bend the bow or throw the tomahawk in contest, or listen to the tale during the long nights round the camp-fire. You have his heart in your keeping. Say, will you not give him yours ? "

Softly the Peace Queen murmured : " I will."

Hand in hand like two joyous children they sought his canoe, which bore them swiftly westward. No longer was Genetaska Peace Queen, for her vows were broken by the power of love.

The two were happy. But not so the men of the Five Nations. They were wroth because the Peace Queen had broken her vows, and knew how foolish they had been to trust to the word of a young and beautiful woman. So with one voice they abolished the office of Peace Queen, and war and tumult returned once more to their own.

# CHAPTER V : SIOUX MYTHS AND LEGENDS

### The Sioux or Dakota Indians

THE Sioux or Dakota Indians dwell north of the Arkansas River on the right bank of the Mississippi, stretching over to Lake Michigan and up the valley of the Missouri. One of their principal tribes is the Iowa.

### The Adventures of Ictinike

Many tales are told by the Iowa Indians regarding Ictinike, the son of the sun-god, who had offended his father, and was consequently expelled from the celestial regions. He possesses a very bad reputation among the Indians for deceit and trickery. They say that he taught them all the evil things they know, and they seem to regard him as a Father of Lies. The Omahas state that he gave them their war-customs, and for one reason or another they appear to look upon him as a species of war-god. A series of myths recount his adventures with several inhabitants of the wild. The first of these is as follows.

One day Ictinike encountered the Rabbit, and hailed him in a friendly manner, calling him 'grandchild,' and requesting him to do him a service. The Rabbit expressed his willingness to assist the god to the best of his ability, and inquired what he wished him to do.

"Oh, grandchild," said the crafty one, pointing upward to where a bird circled in the blue vault above them, "take your bow and arrow and bring down yonder bird."

The Rabbit fitted an arrow to his bow, and the shaft transfixed the bird, which fell like a stone and lodged in the branches of a great tree.

266

# THE ADVENTURES OF ICTINIKE

"Now, grandchild," said Ictinike, "go into the tree and fetch me the game."

This, however, the Rabbit at first refused to do, but at length he took off his clothes and climbed into the tree, where he stuck fast among the tortuous branches.

Ictinike, seeing that he could not make his way down, donned the unfortunate Rabbit's garments, and, highly amused at the animal's predicament, betook himself to the nearest village. There he encountered a chief who had two beautiful daughters, the elder of whom he married. The younger daughter, regarding this as an affront to her personal attractions, wandered off into the forest in a fit of the sulks. As she paced angrily up and down she heard some one calling to her from above, and, looking upward, she beheld the unfortunate Rabbit, whose fur was adhering to the natural gum which exuded from the bark of the tree. The girl cut down the tree and lit a fire near it, which melted the gum and freed the Rabbit. The Rabbit and the chief's daughter compared notes, and discovered that the being who had tricked the one and affronted the other was the same. Together they proceeded to the chief's lodge, where the girl was laughed at because of the strange companion she had brought back with her. Suddenly an eagle appeared in the air above them. Ictinike shot at and missed it, but the Rabbit loosed an arrow with great force and brought it to earth. Each morning a feather of the bird became another eagle, and each morning Ictinike shot at and missed this newly created bird, which the Rabbit invariably succeeded in killing. This went on until Ictinike had quite worn out the Rabbit's clothing and was wearing a very old piece of tent skin; but the Rabbit returned to him the garments he had been forced to don when Ictinike had stolen his. Then the Rabbit commanded the Indians to beat the drums, and each time they were beaten Ictinike jumped so high that every bone in his body was shaken. At length, after a more than usually loud series of beats, he leapt to such a height that when he came down it was found that the fall had broken his neck. The Rabbit was avenged.

## Ictinike and the Buzzard

One day Ictinike, footsore and weary, encountered a buzzard, which he asked to oblige him by carrying him on its back part of the way. The crafty bird immediately consented, and, seating Ictinike between its wings, flew off with him.

They had not gone far when they passed above a hollow tree, and Ictinike began to shift uneasily in his seat as he observed the buzzard hovering over it. He requested the bird to fly onward, but for answer it cast him headlong into the tree-trunk, where he found himself a prisoner. For a long time he lay there in want and wretchedness, until at last a large hunting-party struck camp at the spot. Ictinike chanced to be wearing some racoon skins, and he thrust the tails of these through the cracks in the tree. Three women who were standing near imagined that a number of racoons had become imprisoned in the hollow trunk, and they made a large hole in it for the purpose of capturing them. Ictinike at once emerged, where-upon the women fled. Ictinike lay on the ground pretending to be dead, and as he was covered with the racoon-skins the birds of prey, the eagle, the rook, and the magpie, came to devour him. While they pecked at him the buzzard made his appearance for the purpose of joining in the feast, but Ictinike, rising quickly, tore the feathers from its scalp. That is why the buzzard has no feathers on its head.

## Ictinike and the Creators

In course of time Ictinike married and dwelt in a lodge of his own. One day he intimated to his wife that it was his intention to visit her grandfather the Beaver. On arriving at the Beaver's lodge he found that his grandfather-in-law and his family had been without food for a long time, and were slowly dying of starvation. Ashamed at having no food to place before their guest, one of the young beavers offered himself up to provide a meal for Ictinike, and was duly cooked and served to the visitor. Before Ictinike partook of the dish, however, he was earnestly requested by the Beaver not to break any of the bones of his son, but unwittingly he split one of the toe-bones. Having finished his repast, he lay down to rest, and the Beaver gathered the bones and put them in a skin. This he plunged into the river that flowed beside his lodge, and in a moment the young beaver emerged from the water alive.

" How do you feel, my son ? " asked the Beaver.

" Alas ! father," replied the young beaver, " one of my toes is broken."

From that time every beaver has had one toe—that next to the little one—which looks as if it had been split by biting.

Ictinike shortly after took his leave of the Beavers, and pretended to forget his tobacco-pouch, which he left behind. The Beaver told one of his young ones to run after him with the pouch, but, being aware of Ictinike's treacherous character, he advised his offspring to throw it to the god when at some distance away. The young beaver accordingly took the pouch and hurried after Ictinike, and, obeying his father's instruction, was about to throw it to him from a

considerable distance when Ictinike called to him:
" Come closer, come closer."

The young beaver obeyed, and as Ictinike took the
pouch from him he said : " Tell your father that he
must visit me."

When the young beaver arrived home he acquainted
his father with what had passed, and the Beaver showed
signs of great annoyance.

" I knew he would say that," he growled, " and that
is why I did not want you to go near him."

But the Beaver could not refuse the invitation,
and in due course returned the visit. Ictinike, wishing to pay him a compliment, was about to kill one of
his own children wherewith to regale the Beaver, and
was slapping it to make it cry in order that he might
work himself into a passion sufficiently murderous to
enable him to take its life, when the Beaver spoke to
him sharply and told him that such a sacrifice was
unnecessary. Going down to the stream hard by, the
Beaver found a young beaver by the water, which was
brought up to the lodge, killed and cooked, and duly
eaten.

On another occasion Ictinike announced to his wife
his intention of calling upon her grandfather the
Musk-rat. At the Musk-rat's lodge he met with the
same tale of starvation as at the home of the Beaver,
but the Musk-rat told his wife to fetch some water,
put it in the kettle, and hang the kettle over the fire.
When the water was boiling the Musk-rat upset the
kettle, which was found to be full of wild rice, upon
which Ictinike feasted. As before, he left his tobacco-
pouch with his host, and the Musk-rat sent one of his
children after him with the article. An invitation for
the Musk-rat to visit him resulted, and the call was
duly paid. Ictinike, wishing to display his magical

powers, requested his wife to hang a kettle of water over the fire, but, to his chagrin, when the water was boiled and the kettle upset instead of wild rice only water poured out. Thereupon the Musk-rat had the kettle refilled, and produced an abundance of rice, much to Ictinike's annoyance.

Ictinike then called upon his wife's grandfather the Kingfisher, who, to provide him with food, dived into the river and brought up fish. Ictinike extended a similar invitation to him, and the visit was duly paid. Desiring to be even with his late host, the god dived into the river in search of fish. He soon found himself in difficulties, however, and if it had not been for the Kingfisher he would most assuredly have been drowned.

Lastly, Ictinike went to visit his wife's grandfather the Flying Squirrel. The Squirrel climbed to the top of his lodge and brought down a quantity of excellent black walnuts, which Ictinike ate. When he departed from the Squirrel's house he purposely left one of his gloves, which a small squirrel brought after him, and he sent an invitation by this messenger for the Squirrel to visit him in turn. Wishing to show his cleverness, Ictinike scrambled to the top of his lodge, but instead of finding any black walnuts there he fell and severely injured himself. Thus his presumption was punished for the fourth time.

The four beings alluded to in this story as the Beaver, Musk-rat, Kingfisher, and Flying Squirrel are four of the creative gods of the Sioux, whom Ictinike evidently could not equal so far as reproductive magic was concerned.

## The Story of Wabaskaha

An interesting story is that of Wabaskaha, an Omaha brave, the facts related in which occurred about a

271

century ago. A party of Pawnees on the war-path raided the horses belonging to some Omahas dwelling beside Omaha Creek. Most of the animals were the property of Wabaskaha, who immediately followed on their trail. A few Omahas who had tried to rescue the horses had also been carried off, and on the arrival of the Pawnee party at the Republican River several of the Pawnees proposed to put their prisoners to death. Others, however, refused to participate in such an act, and strenuously opposed the suggestion. A wife of one of the Pawnee chiefs fed the captives, after which her husband gave them permission to depart.

After this incident quite a feeling of friendship sprang up between the two peoples, and the Pawnees were continually inviting the Omahas to feasts and other entertainments, but they refused to return the horses they had stolen. They told Wabaskaha that if he came for his horses in the fall they would exchange them then for a certain amount of gunpowder, and that was the best arrangement he could come to with them. On his way homeward Wabaskaha mourned loudly for the horses, which constituted nearly the whole of his worldly possessions, and called upon Wakanda, his god, to assist and avenge him. In glowing language he recounted the circumstances of his loss to the people of his tribe, and so strong was their sense of the injustice done him that next day a general meeting was held in the village to consider his case. A pipe was filled, and Wabaskaha asked the men of his tribe to place it to their lips if they decided to take vengeance on the Pawnees. All did so, but the premeditated raid was postponed until the early autumn.

After a summer of hunting the braves sought the war-path. They had hardly started when a number of

272

Dakotas arrived at their village, bringing some tobacco. The Dakotas announced their intention of joining the Omaha war-party, the trail of which they took up accordingly. In a few days the Omahas arrived at the Pawnee village, which they attacked at daylight. After a vigorous defence the Pawnees were almost exterminated, and all their horses captured. The Dakotas who had elected to assist the Omaha war-party were, however, slain to a man. Such was the vengeance of Wabaskaha.

This story is interesting as an account of a veritable Indian raid, taken from the lips of Joseph La Flèche, a Dakota Indian.

### The Men-Serpents

Twenty warriors who had been on the war-path were returning homeward worn-out and hungry, and as they went they scattered in search of game to sustain them on their way.

Suddenly one of the braves, placing his ear to the ground, declared that he could hear a herd of buffaloes approaching.

The band was greatly cheered by this news, and the plans made by the chief to intercept the animals were quickly carried into effect.

Nearer and nearer came the supposed herd. The chief lay very still, ready to shoot when it came within range. Suddenly he saw, to his horror, that what approached them was a huge snake with a rattle as large as a man's head. Though almost paralysed with surprise and terror, he managed to shoot the monster and kill it. He called up his men, who were not a little afraid of the gigantic creature, even though it was dead, and for a long time they debated what they should do with the carcass. At length hunger conquered their scruples and made them decide to cook and eat it. To their surprise, they found the meat as savoury as that of a buffalo, which it much resembled. All partook of the fare, with the exception of one boy, who persisted in refusing it, though they pressed him to eat.

When the warriors had finished their meal they lay down beside the camp-fire and fell asleep. Later in the night the chief awoke and was horrified to find that his companions had turned to snakes, and that he himself was already half snake, half man. Hastily he gathered his transformed warriors, and they saw that the boy who had not eaten of the reptile had retained his own form. The lad, fearing that the serpents might attack him, began to weep, but the snake-warriors treated him very kindly, giving him their charms and all they possessed.

At their request he put them into a large robe and carried them to the summit of a high hill, where he set them down under the trees.

"You must return to our lodges," they told him, "and in the summer we will visit our kindred. See that our wives and children come out to greet us."

The boy carried the news to his village, and there was much weeping and lamentation when the friends of the warriors heard of their fate. But in the summer the snakes came and sat in a group outside the village, and all the people crowded round them, loudly venting their grief. The horses which had belonged to the snakes were brought out to them, as well as their moccasins, leggings, whips, and saddles.

"Do not be afraid of them," said the boy to the assembled people. "Do not flee from them, lest something happen to you also." So they let the snakes creep over them, and no harm befell.

In the winter the snakes vanished altogether, and with them their horses and other possessions, and the people never saw them more.

## The Three Tests

There dwelt in a certain village a woman of remarkable grace and attractiveness. The fame of her beauty drew suitors from far and near, eager to display their prowess and win the love of this imperious creature—for, besides being beautiful, she was extremely hard to please, and set such tests for her lovers as none had ever been able to satisfy.

A certain young man who lived at a considerable distance had heard of her great charms, and made up his mind to woo and win her. The difficulty of the task did not daunt him, and, full of hope, he set out on his mission.

As he travelled he came to a very high hill, and on the summit he saw a man rising and sitting down at short intervals. When the prospective suitor drew nearer he observed that the man was fastening large stones to his ankles. The youth approached him, saying: "Why do you tie these great stones to your ankles?"

"Oh," replied the other, "I wish to chase buffaloes, and yet whenever I do so I go beyond them, so I am tying stones to my ankles that I may not run so fast."

"My friend," said the suitor, "you can run some other time. In the meantime I am without a companion: come with me."

The Swift One agreed, and they walked on their way together. Ere they had gone very far they saw two large lakes. By the side of one of them sat a man, who frequently bowed his head to the water and drank. Surprised that his thirst was not quenched, they said to him: "Why do you sit there drinking of the lake?"

"I can never get enough water. When I have finished this lake I shall start on the other."

"My friend," said the suitor, "do not trouble to drink it just now. Come and join us."

The Thirsty One complied, and the three comrades journeyed on. When they had gone a little farther they noticed a man walking along with his face lifted to the sky. Curious to know why he acted thus, they addressed him.

"Why do you walk with your eyes turned skyward?" said they.

"I have shot an arrow," he said, "and I am waiting for it to reappear."

"Never mind your arrow," said the suitor. "Come with us."

"I will come," said the Skilful Archer.

As the four companions journeyed through a forest they beheld a strange sight. A man was lying with his ear to the ground, and if he lifted his head for a moment he bowed it again, listening intently. The four approached him, saying : "Friend, for what do you listen so earnestly?"

"I am listening," said he, "to the plants growing. This forest is full of plants, and I am listening to their breathing."

"You can listen when the occasion arises," they told him. "Come and join us."

He agreed, and so they travelled to the village where dwelt the beautiful maiden.

When they had reached their destination they were quickly surrounded by the villagers, who displayed no small curiosity as to who their visitors were and what object they had in coming so far. When they heard that one of the strangers desired to marry the village beauty they shook their heads over him. Did he not

276

know the difficulties in the way ? Finding that he would not be turned from his purpose, they led him to a huge rock which overshadowed the village, and described the first test he would be required to meet.

"If you wish to win the maiden," they said, "you must first of all push away that great stone. It is keeping the sunlight from us."

"Alas !" said the youth, "it is impossible."

"Not so," said his companion of the swift foot; "nothing could be more easy."

Saying this, he leaned his shoulder against the rock, and with a mighty crash it fell from its place. From the breaking up of it came the rocks and stones that are scattered over all the world.

The second test was of a different nature. The people brought the strangers a large quantity of food and water, and bade them eat and drink. Being very hungry, they succeeded in disposing of the food, but the suitor sorrowfully regarded the great kettles of water.

"Alas !" said he, "who can drink up that ? "

"I can," said the Thirsty One, and in a twinkling he had drunk it all.

The people were amazed at the prowess of the visitors. However, they said, "There is still another test," and they brought out a woman who was a very swift runner, so swift that no one had ever outstripped her in a race.

### The Race

"You must run a race with this woman," said they. "If you win you shall have the hand of the maiden you have come to seek."

Naturally the suitor chose the Swift One for this test. When the runners were started the people hailed them as fairly matched, for they raced together till they were out of sight.

When they reached the turning-point the woman said : " Come, let us rest for a little."

The man agreed, but no sooner had he sat down than he fell asleep. The woman seized her opportunity. Making sure that her rival was sleeping soundly, she set off for the village, running as hard as she could.

Meanwhile the four comrades were anxiously await-ing the return of the competitors, and great was their disappointment when the woman came in sight, while there was yet no sign of their champion.

The man who could hear the plants growing bent his ear to the ground.

" He is asleep," said he; " I can hear him snoring."

The Skilful Archer came forward, and as he bit the point off an arrow he said : " I will soon wake him."

He shot an arrow from the bowstring with such a wonderful aim that it wounded the sleeper's nose, and roused him from his slumbers. The runner started to his feet and looked round for the woman. She was gone. Knowing that he had been tricked, the Swift One put all his energy into an effort to overtake her. She was within a few yards of the winning-post when he passed her. It was a narrow margin, but nevertheless the Swift One had gained the race for his comrade.

The youth was then married to the damsel, whom he found to be all that her admirers had claimed, and more.

### The Snake-Ogre

One day a young brave, feeling at variance with the world in general, and wishing to rid himself of the mood, left the lodges of his people and journeyed into

278

the forest. By and by he came to an open space, in the centre of which was a high hill. Thinking he would climb to the top and reconnoitre, he directed his footsteps thither, and as he went he observed a man coming in the opposite direction and making for the same spot. The two met on the summit, and stood for a few moments silently regarding each other. The stranger was the first to speak, gravely inviting the young brave to accompany him to his lodge and sup with him. The other accepted the invitation, and they proceeded in the direction the stranger indicated.

On approaching the lodge the youth saw with some surprise that there was a large heap of bones in front of the door. Within sat a very old woman tending a pot. When the young man learned that the feast was to be a cannibal one, however, he declined to partake of it. The woman thereupon boiled some corn for him, and while doing so told him that his host was nothing more nor less than a snake-man, a sort of ogre who killed and ate human beings. Because the brave was young and very handsome the old woman took pity on him, bemoaning the fate that would surely befall him unless he could escape from the wiles of the snake-man.

"Listen," said she : " I will tell you what to do. Here are some moccasins. When the morning comes put them on your feet, take one step, and you will find yourself on that headland you see in the distance. Give this paper to the man you will meet there, and he will direct you further. But remember that however far you may go, in the evening the Snake will overtake you. When you have finished with the moccasins take them off, place them on the ground facing this way, and they will return."

" Is that all ? " said the youth.

"No," she replied. "Before you go you must kill me and put a robe over my bones."

### The Magic Moccasins

The young brave forthwith proceeded to carry these instructions into effect. First of all he killed the old woman, and disposed of her remains in accordance with her bidding. In the morning he put on the magic moccasins which she had provided for him, and with one great step he reached the distant headland. Here he met an old man, who received the paper from him, and then, giving him another pair of moccasins, directed him to a far-off point where he was to deliver another piece of paper to a man who would await him there. Turning the first moccasins homeward, the young brave put the second pair to use, and took another gigantic step. Arrived at the second stage of his journey from the Snake's lodge, he found it a repetition of the first. He was directed to another distant spot, and from that to yet another. But when he delivered his message for the fourth time he was treated somewhat differently.

"Down there in the hollow," said the recipient of the paper, "there is a stream. Go toward it, and walk straight on, but do not look at the water."

The youth did as he was bidden, and shortly found himself on the opposite bank of the stream.

He journeyed up the creek, and as evening fell he came upon a place where the river widened to a lake. Skirting its shores, he suddenly found himself face to face with the Snake. Only then did he remember the words of the old woman, who had warned him that in the evening the Snake would overtake him. So he turned himself into a little fish with red fins, lazily moving in the lake.

## The Snake's Quest

The Snake, high on the bank, saw the little creature, and cried : "Little Fish ! have you seen the person I am looking for ? If a bird had flown over the lake you must have seen it, the water is so still, and surely you have seen the man I am seeking ?"

"Not so," replied the Little Fish, "I have seen no one. But if he passes this way I will tell you."

So the Snake continued down-stream, and as he went there was a little grey toad right in his path.

"Little Toad," said he, "have you seen him for whom I am seeking ? Even if only a shadow were here you must have seen it."

"Yes," said the Little Toad, "I have seen him, but I cannot tell you which way he has gone."

The Snake doubled and came back on his trail. Seeing a very large fish in shallow water, he said : "Have you seen the man I am looking for ?"

"That is he with whom you have just been talking," said the Fish, and the Snake turned homeward. Meeting a musk-rat he stopped.

"Have you seen the person I am looking for ?" he said. Then, having his suspicions aroused, he added craftily : "I think that you are he."

But the Musk-rat began a bitter complaint.

"Just now," said he, "the person you seek passed over my lodge and broke it."

So the Snake passed on, and encountered a red-breasted turtle.

He repeated his query, and the Turtle told him that the object of his search was to be met with farther on.

"But beware," he added, "for if you do not recognize him he will kill you."

Following the stream, the Snake came upon a large green frog floating in shallow water.

"I have been seeking a person since morning," he said. "I think that you are he."

The Frog allayed his suspicions, saying : "You will meet him farther down the stream."

The Snake next found a large turtle floating among the green scum on a lake. Getting on the Turtle's back, he said : "You must be the person I seek," and his head rose higher and higher as he prepared to strike.

"I am not," replied the Turtle. "The next person you meet will be he. But beware, for if you do not recognize him he will kill you."

When he had gone a little farther down the Snake attempted to cross the stream. In the middle was an eddy. Crafty as he was, the Snake failed to recognize his enemy, and the eddy drew him down into the water and drowned him. So the youth succeeded in slaying the Snake who had sought throughout the day to kill him.

### The Story of the Salmon

A certain chief who had a very beautiful daughter was unwilling to part with her, but knowing that the time must come when she would marry he arranged a contest for her suitors, in which the feat was to break a pair of elk's antlers hung in the centre of the lodge.

"Whoever shall break these antlers," the old chief declared, "shall have the hand of my daughter."

The quadrupeds came first—the Snail, Squirrel, Otter, Beaver, Wolf, Bear, and Panther ; but all their strength and skill would not suffice to break the antlers. Next came the Birds, but their efforts also were unavailing. The only creature left who had not attempted the feat was a feeble thing covered with sores, whom the mischievous Blue Jay derisively summoned to perform the task. After repeated taunts from the tricky bird, the creature rose, shook itself, and became whole and clean and very good to look upon, and the assembled company saw that it was the Salmon. He grasped the elk's antlers and easily broke them in five pieces. Then, claiming his prize, the chief's daughter, he led her away.

Before they had gone very far the people said : "Let us go and take the chief's daughter back," and they set off in pursuit of the pair along the sea-shore.

When Salmon saw what was happening he created a bay between himself and his pursuers. The people at length reached the point of the bay on which Salmon stood, but he made another bay, and when they looked they could see him on the far-off point of that one. So the chase went on, till Salmon grew tired of exercising his magic powers.

Coyote and Badger, who were in advance of the others, decided to shoot at Salmon. The arrow hit him in the neck and killed him instantly. When the rest of the band came up they gave the chief's daughter to the Wolves, and she became the wife of one of them.

In due time the people returned to their village, and the Crow, who was Salmon's aunt, learnt of his death. She hastened away to the spot where he had been killed, to seek for his remains, but all she could find was one salmon's egg, which she hid in a hole in the river-bank. Next day she found that the egg was much larger, on the third day it was a small trout, and so it grew till it became a full-grown salmon, and at length a handsome youth.

### Salmon's Magic Bath

Leading young Salmon to a mountain pool, his grand-aunt said : " Bathe there, that you may see spirits."

One day Salmon said : " I am tired of seeing spirits. Let me go away."

The old Crow thereupon told him of his father's death at the hands of Badger and Coyote.

"They have taken your father's bow," she said.

The Salmon shot an arrow toward the forest, and the forest went on fire. He shot an arrow toward the prairie, and it also caught fire.

"Truly," muttered the old Crow, "you have seen spirits."

Having made up his mind to get his father's bow, Salmon journeyed to the lodge where Coyote and Badger dwelt. He found the door shut, and the creatures with their faces blackened, pretending to lament the death of old Salmon. However, he was not deceived by their tricks, but boldly entered and demanded his father's bow. Four times they gave him other bows, which broke when he drew them. The fifth time it was really his father's bow he received. Taking Coyote and Badger outside, he knocked them together and killed them.

### The Wolf Lodge

As he travelled across the prairie he stumbled on the habitation of the Wolves, and on entering the lodge he encountered his father's wife, who bade him hide before the monsters returned. By means of strategy he got the better of them, shot them all, and sailed away in a little boat with the woman. Here he fell into a deep sleep, and slept so long that at last his companion ventured to wake him. Very angry at being roused, he turned her into a pigeon and cast her out of the boat, while he himself, as a salmon, swam to the shore.

Near the edge of the water was a lodge, where dwelt five beautiful sisters. Salmon sat on the shore at a little distance, and took the form of an aged man covered with sores. When the eldest sister came down to speak to him he bade her carry him on her back to the lodge, but so loathsome a creature was he that she beat a hasty retreat. The second sister did likewise, and the third, and the fourth. But the youngest sister proceeded to carry him to the lodge, where he became again a young and handsome brave. He married all the sisters, but the youngest was his head-wife and his favourite.

### The Drowned Child

On the banks of a river there dwelt a worthy couple with their only son, a little child whom they loved dearly. One day the boy wandered away from the lodge and fell into the water, and no one was near enough to rescue him. Great was the distress of the parents when the news reached them, and all his kindred were loud in their lamentations, for the child had been a favourite with everybody. The father especially showed signs of the deepest grief, and refused to enter his lodge till he should recover the boy. All night he lay outside on the bare ground, his cheek pillowed on his hand. Suddenly he heard a faint sound, far under the earth. He listened intently : it was the crying of his lost child ! Hastily he gathered all his relatives round him, told them what he had heard, and besought them piteously to dig into the earth and bring back his son. This task they hesitated to undertake, but they willingly collected horses and goods in abundance, to be given to any one who would venture.

Two men came forward who claimed to possess supernatural powers, and to them was entrusted the work of finding the child. The grateful father gave them a pipe filled with tobacco, and promised them all his possessions if their mission should succeed. The two gifted men painted their bodies, one making himself quite black, the other yellow. Going to the neighbouring river, they plunged into its depths, and so arrived at the abode of the Water-god. This being and his wife, having no children of their own, had adopted the Indian's little son who was supposed to have been drowned, and the two men, seeing him alive and well, were pleased to think that their task was as good as accomplished.

"The father has sent for his son," they said. "He has commanded us to bring him back. We dare not return without him."

"You are too late," responded the Water-god. "Had you come before he had eaten of my food he might safely have returned with you. But he wished to eat, and he has eaten, and now, alas! he would die if he were taken out of the water." [1]

Sorrowfully the men rose to the surface and carried the tidings to the father.

"Alas!" they said, "he has eaten in the palace of the Water-god. He will die if we bring him home."

Nevertheless the father persisted in his desire to see the child.

"I must see him," he said, and the two men prepared for a second journey, saying: "If you get him back, the Water-god will require a white dog in payment."

The Indian promised to supply the dog. The two

[1] See p. 129, "The Soul's Journey."

men painted themselves again, the one black, the other yellow. Once more they dived through the limpid water to the palace of the god.

"The father must have his child," they said. "This time we dare not return without him."

So the deity gave up the little boy, who was placed in his father's arms, dead. At the sight the grief of his kindred burst out afresh. However, they did not omit to cast a white dog into the river, nor to pay the men lavishly, as they had promised.

Later the parents lost a daughter in the same manner, but as she had eaten nothing of the food offered her under the water she was brought back alive, on payment by her relatives of a tribute to the Water-god of four white-haired dogs.

## The Snake-Wife

A certain chief advised his son to travel. Idling, he pointed out, was not the way to qualify for chieftainship.

"When I was your age," said he, "I did not sit still. There was hard work to be done. And now look at me : I have become a great chief."

"I will go hunting, father," said the youth. So his father furnished him with good clothing, and had a horse saddled for him.

The young man went off on his expedition, and by and by fell in with some elk. Shooting at the largest beast, he wounded it but slightly, and as it dashed away he spurred his horse after it. In this manner they covered a considerable distance, till at length the hunter, worn out with thirst and fatigue, reined in his steed and dismounted. He wandered about in search of water till he was well-nigh spent, but after a time he came upon a spring, and immediately improvised a song of thanksgiving to the deity,

Wakanda, who had permitted him to find it. His rejoicing was somewhat premature, however, for when he approached the spring a snake started up from it. The youth was badly scared, and retreated to a safe distance without drinking. It seemed as though he must die of thirst after all. Venturing to look back after a time, he saw that the snake had disappeared, and very cautiously he returned. Again the snake darted from the water, and the thirsty hunter was forced to flee. A third return to the spring had no happier results, but when his thirst drove him to a fourth attempt the youth found, instead of a snake, a very beautiful woman. She offered him a drink in a small cup, which she replenished as often as he emptied it. So struck was he by her grace and beauty that he promptly fell in love with her. When it was time for him to return home she gave him a ring, saying : " When you sit down to eat, place this ring on a seat and say, ' Come, let us eat,' and I will come to you."

Having bidden her farewell, the young man turned his steps homeward, and when he was once more among his kindred he asked that food might be placed before him. " Make haste," said he, " for I am very hungry."

Quickly they obeyed him, and set down a variety of dishes. When he was alone the youth drew the ring from his finger and laid it on a seat. " Come," he said, " let us eat."

Immediately the Snake-woman appeared and joined him at his meal. When she had eaten she vanished as mysteriously as she had come, and the disconsolate husband (for the youth had married her) went out of the lodge to seek her. Thinking she might be among the women of the village, he said to his father : " Let the women dance before me."

# THE RING UNAVAILING

An old man was deputed to gather the women together, but not one of them so much as resembled the Snake-woman.

Again the youth sat down to eat, and repeated the formula which his wife had described to him. She ate with him as before, and vanished when the meal was over.

"Father," said the young man, "let the very young women dance before me."

But the Snake-woman was not found among them either.

Another fleeting visit from his wife induced the chief's son to make yet another attempt to find her in the community.

"Let the young girls dance," he said. Still the mysterious Snake-woman was not found.

One day a girl overheard voices in the youth's lodge, and, peering in, saw a beautiful woman sharing his meal. She told the news to the chief, and it soon became known that the chief's son was married to a beautiful stranger.

The youth, however, wished to marry a woman of his own tribe ; but the maiden's father, having heard that the young man was already married, told his daughter that she was only being made fun of.

So the girl had nothing more to do with her wooer, who turned for consolation to his ring. He caused food to be brought, and placed the ring on a seat.

### The Ring Unavailing

"Come," he said, "let us eat."

There was no response ; the Snake-woman would not appear.

The youth was greatly disappointed, and made up his mind to go in search of his wife.

"I am going a-hunting," said he, and again his father gave him good clothes and saddled a horse for him.

When he reached the spot where the Snake-woman had first met him, he found her trail leading up to the spring, and beyond it on the other side. Still following the trail, he saw before him a very dilapidated lodge, at the door of which sat an old man in rags. The youth felt very sorry for the tattered old fellow, and gave him his fine clothes, in exchange for which he received the other's rags.

"You think you are doing me a good turn," said the old man, "but it is I who am going to do you one. The woman you seek has gone over the Great Water. When you get to the other shore talk with the people you shall meet there, and if they do not obey you send them away."

In addition to the tattered garments, the old man gave him a hat, a sword, and a lame old horse.

At the edge of the Great Water the youth prepared to cross, while his companion seated himself on the shore, closed his eyes, and recited a spell. In a moment the young man found himself on the opposite shore. Here he found a lodge inhabited by two aged Thunder-men, who were apparently given to eating human beings. The young stranger made the discovery that his hat rendered him invisible, and he was able to move unseen among the creatures. Taking off his hat for a moment, he took the pipe from the lips of a Thunder-man and pressed it against the latter's hand.

"Oh," cried the Thunder-man, "I am burnt!"

But the youth had clapped on his hat and disappeared.

"It is not well," said the Thunder-man gravely. "A stranger has been here and we have let him escape.

When our brother returns he will not believe us if we tell him the man has vanished."

Shortly after this another Thunder-man entered with the body of a man he had killed. When the brothers told him their story he was quite sceptical.

"If I had been here," said he, "I would not have let him escape."

As he spoke the youth snatched his pipe from him and pressed it against the back of his hand.

"Oh," said the Thunder-man, "I am burnt!"

"It was not I," said one brother.

"It was not I," said the other.

"It was I," said the youth, pulling off his hat and appearing among them. "What were you talking about among yourselves? Here I am. Do as you said."

But the Thunder-men were afraid.

"We were not speaking," they said, and the youth put on his hat and vanished.

"What will our brother say," cried the three in dismay, "when he hears that a man has been here and we have not killed him? Our brother will surely hate us."

In a few minutes another Thunder-man came into the lodge, carrying the body of a child. He was very angry when he heard that they had let a man escape.

The youth repeated his trick on the new-comer— appeared for a moment, then vanished again. The fifth and last of the brothers was also deceived in the same manner.

Seeing that the monsters were now thoroughly frightened, the young man took off his magic hat and talked with them.

### The Finding of the Snake-Wife

"You do wrong," said he, "to eat men like this. You should eat buffaloes, not men. I am going away.

When I come back I will visit you, and if you are eating buffaloes you shall remain, but if you are eating men I shall send you away."

The Thunder-men promised they would eat only buffaloes in future, and the young man went on his way to seek for the Snake-woman. When at last he came to the village where she dwelt he found she had married a man of another tribe, and in a great rage he swung the sword the magician had given him and slew her, and her husband, and the whole village, after which he returned the way he had come. When he reached the lodge of the Thunder-men he saw that they had not kept their promise to eat only buffaloes.

" I am going to send you above," he said. " Hitherto you have destroyed men, but when I have sent you away you shall give them cooling rain to keep them alive."

So he sent them above, where they became the thunder-clouds.

Proceeding on his journey, he again crossed the Great Water with a single stride, and related to the old wizard all that had happened.

" I have sent the Thunder-men above, because they would not stop eating men. Have I done well ? "

" Very well."

" I have killed the whole village where the Snake-woman was, because she had taken another husband. Have I done well ? "

" Very well. It was for that I gave you the sword."

The youth returned to his father, and married a very beautiful woman of his own village.

### A Subterranean Adventure

There lived in a populous village a chief who had two sons and one daughter, all of them unmarried.

# A SUBTERRANEAN ADVENTURE

Both the sons were in the habit of joining the hunters when they went to shoot buffaloes, and on one such occasion a large animal became separated from the herd. One of the chief's sons followed it, and when the pursuit had taken him some distance from the rest of the party the buffalo suddenly disappeared into a large pit. Before they could check themselves man and horse had plunged in after him. When the hunters returned the chief was greatly disturbed to learn that his son was missing. He sent the criers in all directions, and spared no pains to get news of the youth.

"If any person knows the whereabouts of the chief's son," shouted the criers, "let him come and tell."

This they repeated again and again, till at length a young man came forward who had witnessed the accident.

"I was standing on a hill," he said, "and I saw the hunters, and I saw the son of the chief. And when he was on level ground he disappeared, and I saw him no more."

He led the men of the tribe to the spot, and they scattered to look for signs of the youth. They found his trail; they followed it to the pit, and there it stopped.

They pitched their tents round the chasm, and the chief begged his people to descend into it to search for his son.

"If any man among you is brave and stout-hearted," he said, "let him enter."

There was no response.

"If any one will go I will make him rich."

Still no one ventured to speak.

"If any one will go I will give him my daughter in marriage."

There was a stir among the braves and a youth came forward.

293

"I will go," he said simply.

Ropes of hide were made by willing hands, and secured to a skin shaped to form a sort of bucket.

After arranging signals with the party at the mouth of the pit, the adventurous searcher allowed himself to be lowered. Once fairly launched in the Cimmerian depths his eyes became accustomed to the darkness, and he saw first the buffalo, then the horse, then the young brave, quite dead. He put the body of the chief's son into the skin bucket, and gave the signal for it to be drawn up to the surface. But so great was the excitement that when his comrades had drawn up the dead man they forgot about the living one still in the pit, and hurried away.

### Lost Underground

By and by the hero got tired of shouting, and wandered off into the darkness.

He had not gone very far when he met an old woman. Respectfully addressing her, he told her his story and begged her to aid his return to his own country.

"Indeed I cannot help you," she said, "but if you will go to the house of the wise man who lives round the corner you may get what you want."

Having followed the direction she had indicated with a withered finger, the youth shortly arrived at a lodge. Hungry and weary, he knocked somewhat impatiently. Receiving no answer, he knocked again, still more loudly. This time there was a movement inside the lodge, and a woman came to the door. She led him inside, where her husband sat dejectedly, not even rising to greet the visitor. Sadly the woman told him that they were mourning the death of their only son. At a word from his wife the husband looked at the youth. Eagerly he rose and embraced him.

"You are like our lost child," said he. "Come and we will make you our son."

The young brave then told him his story.

"We shall treat you as our child," said the Wise Man. "Whatever you shall ask we will give you, even should you desire to leave us and to return to your own people."

Though he was touched by the kindness of the good folk, there was yet nothing the youth desired so much as to return to his kindred.

"Give me," said he, "a white horse and a white mule."

### The Return to Earth

The old man bade him go to where the horses were hobbled, and there he found what he had asked for. He also received from his host a magic piece of iron, which would enable him to obtain whatever he desired. The rocks even melted away at a touch of this talisman. Thus equipped, the adventurer rode off.

Shortly afterward he emerged in his own country, where the first persons he met were the chief and his wife, to whom he disclosed his identity, as he was by this time very much changed. They were sceptical at first, but soon they came to recognize him, and gave him a very cordial reception.

He married the chief's daughter, and was made head chieftain by his father-in-law. The people built a lodge for him in the centre of the encampment, and brought him many valuable presents of clothing and horses. On his marriage-day the criers were sent out to tell the people that on the following day no one must leave the village or do any work.

On the morrow all the men of the tribe went out to hunt buffaloes, and the young chieftain accompanied them. By means of his magic piece of iron he charmed many buffaloes, and slew more than did the others.

Now it so happened that the chief's remaining son was very jealous of his brother-in-law. He thought his father should have given him the chieftainship, and the honours accorded by the people to his young relative were exceedingly galling to him. So he made up his mind to kill the youth and destroy his beautiful white horse. But the sagacious beast told its master that some one was plotting against his life, and, duly warned, he watched in the stable every night.

On the occasion of a second great buffalo hunt the wicked schemer found his opportunity. By waving his robe he scared the buffaloes and caused them to close in on the youth and trample him to death. But when the herd had scattered and moved away there was no trace of the young brave or of his milk-white steed. They had returned to the Underworld.

### White Feather the Giant-Killer

There once dwelt in the heart of a great forest an old man and his grandchild. So far as he could remember, the boy had never seen any human being but his grandfather, and though he frequently questioned the latter on the subject of his relatives he could elicit no information from him. The truth was that they had perished at the hands of six great giants. The nation to which the boy belonged had wagered their children against those of the giants that they would beat the latter in a race. Unfortunately the giants won, the children of the rash Indians were forfeited, and all were slain with the exception of little Chácopee, whose grandfather had taken charge of him. The child learned to hunt and fish, and seemed quite contented and happy.

One day the boy wandered away to the edge of a prairie, where he found traces of an encampment. Returning, he told his grandfather of the ashes and tent-poles he had seen, and asked for an explanation. Had his grandfather set them there ? The old man responded brusquely that there were no ashes or tent-poles : he had merely imagined them. The boy was sorely puzzled, but he let the matter drop, and next day he followed a different path. Quite suddenly he heard a voice addressing him as " Wearer of the White Feather." Now there had been a tradition in his tribe that a mighty man would arise among them wearing a white feather and performing prodigies of valour. But of this Chácopee as yet knew nothing, so he could only look about him in a startled way. Close by him stood a man, which fact was in itself sufficiently astonishing to the boy, who had never seen any one but his grandfather ; but to his further bewilderment he perceived that the man was made of wood from the breast downward, only the head being of flesh.

" You do not wear the white feather yet," the curious stranger resumed, " but you will by and by. Go home and sleep. You will dream of a pipe, a sack, and a large white feather. When you wake you will see these things by your side. Put the feather on your head and you will become a very great warrior. If you want proof, smoke the pipe and you will see the smoke turn into pigeons."

He then proceeded to tell him who his parents were, and of the manner in which they had perished, and bade him avenge their death on the giants. To aid him in the accomplishment of this feat he gave him a magic vine which would be invisible to the giants, and with which he must trip them up when they ran a race with him.

297

Chácopee returned home, and everything happened as the Man of Wood had predicted. The old grandfather was greatly surprised to see a flock of pigeons issuing from the lodge, from which Chácopee also shortly emerged, wearing on his head a white feather. Remembering the prophecy, the old man wept to think that he might lose his grandchild.

### In Search of the Giants

Next morning Chácopee set off in search of the giants, whom he found in a very large lodge in the centre of the forest. The giants had learned of his approach from the 'little spirits who carry the news.' Among themselves they mocked and scoffed at him, but outwardly they greeted him with much civility, which, however, in nowise deceived him as to their true feelings. Without loss of time they arranged a race between Chácopee and the youngest giant, the winner of which was to cut off the head of the other. Chácopee won, with the help of his magic vine, and killed his opponent. Next morning he appeared again, and decapitated another of his foes. This happened on five mornings. On the sixth he set out as usual, but was met by the Man of Wood, who informed him that on his way to the giants' lodge he would encounter the most beautiful woman in the world.

### Chácopee's Downfall

"Pay no attention to her," he said earnestly. "She is there for your destruction. When you see her turn yourself into an elk, and you will be safe from her wiles."

Chácopee proceeded on his way, and sure enough before long he met the most beautiful woman in the world. Mindful of the advice he had received, he turned himself into an elk, but, instead of passing by, the woman, who was really the sixth giant, came up to him and reproached him with tears for taking the form of an elk when she had travelled so far to become his wife. Chácopee was so touched by her grief and beauty that he resumed his own shape and endeavoured to console her with gentle words and caresses. At last he fell asleep with his head in her lap. The beautiful woman once more became the cruel giant, and, seizing his axe, the monster broke Chácopee's back; then, turning him into a dog, he bade him rise and follow him. The white feather he stuck in his own head, fancying that magic powers accompanied the wearing of it.

In the path of the travellers there lay a certain village in which dwelt two young girls, the daughters of a chief. Having heard the prophecy concerning the wearer of the white feather, each made up her mind that she would marry him when he should appear. Therefore, when they saw a man approaching with a white feather in his hair the elder ran to meet him, invited him into her lodge, and soon after married him. The younger, who was gentle and timid, took the dog into her home and treated him with great kindness.

One day while the giant was out hunting he saw the dog casting a stone into the water. Immediately the stone became a beaver, which the dog caught and killed. The giant strove to emulate this feat, and was successful, but when he went home and ordered his wife to go outside and fetch the beaver only a stone lay by the door. Next day he saw the dog plucking a withered branch and throwing it on the ground, where it became a deer, which the dog slew. The Giant performed this magic feat also, but when his wife went to the door of the lodge to fetch the deer she saw only a piece of rotten wood. Nevertheless the giant had some success in the chase, and his wife repaired to the home of her father to tell him what a skilful hunter her husband was. She also spoke of the dog that lived with her sister, and his skill in the chase.

### The Transformation

The old chief suspected magic, and sent a deputation of youths and maidens to invite his younger daughter and her dog to visit him. To the surprise of the deputation, no dog was there, but an exceedingly handsome warrior. But alas! Chácopee could not speak. The party set off for the home of the old chief, where they were warmly welcomed.

It was arranged to hold a general meeting, so that the wearer of the white feather might show his prowess and magical powers. First of all they took the giant's pipe (which had belonged to Chácopee), and the warriors smoked it one after the other. When it came to Chácopee's turn he signified that the giant should precede him. The giant smoked, but to the disappointment of the assembly nothing unusual happened. Then Chácopee took the pipe, and as the smoke ascended it became a flock of pigeons. At the same moment he recovered his speech, and recounted his strange adventures to the astounded listeners. Their indignation against the giant was unbounded, and the chief ordered that he should be given the form of a dog and stoned to death by the people.

Chácopee gave a further proof of his right to wear the white feather. Calling for a buffalo-hide, he cut it into little pieces and strewed it on the prairie. Next day he summoned the braves of the tribe to a buffalo-hunt, and at no great distance they found a magnificent herd. The pieces of hide had become buffaloes. The

300

people greeted this exhibition of magic art with loud acclamations, and Chácopee's reputation was firmly established with the tribe.

Chácopee begged the chief's permission to take his wife on a visit to his grandfather, which was readily granted, and the old man's gratitude and delight more than repaid them for the perils of their journey.

### How the Rabbit Caught the Sun

Once upon a time the Rabbit dwelt in a lodge with no one but his grandmother to keep him company. Every morning he went hunting very early, but no matter how early he was he always noticed that some one with a very long foot had been before him and had left a trail. The Rabbit resolved to discover the identity of the hunter who forestalled him, so one fine morning he rose even earlier than usual, in the hope of encountering the stranger. But all to no purpose, for the mysterious one had gone, leaving behind him, as was his wont, the trail of the long foot.

This irritated the Rabbit profoundly, and he returned to the lodge to consult with his grandmother.

"Grandmother," he grumbled, "although I rise early every morning and set my traps in the hope of snaring game, some one is always before me and frightens the game away. I shall make a snare and catch him."

"Why should you do so?" replied his grandmother. "In what way has he harmed you?"

"It is sufficient that I hate him," replied the querulous Rabbit, and departed. He secreted himself among the bushes and waited for nightfall. He had provided himself with a stout bowstring, which he arranged as a trap in the place where the footprints were usually to be found. Then he went home, but returned very early to examine his snare.

When he arrived at the spot he discovered that he had caught the intruder, who was, indeed, no less a personage than the Sun. He ran home at the top of his speed to acquaint his grandmother with the news. He did not know what he had caught, so his grandmother bade him seek the forest once more and find out. On returning he saw that the Sun was in a violent passion.

"How dare you snare me!" he cried angrily. "Come hither and untie me at once!"

The Rabbit advanced cautiously, and circled round him in abject terror. At last he ducked his head and, running in, cut the bowstring which secured the Sun with his knife. The Sun immediately soared upward, and was quickly lost to sight. And the reason why the hair between the Rabbit's shoulders is yellow is that he was scorched there by the great heat which came from the Sun-god when he loosed him.

### How the Rabbit Slew the Devouring Hill

In the long ago there existed a hill of ogre-like propensities which drew people into its mouth and devoured them. The Rabbit's grandmother warned him not to approach it upon any account.

But the Rabbit was rash, and the very fact that he had been warned against the vicinity made him all the more anxious to visit it. So he went to the hill, and cried mockingly : "Pahe-Wathahuni, draw me into your mouth! Come, devour me!"

But Pahe-Wathahuni knew the Rabbit, so he took no notice of him.

Shortly afterward a hunting-party came that way, and Pahe-Wathahuni opened his mouth, so that they took it to be a great cavern, and entered. The Rabbit, waiting his chance, pressed in behind them. But when he reached Pahe-Wathahuni's stomach the monster felt that something disagreed with him, and he vomited the Rabbit up.

Later in the day another hunting-party appeared, and Pahe-Wathahuni again opened his capacious gullet. The hunters entered unwittingly, and were devoured. And once more the Rabbit entered, disguised as a man by magic art. This time the cannibal hill did not eject him. Imprisoned in the monster's entrails, he saw in the distance the whitened bones of folk who had been devoured, the still undigested bodies of others, and some who were yet alive.

Mocking Pahe-Wathahuni, the Rabbit said : "Why do you not eat? You should have eaten that very fat heart." And, seizing his knife, he made as if to devour it. At this Pahe-Wathahuni set up a dismal howling ; but the Rabbit merely mocked him, and slit the heart in twain. At this the hill split asunder, and all the folk who had been imprisoned within it went out again, stretched their arms to the blue sky, and hailed the Rabbit as their deliverer ; for it was Pahe-Wathahuni's heart that had been sundered.

The people gathered together and said: "Let us make the Rabbit chief." But he mocked them and told them to be gone, that all he desired was the heap of fat the hill had concealed within its entrails, which would serve him and his old grandmother for food for many a day. With that the Rabbit went homeward, carrying the fat on his back, and he and his grandmother rejoiced exceedingly and were never in want again.

# CHAPTER VI : MYTHS AND LEGENDS OF THE PAWNEES

### The Pawnees, or Caddoan Indians

THE Caddoan stock, the principal representatives of which are the Pawnees, are now settled in Oklahoma and North Dakota. From the earliest period they seem to have been cultivators of the soil, as well as hunters, and skilled in the arts of weaving and pottery-making. They possessed an elaborate form of religious ceremonial. The following myths well exemplify how strongly the Pawnee was gifted with the religious sense.

### The Sacred Bundle

A certain young man was very vain of his personal appearance, and always wore the finest clothes and richest adornments he could procure. Among other possessions he had a down feather of an eagle, which he wore on his head when he went to war, and which possessed magical properties. He was unmarried, and cared nothing for women, though doubtless there was more than one maiden of the village who would not have disdained the hand of the young hunter, for he was as brave and good-natured as he was handsome.

One day while he was out hunting with his companions—the Indians hunted on foot in those days—he got separated from the others, and followed some buffaloes for a considerable distance. The animals managed to escape, with the exception of a young cow, which had become stranded in a mud-hole. The youth fitted an arrow to his bow, and was about to fire, when he saw that the buffalo had vanished and only a young and pretty woman was in sight. The hunter was rather perplexed, for he could not understand where the animal had gone to, nor where the woman had come from. However, he talked to the maiden, and found her so agreeable that he proposed to marry her and return with her to his tribe. She consented to marry him, but only on condition that they remained where they were. To this he agreed, and gave her as a wedding gift a string of blue and white beads he wore round his neck.

One evening when he returned home after a day's hunting he found that his camp was gone, and all round about were the marks of many hoofs. No trace of his wife's body could he discover, and at last, mourning her bitterly, he returned to his tribe.

Years elapsed, and one summer morning as he was playing the stick game with his friends a little boy came toward him, wearing round his neck a string of blue and white beads.

"Father," he said, "mother wants you."

The hunter was annoyed at the interruption.

"I am not your father," he replied. "Go away."

The boy went away, and the man's companions laughed at him when they heard him addressed as 'father,' for they knew he was a woman-hater and unmarried.

However, the boy returned in a little while. He was sent away again by the angry hunter, but one of the players now suggested that he should accompany the child and see what he wanted. All the time the hunter had been wondering where he had seen the beads before. As he reflected he saw a buffalo cow and calf running across the prairie, and suddenly he remembered.

Taking his bow and arrows, he followed the buffaloes, whom he now recognized as his wife and child. A

long and wearisome journey they had.  The woman
was angry with her husband, and dried up every creek
they came to, so that he feared he would die of thirst,
but the strategy of his son obtained food and drink for
him until they arrived at the home of the buffaloes.  The
big bulls, the leaders of the herd, were very angry, and
threatened to kill him.  First, however, they gave him
a test, telling him that if he accomplished it he should
live.  Six cows, all exactly alike, were placed in a row,
and he was told that if he could point out his wife his life
would be spared.  His son helped him secretly, and
he succeeded.  The old bulls were surprised, and much
annoyed, for they had not expected him to distinguish
his wife from the other cows.  They gave him another
test.  He was requested to pick out his son from among
several calves.  Again the young buffalo helped him
to perform the feat.  Not yet satisfied, they decreed
that he must run a race.  If he should win they would
let him go.  They chose their fastest runners, but on
the day set for the race a thin coating of ice covered the
ground, and the buffaloes could not run at all, while the
young Indian ran swiftly and steadily, and won with
ease.

### The Magic Feather

The chief bulls were still angry, however, and determined that they would kill him, even though he
had passed their tests.  So they made him sit on the
ground, all the strongest and fiercest bulls round him.
Together they rushed at him, and in a little while his
feather was seen floating in the air.  The chief bulls
called on the others to stop, for they were sure that he
must be trampled to pieces by this time.  But when
they drew back there sat the Indian in the centre of the
circle, with his feather in his hair.

306

# THE MAGIC FEATHER

It was, in fact, his magic feather to which he owed his escape, and a second rush which the buffaloes made had as little effect on him. Seeing that he was possessed of magical powers, the buffaloes made the best of matters and welcomed him into their camp, on condition that he would bring them gifts from his tribe. This he agreed to do.

When the Indian returned with his wife and son to the village people they found that there was no food to be had ; but the buffalo-wife produced some meat from under her robe, and they ate of it. Afterward they went back to the herd with gifts, which pleased the buffaloes greatly. The chief bulls, knowing that the people were in want of food, offered to return with the hunter. His son, who also wished to return, arranged to accompany the herd in the form of a buffalo, while his parents went ahead in human shape. The father warned the people that they must not kill his son when they went to hunt buffaloes, for, he said, the yellow calf would always return leading more buffaloes.

By and by the child came to his father saying that he would no more visit the camp in the form of a boy, as he was about to lead the herd eastward. Ere he went he told his father that when the hunters sought the chase they should kill the yellow calf and sacrifice it to Atíus Tiráwa, tan its hide, and wrap in the skin an ear of corn and other sacred things. Every year they should look out for another yellow calf, sacrifice it, and keep a piece of its fat to add to the bundle. Then when food was scarce and famine threatened the tribe the chiefs should gather in council and pay a friendly visit to the young buffalo, and he would tell Tiráwa of their need, so that another yellow calf might be sent to lead the herd to the people.

When he had said this the boy left the camp. All

was done as he had ordered. Food became plentiful, and the father became a chief, greatly respected by his people. His buffalo-wife, however, he almost forgot, and one night she vanished. So distressed was the chief, and so remorseful for his neglect of her, that he never recovered, but withered away and died. But the sacred bundle was long preserved in the tribe as a magic charm to bring the buffalo.

Their sacred bundles were most precious to the Indians, and were guarded religiously. In times of famine they were opened by the priests with much ceremony. The above story is given to explain the origin of that belonging to the Pawnee tribe.

### The Bear-Man

There was once a boy of the Pawnee tribe who imitated the ways of a bear; and, indeed, he much resembled that animal. When he played with the other boys of his village he would pretend to be a bear, and even when he grew up he would often tell his companions laughingly that he could turn himself into a bear whenever he liked.

His resemblance to the animal came about in this manner. Before the boy was born his father had gone on the war-path, and at some distance from his home had come upon a tiny bear-cub. The little creature looked at him so wistfully and was so small and help-less that he could not pass by without taking notice of it. So he stooped and picked it up in his arms, tied some Indian tobacco round its neck, and said : " I know that the Great Spirit, Tiráwa, will care for you, but I cannot go on my way without putting these things round your neck to show that I feel kindly toward you. I hope that the animals will take care of my son when he is born, and help him to grow up

308

a great and wise man." With that he went on his way.

On his return he told his wife of his encounter with the Little Bear, told her how he had taken it in his arms and looked at it and talked to it. Now there is an Indian superstition that a woman, before a child is born, must not look fixedly at or think much about any animal, or the infant will resemble it. So when the warrior's boy was born he was found to have the ways of a bear, and to become more and more like that animal the older he grew. The boy, quite aware of the resemblance, often went away by himself into the forest, where he used to pray to the Bear.

### The Bear-Man Slain

On one occasion, when he was quite grown up, he accompanied a war party of the Pawnees as their chief. They travelled a considerable distance, but ere they arrived at any village they fell into a trap prepared for them by their enemies, the Sioux. Taken completely off their guard, the Pawnees, to the number of about forty, were slain to a man. The part of the country in which this incident took place was rocky and cedar-clad and harboured many bears, and the bodies of the dead Pawnees lay in a ravine in the path of these animals. When they came to the body of the Bear-man a she-bear instantly recognized it as that of their benefactor, who had sacrificed smokes to them, made songs about them, and done them many a good turn during his lifetime. She called to her companion and begged him to do something to bring the Bear-man to life again. The other protested that he could do nothing. "Nevertheless," he added, "I will try. If the sun were shining I might succeed, but when it is dark and cloudy I am powerless."

### The Resuscitation of the Bear-Man

The sun was shining but fitfully that day, however. Long intervals of gloom succeeded each gleam of sunlight. But the two bears set about collecting the remains of the Bear-man, who was indeed sadly mutilated, and, lying down on his body, they worked over him with their magic medicine till he showed signs of returning life. At length he fully regained consciousness, and, finding himself in the presence of two bears, was at a loss to know what had happened to him. But the animals related how they had brought him to life, and the sight of his dead comrades lying around him recalled what had gone before. Gratefully acknowledging the service the bears had done him, he accompanied them to their den. He was still very weak, and frequently fainted, but ere long he recovered his strength and was as well as ever, only he had no hair on his head, for the Sioux had scalped him. During his sojourn with the bears he was taught all the things that they knew—which was a great deal, for all Indians know that the bear is one of the wisest of animals. However, his host begged him not to regard the wonderful things he did as the outcome of his own strength, but to give thanks to Tiráwa, who had made the bears and had given them their wisdom and greatness. Finally he told the Bear-man to return to his people, where he would become a very great man, great in war and in wealth. But at the same time he must not forget the bears, nor cease to imitate them, for on that would depend much of his success.

"I shall look after you," he concluded. "If I die, you shall die; if I grow old, you shall grow old along with me. This tree"—pointing to a cedar—"shall be a protector to you. It never becomes old; it is always
310

fresh and beautiful, the gift of Tiráwa. And if a thunderstorm should come while you are at home throw some cedar-wood on the fire and you will be safe."

Giving him a bear-skin cap to hide his hairless scalp, the Bear then bade him depart.

Arrived at his home, the young man was greeted with amazement, for it was thought that he had perished with the rest of the war party. But when he convinced his parents that it was indeed their son who visited them, they received him joyfully. When he had embraced his friends and had been congratulated by them on his return, he told them of the bears, who were waiting outside the village. Taking presents of Indian tobacco, sweet-smelling clay, buffalo-meat, and beads, he returned to them, and again talked with the he-bear. The latter hugged him, saying : " As my fur has touched you, you will be great ; as my hands have touched your hands, you will be fearless ; and as my mouth touches your mouth, you will be wise." With that the bears departed.

True to his words, the animal made the Bear-man the greatest warrior of his tribe. He was the originator of the Bear Dance, which the Pawnees still practise. He lived to an advanced age, greatly honoured by his people.

# CHAPTER VII : MYTHS AND LEGENDS OF THE NORTHERN AND NORTH-WESTERN INDIANS

## Haida Demi-Gods

THERE is a curious Haida story told of the origin of certain supernatural people, who are supposed to speak through the *shamans*, or medicine-men, and of how they got their names.

Ten brothers went out to hunt with their dogs. While they were climbing a steep rocky mountain a thick mist enveloped them, and they were compelled to remain on the heights. By and by they made a fire, and the youngest, who was full of mischief, cast his bow in it. When the bow was burnt the hunters were astonished to see it on the level ground below. The mischievous brother thereupon announced his intention of following his weapon, and by the same means. Though the others tried hard to dissuade him, he threw himself on the blazing fire, and was quickly consumed. His brothers then beheld him on the plain vigorously exhorting them to follow his example. One by one they did so, some boldly, some timorously, but all found themselves at last on the level ground.

As the brothers travelled on they heard a wren chirping, and they saw that one of their number had a blue hole in his heart. Farther on they found a hawk's feather, which they tied in the hair of the youngest. They came at length to a deserted village on the shores of an inlet, and took possession of one of the huts. For food they ate some mussels, and having satisfied their hunger they set out to explore the settlement. Nothing rewarded their search but an old canoe, moss-grown and covered with nettles. When they had removed the weeds and scraped off the moss they repaired it, and the mischievous one who had led them into the fire made a bark bailer for it, on which he carved the representation of a bird. Another, who had in his hair a bunch of feathers, took a pole and jumped into the canoe. The rest followed, and the canoe slid away from the shore. Soon they came in sight of a village where a *shaman* was performing.

Attracted by the noise and the glow of the fire, the warrior at the bow stepped ashore and advanced to see what was going on. "Now," he heard the *shaman* say, "the chief Supernatural-being-who-keeps-the-bow-off is coming ashore." The Indian was ashamed to hear himself thus mistakenly, as he thought, referred to as a supernatural being, and returned to the canoe. The next one advanced to the village. "Chief Hawk-hole is coming ashore," said the *shaman*. The Indian saw the blue hole at his heart, and he also was ashamed, and returned to his brothers. The third was named Supernatural-being-on-whom-the-daylight-rests, the fourth Supernatural-being-on-the-water-on-whom-is-sunshine, the fifth Supernatural-puffin-on-the-water, the sixth Hawk-with-one-feather-sticking-out-of-the-water, the seventh Wearing-clouds-around-his-neck, the eighth Supernatural-being-with-the-big-eyes, the ninth Supernatural-being-lying-on-his-back-in-the-canoe, and the eldest, and last, Supernatural-being-half-of-whose-words-are-raven. Each as he heard his name pronounced returned to the canoe. When they had all heard the *shaman*, and were assembled once more, the eldest brother said, "We have indeed become supernatural people," which was quite true, for by burning themselves in the fire they had reached the Land of Souls.[1]

[1] This myth would appear to explain the fancied resemblance between smoke and the shadowy or vaporous substance of which spirits or ghosts are supposed to be composed.

### The Supernatural Sister

The ten brothers floated round the coast till they reached another village. Here they took on board a woman whose arms had been accidentally burned by her husband, who mistook them for the arms of some one embracing his wife. The woman was severely burned and was in great distress. The supernatural brothers made a crack in the bottom of the canoe and told the woman to place her hands in it. Her wounds were immediately healed. They called her their sister, and seated her in the canoe to bail out the water. When they came to the Djū, the stream near which dwelt Fine-weather-woman,[1] the latter came and talked to them, repeating the names which the *shaman* had given them, and calling their sister Supernatural-woman-who-does-the-bailing.

" Paddle to the island you see in the distance," she added. " The wizard who lives there is he who paints those who are to become supernatural beings. Go to him and he will paint you. Dance four nights in your canoe and you will be finished."

They did as she bade them, and the wizard dressed them in a manner becoming to their position as supernatural beings. He gave them dancing hats, dancing skirts, and puffin-beak rattles, and drew a cloud over the outside of their canoe.

### The Birth of Sīñ

The Haida of British Columbia and the Queen Charlotte Islands possess a striking myth relating to the incarnation of the Sky-god, their principal deity. The daughter of a certain chief went one day to dig in the beach. After she had worked some time she dug

[1] See page 316.

up a cockle-shell. She was about to throw it to one side when she thought she heard a sound coming from it like that of a child crying. Examining the shell, she found a small baby inside. She carried it home and wrapped it in a warm covering, and tended it so carefully that it grew rapidly and soon began to walk.

She was sitting beside the child one day when he made a movement with his hand as if imitating the drawing of a bowstring, so to please him she took a copper bracelet from her arm and hammered it into the shape of a bow, which she strung and gave him along with two arrows. He was delighted with the tiny weapon, and immediately set out to hunt small game with it. Every day he returned to his foster-mother with some trophy of his skill. One day it was a goose, another a woodpecker, and another a blue jay.

One morning he awoke to find himself and his mother in a fine new house, with gorgeous door-posts splendidly carved and illuminated in rich reds, blues, and greens. The carpenter who had raised this fine building married his mother, and was very kind to him. He took the boy down to the sea-shore, and caused him to sit with his face looking toward the expanse of the Pacific. And so long as the lad looked across the boundless blue there was fair weather.

His father used to go fishing, and one day SĭŇ—for such was the boy's name—expressed a wish to accompany him. They obtained devil-fish for bait, and proceeded to the fishing-ground, where the lad instructed his father to pronounce certain magical formulæ, the result of which was that their fishing-line was violently agitated and their canoe pulled round an adjacent island three times. When the disturbance stopped at last they pulled in the line and dragged out a monster covered with piles of halibut.

One day Sîñ went out wearing a wren-skin. His mother beheld him rise in stature until he soared above her and brooded like a bank of shining clouds over the ocean. Then he descended and donned the skin of a blue jay. Again he rose over the sea, and shone resplendently. Once more he soared upward, wearing the skin of a woodpecker, and the waves reflected a colour as of fire.

Then he said : "Mother, I shall see you no more. I am going away from you. When the sky looks like my face painted by my father there will be no wind. Then the fishing will be good."

His mother bade him farewell, sadly, yet with the proud knowledge that she had nurtured a divinity. But her sorrow increased when her husband intimated that it was time for him to depart as well. Her supernatural son and husband, however, left her a portion of their power. For when she sits by the inlet and loosens her robe the wind scurries down between the banks and the waves are ruffled with tempest; and the more she loosens the garment the greater is the storm. They call her in the Indian tongue Fine-weather-woman. But she dwells mostly in the winds, and when the cold morning airs draw up from the sea landward she makes an offering of feathers to her glorious son. The feathers are flakes of snow, and they serve to remind him that the world is weary for a glimpse of his golden face.

## Master-Carpenter and South-East

A Haida myth relates how Master-carpenter, a supernatural being, went to war with South-east (the south-east wind) at Sqa-i, the town lying farthest south on the Queen Charlotte Islands. The south-east wind is particularly rude and boisterous on that coast, and it

316

was with the intention of punishing him for his violence that Master-carpenter challenged him. First of all, however, he set about building a canoe for himself. The first one he made split, and he was obliged to throw it away. The second also split, notwithstanding the fact that he had made it stouter than the other. Another and another he built, making each one stronger than the last, but every attempt ended in failure, and at last, exceedingly vexed at his unskilfulness, he was on the point of giving the task up. He would have done so, indeed, but for the intervention of Greatest Fool. Hitherto Master-carpenter had been trying to form two canoes from one log by means of wedges. Greatest Fool stood watching him for a time, amused at his clumsiness, and finally showed him that he ought to use bent wedges. And though he was perhaps the last person from whom Master-carpenter might expect to learn anything, the unsuccessful builder of canoes adopted the suggestion, with the happiest results. When at length he was satisfied that he had made a good canoe he let it down into the water, and sailed off in search of South-east.

By and by he floated right down to his enemy's abode, and when he judged himself to be above it he rose in the canoe and flung out a challenge. There was no reply. Again he called, and this time a rapid current began to float past him, bearing on its surface a quantity of seaweed. The shrewd Master-carpenter fancied he saw the matted hair of his enemy floating among the seaweed. He seized hold of it, and after it came South-east. The latter in a great passion began to call on his nephews to help him. The first to be summoned was Red-storm-cloud. Immediately a deep red suffused the sky. Then the stormy tints died away, and the wind rose with a harsh murmur.

317

When this wind had reached its full strength another was summoned, Taker-off-of-the-tree-tops. The blast increased to a hurricane, and the tree-tops were blown off and carried away and fell thickly about the canoe, where Master-carpenter was making use of his magic arts to protect himself. Again another wind was called up, Pebble-rattler, who set the stones and sand flying about as he shrieked in answer to the summons. Maker-of-the-thick-sea-mist came next, the spirit of the fog which strikes terror into the hearts of those at sea, and he was followed by a numerous band of other nephews, each more to be dreaded than the last. Finally Tidal-wave came and covered Master-carpenter with water, so that he was obliged to give in. Relinquishing his hold on South-east, he managed to struggle to the shore. It was said by some that South-east died, but the *shamans*, who ought to know, say that he returned to his own place.

South-east's mother was named To-morrow, and the Indians say that if they utter that word they will have bad weather, for South-east does not like to hear his mother's name used by any one else.

### The Beaver and the Porcupine

This is the tale of a feud between the beavers and the porcupines. Beaver had laid in a plentiful store of food, but Porcupine had failed to do so, and one day when the former was out hunting the latter went to his lodge and stole his provision. When Beaver returned he found that his food was gone, and he questioned Porcupine about the matter.

"Did you steal my food?" he asked.

"No," answered Porcupine. "One cannot steal food from supernatural beings, and you and I both possess supernatural powers."

318

# THE BEAVER AND THE PORCUPINE

Of course this was mere bluff on the part of Porcupine, and it in nowise deceived his companion.

"You stole my food!" said Beaver angrily, and he tried to seize Porcupine with his teeth. But the sharp spines of the latter disconcerted him, though he was not easily repulsed. For a time he fought furiously, but at length he was forced to retreat, with his face covered with quills from his spiny adversary. His friends and relatives greeted him sympathetically. His father summoned all the Beaver People, told them of the injuries his son had received, and bade them avenge the honour of their clan. The people at once repaired to the abode of Porcupine, who, from the fancied security of his lodge, heaped insults and abuse on them. The indignant Beaver People pulled his house down about his ears, seized him, and carried him, in spite of his threats and protests, to a desolate island, where they left him to starve.

It seemed to Porcupine that he had not long to live. Nothing grew on the island save two trees, neither of which was edible, and there was no other food within reach. He called loudly to his friends to come to his assistance, but there was no answer. In vain he summoned all the animals who were related to him. His cries never reached them.

When he had quite given up hope he fancied he heard something whisper to him: "Call upon Cold-weather, call upon North-wind." At first he did not understand, but thought his imagination must be playing tricks with him. Again the voice whispered to him: "Sing North songs, and you will be saved." Wondering much, but with hope rising in his breast, Porcupine did as he was bidden, and raised his voice in the North songs. "Let the cold weather come," he sang, "let the water be smooth."

## The Finding of Porcupine

After a time the weather became very cold, a strong wind blew from the north, and the water became smooth with a layer of ice. When it was sufficiently frozen to bear the weight of the Porcupine People they crossed over to the island in search of their brother. They were greatly rejoiced to see him, but found him so weak that he could hardly walk, and he had to be carried to his father's lodge.

When they wanted to know why Beaver had treated him so cruelly he replied that it was because he had eaten Beaver's food. The Porcupine People, thinking this a small excuse, were greatly incensed against the beavers, and immediately declared war on them. But the latter were generally victorious, and the war by and by came to an inglorious end for the porcupines. The spiny tribe still, however, imagined that they had a grievance against Beaver, and plotted to take his life. They carried him to the top of a tall tree, thinking that as the beavers could not climb he would be in the same plight as their brother had been on the island. But by the simple expedient of eating the tree downward from the top Beaver was enabled to return to his home.

## The Devil-Fish's Daughter

A Haida Indian was sailing in his canoe with his two children and his wife at low tide. They had been paddling for some time, when they came to a place where some devil-fish stones lay, and they could discern the devil-fish's tracks and see where its food was lying piled up. The man, who was a *shaman*, landed upon the rocks with the intention of finding and killing the devil-fish, but while he was searching

320

for it the monster suddenly emerged from its hole and dragged him through the aperture into its den. His wife and children, believing him to be dead, paddled away.

The monster which had seized the man was a female devil-fish, and she dragged him far below into the precincts of the town where dwelt her father, the devil-fish chief, and there he married the devil-fish which had captured him. Many years passed, and at length the man became home-sick and greatly desired to see his wife and family once more. He begged the chief to let him go, and after some demur his request was granted.

The *shaman* departed in one canoe, and his wife, the devil-fish's daughter, in another. The canoes were magical, and sped along of themselves. Soon they reached his father's town by the aid of the enchanted craft. He had brought much wealth with him from the devil-fish kingdom, and with this he traded and became a great chief. Then his children found him and came to him. They were grown up, and to celebrate his home-coming he held a great feast. Five great feasts he held, one after another, and at each of them his children and his human wife were present.

But the devil-fish wife began to pine for the sea-life. One day while her husband and she sat in his father's house he began to melt. At the same time the devil-fish wife disappeared betwixt the planks of the flooring. Her husband then assumed the devil-fish form, and a second soft, slimy body followed the first through the planks. The devil-fish wife and her husband had returned to her father's realm.

This myth, of course, approximates to those of the seal-wives who escape from their mortal husbands, and the swan- and other bird-brides who, pining for their natural environment, take wing one fine day and leave their earth-mates.

### Chinook Tales

The Chinooks formerly dwelt on Columbia River, from the Dalles to its mouth, and on the Lower Willamette. With the exception of a few individuals, they are now extinct, but their myths have been successfully collected and preserved. They were the natives of the north-west coast, cunning in bargaining, yet dwelling on a communal plan. Their chief physical characteristic was a high and narrow forehead artificially flattened. Concerning this people Professor Daniel Wilson says :

"The Chinooks are among the most remarkable of the flat-headed Indians, and carry the process of cranial distortion to the greatest excess. They are in some respects a superior race, making slaves of other tribes, and evincing considerable skill in such arts as are required in their wild forest and coast life. Their chief war-implements are bows and arrows, the former made from the yew-tree, and the latter feathered and pointed with bone. Their canoes are hollowed out of the trunk of the cedar-tree, which attains to a great size in that region, and are frequently ornamented with much taste and skill. In such a canoe the dead Chinook chief is deposited, surrounded with all the requisites for war, or the favourite occupations of life : presenting a correspondence in his sepulchral rites to the ancient pagan viking, who, as appears alike from the contents of the Scandinavian *Skibssaetninger* and from the narratives of the sagas, was interred or consumed in his war-galley, and the form of that favourite scene of ocean triumphs perpetuated in the earth-work that covered his ashes."

### The Story of Blue Jay and Ioi

The Chinooks tell many stories of Blue Jay, the tricky, mischievous totem-bird, and among these tales there are three which are concerned with his sister Ioi. Blue Jay, whose disposition resembled that of the bird he symbolized, delighted in tormenting Ioi by deliberately misinterpreting her commands, and by repeating at every opportunity his favourite phrase, " Ioi is always telling lies."

In the first of the trilogy Ioi requested her brother to take a wife from among the dead, to help her with her work in house and field. To this Blue Jay readily assented, and he took for his spouse a chieftain's daughter who had been recently buried. But Ioi's request that his wife should be an old one he disregarded.

"Take her to the Land of the Supernatural People," said Ioi, when she had seen her brother's bride, " and they will restore her to life."

Blue Jay set out on his errand, and after a day's journey arrived with his wife at a town inhabited by the Supernatural Folk.

"How long has she been dead?" they asked him, when he stated his purpose in visiting them.

" A day," he replied.

The Supernatural People shook their heads.

"We cannot help you," said they. "You must travel to the town where people are restored who have been dead for a day."

Blue Jay obediently resumed his journey, and at the end of another day he reached the town to which he had been directed, and told its inhabitants why he had come.

"How long has she been dead?" they asked.

" Two days," said he.

" Then we can do nothing," replied the Supernatural Folk, " for we can only restore people who have been dead one day. However, you can go to the town where those are brought to life who have been dead two days."

Another day's journey brought Blue Jay and his wife to the third town. Again he found himself a day late, and was directed to a fourth town, and from that one to yet another. At the fifth town, however, the Supernatural People took pity on him, and recovered his wife from death. Blue Jay they made a chieftain among them, and conferred many honours upon him.

After a time he got tired of living in state among the Supernatural People, and returned home.

When he was once more among his kindred his young brother-in-law, the chief's son, learnt that his sister was alive and married to Blue Jay.

Hastily the boy carried the news to his father, the old chief, who sent a message to Blue Jay demanding his hair in payment for his wife. The messenger received no reply, and the angry chief gathered his people round him and led them to Blue Jay's lodge. On their approach Blue Jay turned himself into a bird and flew away, while his wife swooned. All the efforts of her kindred could not bring the woman round, and they called on her husband to return. It was in vain, however: Blue Jay would not come back, and his wife journeyed finally to the Land of Souls.

### The Marriage of Ioi

The second portion of the trilogy relates how the Ghost-people, setting out one night from the Shadowland to buy a wife, took Ioi, the sister of Blue Jay, who disappeared before morning. After a year had elapsed her brother decided to go in search of her. But though he inquired the way to the Ghost-country from all manner of birds and beasts, he got a satisfactory answer from none of them, and would never have arrived at his destination at all had he not been carried thither at last by supernatural means.

In the Ghost-country he found his sister, surrounded by heaps of bones, which she introduced to him as his relatives by marriage. At certain times these relics would attain a semblance of humanity, but instantly became bones again at the sound of a loud voice.

### A Fishing Expedition in Shadow-land

At his sister's request Blue Jay went fishing with his young brother-in-law. Finding that when he spoke in a loud tone he caused the boy to become a heap of bones in the canoe, Blue Jay took a malicious pleasure in reducing him to that condition. It was just the sort of trick he loved to play.

The fish they caught were nothing more than leaves and branches, and Blue Jay, in disgust, threw them back into the water. But, to his chagrin, when he returned his sister told him that they were really fish, and that he ought not to have flung them away. However, he consoled himself with the reflection, " Ioi is always telling lies."

Besides teasing Ioi, he played many pranks on the inoffensive Ghosts. Sometimes he would put the skull of a child on the shoulders of a man, and *vice versa*, and take a mischievous delight in the ludicrous result when they came 'alive.'

On one occasion, when the prairies were on fire, Ioi bade her brother extinguish the flames. For this purpose she gave him five buckets of water, warning him that he must not pour it on the burning prairies until he came to the fourth of them. Blue Jay disobeyed her, as he was wont to do, and with dire results, for when he reached the fifth prairie he found he had no water to pour on it. While endeavouring to beat out the flames he was so seriously burned that he died, and returned to the Ghosts as one of themselves, but without losing his mischievous propensities.

### Blue Jay and Ioi Go Visiting

The third tale of the trilogy tells how Blue Jay and Ioi went to visit their friends. The Magpie was the first to receive the visitors, and by means of magic he provided food for them. Putting a salmon egg into a kettle of boiling water, he placed the kettle on the fire, and immediately it was full of salmon eggs, so that when they had eaten enough Blue Jay and Ioi were able to carry a number away.

On the following day the Magpie called for the kettle they had borrowed. Blue Jay tried to entertain his visitor in the same magical fashion as the latter had entertained him. But his attempt was so ludicrous that the Magpie could not help laughing at him.

The pair's next visit was to the Duck, who obtained food for them by making her children dive for trout. Again there was twice as much as they could eat, and Blue Jay and Ioi carried away the remainder on a mat. During the return visit of the Duck Blue Jay tried to emulate this feat also, using Ioi's children instead of the ducklings. His attempt was again unsuccessful.

The two visited in turn the Black Bear, the Beaver, and the Seal, all of whom similarly supplied refreshment for them in a magical manner. But Blue Jay's attempts at imitating these creatures were futile.

326

A visit to the Shadows concluded the round, and the adventurers returned home.

### The Heaven-sought Bride

A brother and sister left destitute by the death of their father, a chief of the Chinooks, were forced to go hunting sea-otters every day to obtain a livelihood. As they hunted the mists came down, and with them the Supernatural People, one of whom became enamoured of the girl. The ghostly husband sent his wife gifts of stranded timber and whale-meat, so that when her son was born she might want for nothing. The mischievous Blue Jay, hearing of the abundance of meat in the young chief's house, apprised his own chief of the circumstance and brought all the village to share it. The Supernatural People, annoyed that their bounty should be thus misused, abducted the young chief's sister, along with her child.

The woman's aunt, the Crow, gathered many potentilla and other roots, placed them in her canoe, and put out to sea. She came to the country of the Supernatural Folk, and when they saw her approaching they all ran down to the beach to greet her. They greedily snatched at the roots she had brought with her and devoured them, eating the most succulent and throwing away those that were not so much to their taste. The Crow soon found her niece, who laughed at her for bringing such fare to such a land.

"Do you think they are men that you bring them potentilla roots?" she cried. "They only eat certain of the roots you have fetched hither because they have magical properties. The next time you come bring the sort of roots they seized upon—and you can also bring a basket of potentilla roots for me."

### The Whale-catcher

She then called upon a dog which was gambolling close at hand.

"Take this dog," she said to the Crow. "It belongs to your grand-nephew. When you come near the shore say, 'Catch a whale, dog,' and see what happens."

The Crow bade farewell to her niece, and, re-entering her canoe, steered for the world of mortals again. The dog lay quietly in the stern. When about half-way across the Crow recollected her niece's advice.

"Catch a whale, good dog," she cried encouragingly.

The dog arose, and at that moment a whale crossed the path of the canoe. The dog sank his teeth in the great fish, and the frail bark rocked violently.

"Hold him fast, good fellow!" cried the Crow excitedly. "Hold him fast!" But the canoe tossed so dangerously and shipped so much water that in a great fright she bade the dog let go. He did so, and lay down in the stern again.

The Crow arrived at the world of men once more, and after landing turned round to call her wonderful dog ashore. But no trace of him was visible. He had disappeared.

Once more the Crow gathered many roots and plants, taking especial care to collect a good supply of the sort the Supernatural People were fond of, and gathering only a small basket of potentilla. For the second time she crossed over to the land of the Divine Beings, who, on espying her succulent cargo, devoured it at once. She carried the potentilla roots to her niece, and when in her house noticed the dog she had received and lost. Her niece informed her that she should not have ordered the animal to seize

328

the whale in mid-ocean, but should have waited until she was nearer the land. The Crow departed once more, taking the dog with her.

When they approached the land of men the Crow called to the animal to catch a whale, but it stirred not. Then the Crow poured some water over him, and he started up and killed a large whale, the carcass of which drifted on to the beach, when the people came down and cut it up for food.

### The Chinooks Visit the Supernaturals

Some time after this the young chief expressed a desire to go to see his sister, so his people manned a large canoe and set forth. The chief of the Supernatural People, observing their approach, warned his subjects that the mortals might do something to their disadvantage, and by means of magic he covered the sea with ice. The air became exceedingly cold, so cold, indeed, that Blue Jay, who had accompanied the young chief, leapt into the water. At this one of the Supernatural People on shore laughed and cried out: " Ha, ha ! Blue Jay has drowned himself ! " At this taunt the young chief in the canoe arose, and, taking the ice which covered the surface of the sea, cast it away. At sight of such power the Supernatural Folk became much alarmed.

The chief and his followers now came to land, and, walking up the beach, found it deserted. Not a single Supernatural Person was to be seen. Espying the chier's house, however, the Chinooks approached it. It was guarded by sea-lions, one at each side of the door. The chief cautiously warned his people against attempting an entrance. But the irrepressible Blue Jay tried to leap past the sea-lions, and got severely bitten for his pains. Howling dismally, he rushed seaward.

The young chief, annoyed that the Divine Beings should have cause for laughter against any of his people, now darted forward, seized the monsters one in each hand, and hurled them far away.

At this second feat the Supernatural Folk set up a hubbub of rage and dismay, which was turned to loud laughter when Blue Jay claimed the deed as his, loudly chanting his own praises. The Chinooks, taking heart, entered the lodge. But the Supernatural Folk vanished, leaving only the chief's sister behind.

The Chinooks had had nothing to eat since leaving their own country, and Blue Jay, who, like most worthless folk, was always hungry, complained loudly that he was famished. His brother Robin sullenly ordered him to be silent. Suddenly a Supernatural Being with a long beak emerged from under the bed, and, splitting wood with his beak, kindled a large fire.

"Robin," said Blue Jay, "that is the spirit of our great-grandfather's slave."

Soon the house was full of smoke, and a voice was heard calling out for the Smoke-eater. An individual with an enormous belly made his appearance, and swallowed all the smoke, so that the house became light. A small dish was brought, containing only one piece of meat. But the mysterious voice called for the Whale-meat-cutter, who appeared, and sliced the fragment so with his beak that the plate was full to overflowing. Then he blew upon it, and it became a large canoe full of meat, which the Chinooks finished, much to the amazement of the Supernatural People.

### The Four Tests

After a while a messenger from the Divine People approached and asked to be told whether the Indians would accept a challenge to a diving contest, the defeated to lose their lives. This was agreed to, and Blue Jay was selected to dive for the Chinooks. He had taken the precaution of placing some bushes in his canoe, which he threw into the water before diving with his opponent, a woman. When his breath gave out he came to the surface, concealing his head under the floating bushes. Then he sank into the water again, and cried to his opponent : " Where are you ? " " Here I am," she replied. Four times did Blue Jay cunningly come up for breath, hidden beneath the bushes, and on diving for the last time he found the woman against whom he was pitted lying at the bottom of the sea, almost unconscious. He took his club, which he had concealed beneath his blanket, and struck her on the nape of the neck. Then he rose and claimed the victory.

The Supernatural People, much chagrined, suggested a climbing contest, to which Blue Jay readily agreed, but he was warned that if he was beaten he would be dashed to pieces. He placed upright a piece of ice which was so high that it reached the clouds. The Supernaturals matched a chipmunk against him. When the competitors had reached a certain height Blue Jay grew tired, so he used his wings and flew upward. The chipmunk kept her eyes closed and did not notice the deception. Blue Jay hit her on the neck with his club, so that she fell, and Blue Jay was adjudged the winner.

A shooting match was next proposed by the exasperated Supernaturals, in which the persons engaged were to shoot at one another. This the Chinooks won by taking a beaver as their champion and tying a millstone in front of him. A sweating match was also won by the Chinooks taking ice with them into the superheated caves where the contest took place.

As a last effort to shame the Chinooks the Divine

331

People suggested that the two chiefs should engage in a whale-catching contest. This was agreed to, and the Supernatural chief's wife, after warning them, placed Blue Jay and Robin under her armpits to keep them quiet. As they descended to the beach, she said to her brother : "Four whales will pass you, but do not harpoon any until the fifth appears."

Robin did as he was bid, but the woman had a hard time in keeping the curious Blue Jay hidden. The four whales passed, but the young chief took no heed. Then the fifth slid by. He thrust his harpoon deep into its blubber, and cast it ashore. The Supernatural chief was unsuccessful in his attempts, and so the Chinooks won again. On the result being known Blue Jay could no longer be restrained, and, falling from under the woman's arm, he was drowned.

On setting out for home the chief was advised to tie Robin's blanket to a magical rope with which his sister provided him. When the Chinooks were in the middle of the ocean the Supernatural People raised a great storm to encompass their destruction. But the charm the chief's sister had given them proved efficacious, and they reached their own land in safety.

Blue Jay's death may be regarded as merely figurative, for he appears in many subsequent Chinook tales.

This myth is undoubtedly one of the class which relates to the ' harrying of Hades.' See the remarks at the conclusion of the myth of " The Thunderer's Son-in-law."

### The Thunderer's Son-in-Law

There were five brothers who lived together. Four of them were accustomed to spend their days in hunting elk, while the fifth, who was the youngest, was always compelled to remain at the camp. They lived amicably enough, save that the youngest grumbled at never being able to go to the hunting. One day as the youth sat brooding over his grievance the silence was suddenly broken by a hideous din which appeared to come from the region of the doorway. He was at a loss to understand the cause of it, and anxiously wished for the return of his brothers. Suddenly there appeared before him a man of gigantic size, strangely apparelled. He demanded food, and the frightened boy, remembering that they were well provided, hastily arose to satisfy the stranger's desires. He brought out an ample supply of meat and tallow, but was astonished to find that the strange being lustily called for more. The youth, thoroughly terrified, hastened to gratify the monster's craving, and the giant ate steadily on, hour after hour, until the brothers returned at the end of the day to discover the glutton devouring the fruits of their hunting. The monster appeared not to heed the brothers, but, anxious to satisfy his enormous appetite, he still ate. A fresh supply of meat had been secured, and this the brothers placed before him. He continued to gorge himself throughout the night and well into the next day. At last the meat was at an end, and the brothers became alarmed. What next would the insatiable creature demand? They approached him and told him that only skins remained, but he replied : " What shall I eat, grandchildren, now that there are only skins and you ? " They did not appear to understand him until they had questioned him several times. On realizing that the glutton meant to devour them, they determined to escape, so, boiling the skins, which they set before him, they fled through a hole in the hut. Outside they placed a dog, and told him to send the giant in the direction opposite to that which they had taken. Night fell, and the monster slept, while the dog kept a weary vigil over the exit by which his masters had escaped. Day dawned as the giant crept through the gap. He asked the dog: "Which way went your masters?" The animal replied by setting his head in the direction opposite to the true one. The giant observed the sign, and went on the road the dog indicated. After proceeding for some distance he found that the young men could not have gone that way, so he returned to the hut, to find the dog still there. Again he questioned the animal, who merely repeated his previous movement. The monster once more set out, but, unable to discover the fugitives, he again returned. Three times he repeated these fruitless journeys. At last he succeeded in getting on to the right path, and shortly came within sight of the brothers.

## The Thunderer

Immediately they saw their pursuer they endeavoured to outrun him, but without avail. The giant gained ground, and soon overtook the eldest, whom he slew. He then made for the others, and slew three more. The youngest only was left. The lad hurried on until he came to a river, on the bank of which was a man fishing, whose name was the Thunderer. This person he implored to convey him to the opposite side. After much hesitation the Thunderer agreed, and, rowing him over the stream, he commanded the fugitive to go to his hut, and returned to his nets. By this time the monster had gained the river, and on seeing the fisherman he asked to be ferried over also. The Thunderer at first refused, but was eventually persuaded by the offer of a piece of twine. Afraid that the boat might capsize, the Thunderer stretched himself across the river, and commanded the giant to walk over his body.

The monster, unaware of treachery, readily responded, but no sooner had he reached the Thunderer's legs than the latter set them apart, thus precipitating him into the water. His hat also fell in after him. The Thunderer now gained his feet, and watched the giant drifting helplessly down the stream. He did not wish to save the monster, for he believed him to be an evil spirit. "Okulam [Noise of Surge] will be your name," he said. "Only when the storm is raging will you be heard. When the weather is very bad your hat will also be heard." As he concluded this prophecy the giant disappeared from sight. The Thunderer then gathered his nets together and went to his hut. The youth whom he had saved married his daughter, and continued to remain with him. One day the youth desired to watch his father-in-law fishing for whales. His wife warned him against doing so. He paid no heed to her warning, however, but went to the sea, where he saw the Thunderer struggling with a whale. His father-in-law flew into a great rage, and a furious storm arose. The Thunderer looked toward the land, and immediately the storm increased in fury, with thunder and lightning, so he threw down his dip-net and departed for home, followed by his son-in-law.

## Storm-Raising

On reaching the house the young man gathered some pieces of coal and climbed a mountain. There he blackened his face, and a high wind arose which carried everything before it. His father-in-law's house was blown away, and the Thunderer, seeing that it was hopeless to attempt to save anything from the wreck, commanded his daughter to seek for her husband. She hurried up the mountain-side, where she found him, and told him he was the cause of all the destruction,

335

but concluded : " Father says you may look at him to-morrow when he catches whales." He followed his wife back to the valley and washed his face. Immediately he had done so the storm abated. Going up to his father-in-law, he said : "To-morrow I shall go down to the beach, and you shall see me catching whales." Then the Thunderer and he rebuilt their hut. On the following morning they went down to the sea-shore together. The young man cast his net into the sea. After a little while a whale entered the net. The youth quickly pulled the net toward him, reached for the whale, and flung it at the feet of his father-in-law. Thunderer was amazed, and called to him : " Ho, ho, my son-in-law, you are just as I was when I was a young man."

### The Beast Comrades

Soon after this the Thunderer's daughter gave birth to two sons. The Thunderer sent the young man into the woods to capture two wolves with which he used to play when a boy. The son-in-law soon returned with the animals, and threw them at the feet of the Thunderer. But they severely mauled the old man, who, seeing that they had forgotten him, cried piteously to his son-in-law to carry them back to the forest. Shortly after this he again despatched his son-in-law in search of two bears with which he had also been friendly. The young man obeyed. But the bears treated the old man as the wolves had done, so he likewise returned them to their native haunts. For the third time the son-in-law went into the forest, for two grizzly bears, and when he saw them he called : " I come to carry you away." The bears instantly came toward him and suffered themselves to be carried before the Thunderer. But they also had forgotten their former

336

playmate, and immediately set upon him, so that the young man was compelled to return with them to the forest. Thunderer had scarcely recovered from this last attack when he sent his son-in-law into the same forest after two panthers, which in his younger days had also been his companions. Without the slightest hesitation the young man arose and went into the wood, where he met the panthers. He called to them in the same gentle manner : "I come to take you away." The animals seemed to understand, and followed him. But Thunderer was dismayed when he saw how wild they had grown. They would not allow him to tame them, and after suffering their attack he sent them back to the forest. This ended the Thunderer's exciting pastime.

### The Tests

The Thunderer then sent his son-in-law to split a log of wood. When this had been done he put the young man's strength to the test by placing him within the hollow trunk and closing the wood around him. But the young man succeeded in freeing himself, and set off for the hut carrying the log with him. On reaching his home he dropped the wood before the door, and caused the earth to quake. The Thunderer jumped up in alarm and ran to the door rejoicing in the might of his son-in-law. "Oh, my son-in-law," he cried, "you are just as I was when I was young ! " The two continued to live together and the young man's sons grew into manhood. One day the Thunderer approached his son-in-law and said : "Go to the Supernatural Folk and bring me their hoops."

### The Spirit-land

The son-in-law obeyed. He travelled for a long distance, and eventually reached the land of the spirits.

337

They stood in a circle, and he saw that they played with a large hoop. He then remembered that he must secure the hoop. But he was afraid to approach them, as the light of the place dazzled him. He waited until darkness had set in, and, leaving his hiding-place, dashed through the circle and secured the hoop. The Supernatural People pursued him with torches. Just as this was taking place his wife remembered him. She called to her children : " Now whip your grand-father." This they did, while the old man wept. This chastisement brought rain upon the Supernatural People and extinguished their torches. They dared not pursue the young man farther, so they returned to their country. The adventurer was now left in peace to continue his homeward journey. He handed over the hoop to Thunderer, who now [sent him to capture the targets of the Spirit Folk. The son-in-law gladly undertook the journey, and again entered the bright region of Spirit-land. He found the Super-naturals shooting at the targets, and when night had fallen he picked them up and ran away. The spirits lit their torches and followed him. His wife once more was reminded of her absent husband, and com-manded her sons to repeat the punishment upon their grandfather. The rain recommenced and the torches of the pursuers were destroyed. The young man returned in peace to his dwelling and placed the targets before his father-in-law. He had not been long home before a restless spirit took possession of him. He longed for further adventure, and at last decided to set out in quest of it. Arraying himself in his fine necklaces of teeth and strapping around his waist two quivers of arrows, he bade farewell to his wife and sons. He journeyed until he reached a large village, which consisted of five rows of houses. These

338

he carefully inspected. The last house was very small, but he entered it. He was met by two old women, who were known as the Mice. Immediately they saw him they muttered to each other: " Oh, now Blue Jay will make another chief unhappy." On the young man's arrival in the village Blue Jay became conscious of a stranger in the midst of the people. He straightway betook himself to the house of the Mice. He then returned to his chief, saying that a strange chief wished to hold a shooting match. Blue Jay's chief seemed quite willing to enter into the contest with the stranger, so he sent Blue Jay back to the house to inform the young chief of his willingness. Blue Jay led the stranger down to the beach where the targets stood. Soon the old chief arrived and the shooting match began. But the adventurer's skill could not compare with the old chief's, who finally defeated him. Blue Jay now saw his opportunity. He sprang upon the stranger, tore out his hair, cut off his head, and severed the limbs from his body. He carried the pieces to the house and hung up the head. At nightfall the Mice fed the head and managed to keep it alive. This process of feeding went on for many months, the old women never tiring of their task. A full year had passed, and the unfortunate adventurer's sons began to fear for his safety. They decided to search for him. Arming themselves, they made their way to the large village in which their father was imprisoned. They entered the house of the Mice, and there saw the two old women, who asked : " Oh, chiefs, where did you come from ? "

"We search for our father," they replied. But the old women warned them of Blue Jay's treachery, and advised them to depart. The young men would not heed the advice, and succeeded in drawing from the women the story of their father's fate. When they heard that Blue Jay had used their father so badly they were very angry. Blue Jay, meanwhile, had become aware of the arrival of two strangers, and he went to the small house to smell them out. There he espied the youths, and immediately returned to inform his chief of their presence in the village. The chief then sent him back to invite the strangers to a shooting match, but they ignored the invitation. Three times Blue Jay made the journey, and at last the youths looked upon him, whereupon his hair immediately took fire. He ran back to his chief and said : " Oh, these strangers are more powerful than we are. They looked at me and my hair caught fire." The chief was amazed, and went down to the beach to await the arrival of the strangers. When the young men saw the targets they would not shoot, and declared that they were bad. They immediately drew them out of the ground and replaced them by their own, the brilliance of which dazzled the sight of their opponent. The chief was defeated. He lost his life and the people were subdued. The youths then cast Blue Jay into the river, saying as they did so : "Green Sturgeon shall be your name. Henceforth you shall not make chiefs miserable. You shall sing ' Watsetsetsetsetse,' and it shall be a bad omen." This performance over, they restored their father from his death-slumber, and spoke kindly to the Mice, saying : "Oh, you pitiful ones, you shall eat everything that is good. You shall eat berries." Then, after establishing order in this strange land, they returned to their home, accompanied by their father.

This curious story is an example of what is known in mythology as the ' harrying of Hades.' The land of the supernatural or subterranean beings always exercises a profound fascination over the minds of all people, and such tales are invented by their story-tellers for the purpose of minimizing the terrors which await them when they themselves must enter the strange country by death. The incident of the glutton would seem to show that two tales have been amalgamated, a not uncommon circumstance in oral story-telling. In these stories the evil or supernatural power is invariably defeated, and it is touching to observe the child-like attempts of the Indian to quench the dread of death, common to all mankind, by creating amusement at the ludicrous appearance of the dreadful beings whom he fears. The sons of the Thunderer are, of course, hero-gods whose effulgence confounds the powers of darkness, and to some extent they resemble the Hun-Apu and Xbalanque of the Central American *Popol Vuh*, who travel to the dark kingdom of Xibalba to rescue their father and uncle, and succeed in overthrowing its hideous denizens.[1]

### The Myth of Stikŭa

As an example of a myth as taken from the lips of the Indian by the collector we append to this series of Chinook tales the story of Stikŭa in all its pristine ingenuousness. Such a tale well exemplifies the difference of outlook between the native and the Western mind, and exhibits the many difficulties with which collectors of such myths have to contend.

Many people were living at Nakotat. Now their chief died. He had [left] a son who was almost grown up. It was winter and the people were hungry. They had only mussels and roots to eat. Once upon a time a hunter said : "Make yourselves ready." All the men made themselves ready, and went seaward in two canoes.

[1] See the author's *Myths of Mexico and Peru*, in this series, p. 220.

Then the hunter speared a sea-lion. It jumped and drifted on the water [dead]. They hauled it ashore. Blue Jay said : "Let us boil it here." They made a fire and singed it. They cut it and boiled it. Blue Jay said : "Let us eat it here, let us eat all of it." Then the people ate. Raven tried to hide a piece of meat in his mat, and carried it to the canoe. [But] Blue Jay had already seen it ; he ran [after him] took it and threw it into the fire. He burned it. Then they went home. They gathered large and small mussels. In the evening they came home. Then Blue Jay shouted : " Stikŭa, fetch your mussels." Stikŭa was the name of Blue Jay's wife. Then noise of many feet [was heard], and Stikŭa and the other women came running down to the beach. They went to fetch mussels. The women came to the beach and carried the mussels to the house. Raven took care of the chief's son. The boy said : "To-morrow I shall accompany you." Blue Jay said to him : "What do you want to do ? The waves will carry you away, you will drift away ; even I almost drifted away."

The next morning they made themselves ready. They went into the canoe, and the boy came down to the beach. He wanted to accompany them, and held on to the canoe. "Go to the house, go to the house," said Blue Jay. The boy went up, but he was very sad. Then Blue Jay said : "Let us leave him." The people began to paddle. Then they arrived at the sea-lion island. The hunter went ashore and speared a sea-lion. It jumped and drifted on the water [dead]. They hauled it ashore and pulled it up from the water. Blue Jay said : "Let us eat it here ; let us eat all of it, else our chief's son would always want to come here." They singed it, carved it, and boiled it there. When it was done they ate it all. Raven tried to hide a piece in his hair, but Blue Jay took it out immediately and burned it. In the evening they gathered large and small mussels, and then they went home. When they approached the beach Blue Jay shouted : "Stikŭa, fetch your mussels !" Then noise of many feet [was heard]. Stikŭa and her children and all the other women came running down to the beach and carried the mussels up to the house. Blue Jay had told all those people : "Don't tell our chief's son, else he will want to accompany us." In the evening the boy said : "To-morrow I shall accompany you." But Blue Jay said : "What do you want to do ? The waves will carry you away." But the boy replied : "I must go."

In the morning they made themselves ready for the third time. The boy went down to the beach and took hold of the canoe. But Blue Jay pushed him aside and said : "What do you want here ? Go to the house." The boy cried and went up to the house. [When he turned back] Blue Jay said : "Now paddle away. We will leave him." The people began to paddle, and soon they reached the sea-lion island. The hunter went ashore and speared one large sea-lion. It jumped and drifted on the water [dead]. They hauled it toward the shore, landed, pulled it up and singed it. They finished singeing it. Then they carved it and boiled it, and when it was done they began to eat. Blue Jay said : "Let us eat it all. Nobody must speak about it, else our chief's son will always want to accompany us." A little [meat] was still left when they had eaten enough. Raven tried to take a piece with him. He tied it to his leg and said his leg was broken. Blue Jay burned all that was left over. Then he said to Raven : "Let me see your leg." He jumped at it, untied it, and found the piece of meat at Raven's leg. He took it and burned it. In the evening they gathered large and small mussels. Then they went home. When they were near home Blue Jay shouted : "Stikŭa, fetch your mussels ! " Then noise of many feet [was heard], and Stikŭa [her children and the other women] came down to the beach and carried the mussels up to the house. The [women and children] and the chief's son ate the mussels all night. Then that boy said : "To-morrow I shall accompany you." Blue Jay said : "What do you want to do ? You will drift away. If I had not taken hold of the canoe I should have drifted away twice."

On the next morning they made themselves ready for the fourth time. The boy rose and made himself ready also. The people hauled their canoes into the water and went aboard. The boy tried to board a canoe also, but Blue Jay took hold of him and threw him into the water. He stood in the water up to his waist. He held the canoe, but Blue Jay struck his hands. There he stood. He cried, and cried, and went up to the house. The people went; they paddled, and soon they reached the sea-lion island. The hunter went ashore and speared a sea-lion. It jumped and drifted on the water [dead]. Again they towed it to the island, and pulled it ashore. They singed it. When they had finished singeing it they carved it and boiled it. When it was done Blue Jay said : "Let us eat it here." They ate half of it and were satiated. They slept because they had eaten too much. Blue Jay awoke first, and burned all that was left. In the evening they gathered large and small mussels and went home. When they were near the shore he shouted : "Stikŭa, fetch your mussels ! " Noise of many feet [was heard] and Stikŭa [her children and the other women] came running down to the beach and carried up the mussels. The boy said: "To-morrow I shall accompany you." But Blue Jay said: "What do you want to do? We might capsize and you would be drowned."

Early on the following morning the people made themselves ready. The boy arose and made himself ready also. Blue Jay and the people hauled their canoes down to the water. The boy tried to board, but Blue Jay threw him into the water. He tried to hold the canoe. The water reached up to his arm-pits. Blue Jay struck his hands [until he let go]. Then the boy cried and cried. Blue Jay and the other people went away.

After some time the boy went up from the beach. He took his arrows and walked round a point of land. There he met a young eagle and shot it. He skinned it and tried to put the skin on. It was too small; it reached scarcely to his knees. Then he took it off, and went on. After a while he met another eagle. He shot it and it fell down. It was a white-headed eagle. He skinned it and tried the skin on, but it was too small; it reached a little below his knees. He took it off, left it, and went on. Soon he met a bald-headed eagle. He shot it twice and it fell down. He skinned it and put the skin on. It was nearly large enough for him, and he tried to fly. He could fly downward only. He did not rise. He turned back, and now he could fly. Now he went round the point seaward from Nakotat. When he had nearly gone round he smelled smoke of burning fat. When he came round the point he saw the people of his town. He alighted on top of a tree and looked down. [He saw that] they had boiled a sea-lion and that they ate it. When they had nearly finished eating he flew up. He thought: "Oh, I wish Blue Jay would see me." Then Blue Jay looked up [and saw] the bird flying about. "Ah, a bird came to get food from us." Five times the eagle circled over the fire; then it descended. Blue Jay took a piece of blubber and said: "I will give you this to eat." The bird came down, grasped the piece of meat, and flew away. "Ha!" said Blue Jay, "that bird has feet like a man." When the people had eaten enough they slept. Raven again hid a piece of meat. Toward evening they awoke and ate again; then Blue Jay burned the rest of their food. In the evening they gathered large and small mussels and went home. When the boy came home he lay down at once. They approached the village, and Blue Jay shouted : "Fetch your mussels, Stikŭa!" Noise of many feet [was heard] and Stikŭa [and the other women] ran down to the beach and carried up the mussels. They tried to rouse the boy, but he did not arise.

The next morning the people made themselves ready and launched their canoe. The chief's son stayed in bed and did not attempt to accompany them. After sunrise he rose and called the women and children and said: "Wash yourselves; be quick." The women obeyed and washed themselves. He continued: "Comb your hair." Then he put down a plank, took a piece of meat out [from under his blanket, showed it to the women, and said]: "Every day your husbands eat this." He put two pieces side by side on the plank, cut them to pieces, and greased the heads of all the women and children. Then he pulled the planks forming the walls of the houses out of the ground. He sharpened them [at one end, and] those which were very wide he split in two. He sharpened all of them. The last house of the village was that of the Raven. He did not pull out its wall-planks. He put the planks on to the backs of the women and children

and said : "Go down to the beach. When you go
seaward swim five times round that rock. Then go seaward. When you see sea-lions you shall kill them.
But you shall not give anything to stingy people. I
shall take these children down. They shall live on the
sea and be my relatives."

Then he split sinews. The women went into the
water and began to jump [out of the water]. They
swam five times back and forth in front of the village.
Then they went seaward to the place where Blue Jay
and the men were boiling. Blue Jay said to the men :
"What is that ?" The men looked and saw the girls
jumping. Five times they swam round Blue Jay's
rock. Then they went seaward. After a while birds
came flying to the island. Their bills were [as red] as
blood. They followed [the fish]. "Ah !" said Blue
Jay, "do you notice them ? Whence come these
numerous birds ?" The Raven said : "Ha, squint-
eye, they are your children ; do you not recognize
them ?" Five times they went round the rock. Now
[the boy] threw the sinews down upon the stones and
said : "When Blue Jay comes to gather mussels they
shall be fast [to the rocks]." And he said to the
women, turning toward the sea : "Whale-Killer will
be your name. When you catch a whale you will eat
it, but when you catch a sea-lion you will throw it
away ; but you shall not give anything to stingy
people."

Blue Jay and the people were eating. Then that
hunter said : "Let us go home. I am afraid we have
seen evil spirits ; we have never seen anything like that
on this rock." Now they gathered mussels and carried
along the meat which they had left over. In the
evening they came near their home. [Blue Jay shouted :]
"Stikŭa, fetch your mussels !" There was no sound

of people. Five times he called. Now the people went ashore and [they saw that] the walls of the houses had disappeared. The people cried. Blue Jay cried also, but somebody said to him: "Be quiet, Blue Jay; if you had not been bad our chief's son would not have done so." Now they all made one house. Only Raven had one house [by himself]. He went and searched for food on the beach. He found a sturgeon. He went again to the beach and found a porpoise. Then Blue Jay went to the beach and tried to search for food. [As soon as he went out] it began to hail; the hailstones were so large [*indicating*]. He tried to gather mussels and wanted to break them off, but they did not come off. He could not break them off. He gave it up. Raven went to search on the beach and found a seal. The others ate roots only. Thus their chief took revenge on them.

### Beliefs of the Californian Tribes

The tribes of California afford a strange example of racial conglomeration, speaking as they do a variety of languages totally distinct from one another, and exhibiting many differences in physical appearance and custom. Concerning their mythological beliefs Bancroft says :

"The Californian tribes, taken as a whole, are pretty uniform in the main features of their theogonic beliefs. They seem, without exception, to have had a hazy conception of a lofty, almost supreme being ; for the most part referred to as a Great Man, the Old Man Above, the One Above ; attributing to him, however, as is usual in such cases, nothing but the vaguest and most negative functions and qualities. The real practical power that most interested them, who had most to do with them and they with him, was a demon,

348

or body of demons, of a tolerably pronounced character. In the face of divers assertions to the effect that no such thing as a devil proper has ever been found in savage mythology, we would draw attention to the following extract from the *Pomo* manuscript of Mr. Powers—a gentleman who, both by his study and by personal investigation, has made himself one of the best qualified authorities on the belief of the native Californian, and whose dealings have been for the most part with tribes that have never had any friendly intercourse with white men. Of course the thin and meagre imagination of the American savages was not equal to the creation of Milton's magnificent imperial Satan, or of Goethe's Mephistopheles, with his subtle intellect, his vast powers, his malignant mirth ; but in so far as the Indian fiends or devils have the ability, they are wholly as wicked as these. They are totally bad, they have no good thing in them, they think only evil ; but they are weak and undignified and absurd ; they are as much beneath Satan as the 'Big Indians' who invent them are inferior in imagination to John Milton.

"A definite location is generally assigned to the evil one as his favourite residence or resort ; thus the Californians in the county of Siskiyou give over Devil's Castle, its mount and lake, to the malignant spirits, and avoid the vicinity of these places with all possible care.

"The coast tribes of Del Norte County, California, live in constant terror of a malignant spirit that takes the form of certain animals, the form of a bat, of a hawk, of a tarantula, and so on, but especially delights in and affects that of a screech-owl. The belief of the Russian river tribes and others is practically identical with this.

"The Cahrocs have some conception of a great

deity called Chareya, the Old Man Above; he is wont
to appear upon earth at times to some of the most
favoured sorcerers; he is described as wearing a close
tunic, with a medicine-bag, and as having long white
hair that falls venerably about his shoulders. Practically,
however, the Cahrocs, like the majority of Californian
tribes, venerate chiefly the Coyote. Great dread is also
had of certain forest-demons of nocturnal habits; these,
say the Cahrocs, take the form of bears, and shoot
arrows at benighted wayfarers.

"Between the foregoing outlines of Californian
belief and those connected with the remaining tribes,
passing south, we can detect no salient difference
till we reach the Olchones, a coast tribe between San
Francisco and Monterey; the sun here begins to be
connected, or identified by name, with that great spirit,
or rather, that Big Man, who made the earth and who
rules in the sky. So we find it again both around
Monterey and around San Luis Obispo; the first fruits
of the earth were offered in these neighbourhoods to
the great light, and his rising was greeted with cries
of joy."

Father Gerónimo Boscana gives us the following account of the faith and worship of the Acagchemem tribes,
who inhabit the valley and neighbourhood of San Juan
Capistrano, California. We give first the version held
by the *serranos*, or highlanders, of the interior country,
three or four leagues inland from San Juan Capistrano :

"Before the material world at all existed there lived
two beings, brother and sister, of a nature that cannot
be explained; the brother living above, and his name
meaning the Heavens, the sister living below, and her
name signifying Earth. From the union of these two
there sprang a numerous offspring. Earth and sand
were the first-fruits of this marriage; then were born

350

rocks and stones ; then trees, both great and small ; then grass and herbs ; then animals ; lastly was born a great personage called Ouiot, who was a 'grand captain.' By some unknown mother many children of a medicine race were born to this Ouiot. All these things happened in the north ; and afterwards when men were created they were created in the north ; but as the people multiplied they moved toward the south, the earth growing larger also and extending itself in the same direction.

" In process of time, Ouiot becoming old, his children plotted to kill him, alleging that the infirmities of age made him unfit any longer to govern them or attend to their welfare. So they put a strong poison in his drink, and when he drank of it a sore sickness came upon him; he rose up and left his home in the mountains, and went down to what is now the sea-shore, though at that time there was no sea there. His mother, whose name is the Earth, mixed him an antidote in a large shell, and set the potion out in the sun to brew ; but the fragrance of it attracted the attention of the Coyote, who came and overset the shell. So Ouiot sickened to death, and though he told his children that he would shortly return and be with them again, he has never been seen since. All the people made a great pile of wood and burnt his body there, and just as the ceremony began the Coyote leaped upon the body, saying that he would burn with it ; but he only tore a piece of flesh from the stomach and ate it and escaped. After that the title of the Coyote was changed from Eyacque, which means Sub-captain, to Eno, that is to say, Thief and Cannibal.

" When now the funeral rites were over, a general council was held and arrangements made for collecting animal and vegetable food; for up to this time the

351

children and descendants of Ouiot had nothing to eat but a kind of white clay. And while they consulted together, behold a marvellous thing appeared before them, and they spoke to it, saying: 'Art thou our captain, Ouiot?' But the spectre said: 'Nay, for I am greater than Ouiot; my habitation is above, and my name is Chinigchinich.' Then he spoke further, having been told for what they were come together: 'I create all things, and I go now to make man, another people like unto you; as for you, I give you power, each after his kind, to produce all good and pleasant things. One of you shall bring rain, and another dew, and another make the acorn grow, and others other seeds, and yet others shall cause all kinds of game to abound in the land; and your children shall have this power for ever, and they shall be sorcerers to the men I go to create, and shall receive gifts of them, that the game fail not and the harvests be sure.' Then Chinigchinich made man; out of the clay of the lake he formed him, male and female; and the present Californians are the descendants of the one or more pairs there and thus created.

"So ends the known tradition of the mountaineers; we must now go back and take up the story anew at its beginning, as told by the *playanos*, or people of the valley of San Juan Capistrano. These say that an invisible, all-powerful being, called Nocuma, made the world and all that it contains of things that grow and move. He made it round like a ball and held it in his hands, where it rolled about a good deal at first, till he steadied it by sticking a heavy black rock called Tosaut into it, as a kind of ballast. The sea was at this time only a little stream running round the world, and so crowded with fish that their twinkling fins had no longer room to move; so great was the press that

352

some of the more foolish fry were for effecting a landing and founding a colony upon the dry land, and it was only with the utmost difficulty that they were persuaded by their elders that the killing air and baneful sun and the want of feet must infallibly prove the destruction before many days of all who took part in such a desperate enterprise. The proper plan was evidently to improve and enlarge their present home ; and to this end, principally by the aid of one very large fish, they broke the great rock Tosaut in two, finding a bladder in the centre filled with a very bitter substance. The taste of it pleased the fish, so they emptied it into the water, and instantly the water became salt and swelled up and overflowed a great part of the old earth, and made itself the new boundaries that remain to this day.

" Then Nocuma created a man, shaping him out of the soil of the earth, calling him Ejoni. A woman also the great god made, presumably out of the same material as the man, calling her Aé. Many children were born to this first pair, and their descendants multiplied over the land. The name of one of these last was Sirout, that is to say, Handful of Tobacco, and the name of his wife was Ycaiut, which means Above ; and to Sirout and Ycaiut was born a son, while they lived in a place north-east about eight leagues from San Juan Capistrano. The name of this son was Ouiot, that is to say, Dominator ; he grew a fierce and redoubtable warrior ; haughty, ambitious, tyrannous, he extended his lordship on every side, ruling everywhere as with a rod of iron ; and the people conspired against him. It was determined that he should die by poison ; a piece of the rock Tosaut was ground up in so deadly a way that its mere external application was sufficient to cause death. Ouiot, notwithstanding that

353

he held himself constantly on the alert, having been warned of his danger by a small burrowing animal called the *cucumel*, was unable to avoid his fate ; a few grains of the cankerous mixture were dropped upon his breast while he slept, and the strong mineral ate its way to the very springs of his life. All the wise men of the land were called to his assistance ; but there was nothing for him save to die. His body was burned on a great pile with songs of joy and dances, and the nation rejoiced.

" While the people were gathered to this end, it was thought advisable to consult on the feasibility of procuring seed and flesh to eat instead of the clay which had up to this time been the sole food of the human family. And while they yet talked together, there appeared to them, coming they knew not whence, one called Attajen, 'which name implies man, or rational being.' And Attajen, understanding their desires, chose out certain of the elders among them, and to these gave he power ; one that he might cause rain to fall, to another that he might cause game to abound, and so with the rest, to each his power and gift, and to the successors of each for ever. These were the first medicine-men."

Many years having elapsed since the death of Ouiot, there appeared in the same place one called Ouiamot, reputed son of Tacu and Auzar—people unknown, but natives, it is thought by Boscana, of "some distant land." This Ouiamot is better known by his great name Chinigchinich, which means Almighty. He first manifested his powers to the people on a day when they had met in congregation for some purpose or other ; he appeared dancing before them crowned with a kind of high crown made of tall feathers stuck into a circlet of some kind, girt with a

354

kind of petticoat of feathers, and having his flesh
painted black and red. Thus decorated he was called
the *tobet*. Having danced some time, Chinigchinich
called out the medicine-men, or *puplems*, as they were
called, among whom it would appear the chiefs are
always numbered, and confirmed their power ; telling
them that he had come from the stars to instruct them
in dancing and all other things, and commanding that
in all their necessities they should array themselves in
the *tobet*, and so dance as he had danced, supplicating
him by his great name, that thus they might be granted
their petitions. He taught them how to worship him,
how to build *vanquechs*, or places of worship, and
how to direct their conduct in various affairs of life.
Then he prepared to die, and the people asked him if
they should bury him ; but he warned them against
attempting such a thing. "If ye buried me," he said,
"ye would tread upon my grave, and for that my hand
would be heavy upon you ; look to it, and to all your
ways, for lo, I go up where the high stars are, where
mine eyes shall see all the ways of men ; and who-
soever will not keep my commandments nor observe
the things I have taught, behold, disease shall plague
all his body, and no food shall come near his lips, the
bear shall rend his flesh, and the crooked tooth of the
serpent shall sting him."

In Lower California the Pericues were divided into
two *gentes*, each of which worshipped a divinity which
was hostile to the other. The tradition explains that
there was a great lord in heaven, called Niparaya, who
made earth and sea, and was almighty and invisible.
His wife was Anayicoyondi, a goddess who, though
possessing no body, bore him in a divinely mysterious manner three children, one of whom, Quaayayp,
was a real man and born on earth, on the Acaragui

mountains. Very powerful this young god was, and for a long time he lived with the ancestors of the Periçues, whom it is almost to be inferred that he created; at any rate we are told that he was able to make men, drawing them up out of the earth. The men at last killed their great hero and teacher, and put a crown of thorns upon his head. Somewhere or other he remains lying dead to this day; and he remains constantly beautiful, neither does his body know corruption. Blood drips constantly from his wounds; and though he can speak no more, being dead, yet there is an owl that speaks to him.

The other god was called Wac, or Tuparan. According to the Niparaya sect, this Wac had made war on their favourite god, and had been by him defeated and cast forth from heaven into a cave under the earth, of which cave the whales of the sea were the guardians. With a perverse, though not unnatural, obstinacy, the sect that took Wac or Tuparan for their great god persisted in holding ideas peculiar to themselves with regard to the truth of the foregoing story, and their account of the great war in heaven and its results differed from the other as differ the creeds of heterodox and orthodox everywhere; they ascribe, for example, part of the creation to other gods besides Niparaya.

## Myths of the Athapascans

The great Athapascan family, who inhabit a vast extent of territory stretching north from the fifty-fifth parallel nearly to the Arctic Ocean, and westward to the Pacific, with cognate ramifications to the far south, are weak in mythological conceptions. Regarding them Bancroft says : [1]

[1] *The Native Races of the Pacific States*, vol. iii.

# MYTHS OF THE ATHAPASCANS

" They do not seem in any of their various tribes to have a single expressed idea with regard to a supreme power. The Loucheux branch recognize a certain personage, resident in the moon, whom they supplicate for success in starting on a hunting expedition. This being once lived among them as a poor ragged boy that an old woman had found and was bringing up ; and who made himself ridiculous to his fellows by making a pair of very large snow-shoes ; for the people could not see what a starveling like him should want with shoes of such unusual size. Times of great scarcity troubled the hunters, and they would often have fared badly had they not invariably on such occasions come across a new broad trail that led to a head or two of freshly killed game. They were glad enough to get the game and without scruples as to its appropriation ; still they felt curious as to whence it came and how. Suspicion at last pointing to the boy and his great shoes as being in some way implicated in the affair, he was watched. It soon became evident that he was indeed the benefactor of the Loucheux, and the secret hunter whose quarry had so often replenished their empty pots ; yet the people were far from being adequately grateful, and continued to treat him with little kindness or respect. On one occasion they refused him a certain piece of fat—him who had so often saved their lives by his timely bounty ! That night the lad disappeared, leaving only his clothes behind, hanging on a tree. He returned to them in a month, however, appearing as a man, and dressed as a man. He told them that he had taken up his home in the moon ; that he would always look down with a kindly eye to their success in hunting ; but he added that as a punishment for their shameless greed and ingratitude in refusing him the piece of fat, all animals should be lean the long winter through, and fat only in summer ; as has since been the case.

" According to Hearne, the Tinneh believe in a kind of spirits, or fairies, called *nantena*, which people the earth, the sea, and the air, and are instrumental for both good and evil. Some of them believe in a good spirit called Tihugun, 'my old friend,' supposed to reside in the sun and in the moon ; they have also a bad spirit, Chutsain, apparently only a personification of death, and for this reason called bad.

" They have no regular order of *shamans*; any one when the spirit moves him may take upon himself their duties and pretensions, though some by happy chances, or peculiar cunning, are much more highly esteemed in this regard than others, and are supported by voluntary contributions. The conjurer often shuts himself in his tent and abstains from food for days till his earthly grossness thins away, and the spirits and things unseen are constrained to appear at his behest. The young Tinneh care for none of these things ; the strong limb and the keen eye, holding their own well in the jostle of life, mock at the terrors of the invisible ; but as the pulses dwindle with disease or age, and the knees strike together in the shadow of impending death, the *shaman* is hired to expel the evil things of which a patient is possessed. Among the Tacullies a confession is often resorted to at this stage, on the truth and accuracy of which depend the chances of a recovery."

## Conclusion

In concluding this survey of representative myths of the Red Race of North America, the reader will probably be chiefly impressed with the circumstance that although many of these tales exhibit a striking

# CONCLUSION

resemblance to the myths of European and Asiatic peoples they have yet an atmosphere of their own which strongly differentiates them from the folk-tales of all other races. It is a truism in mythology that although the tales and mythological systems of peoples dwelling widely apart may show much likeness to one another, such a resemblance cannot be advanced as a proof that the divergent races at some distant period possessed a common mythology. Certain tribes in Borneo live in huts built on piles driven into lake-beds and use blow-pipes; so do some Indians of Guiana and contiguous countries; yet no scientist of experience would be so rash as to advance the theory that these races possessed a common origin. It is the same with mythological processes, which may have been evolved separately at great distances, but yet exhibit a marked likeness. These resemblances arise from the circumstance that the mind of man, whether he be situated in China or Peru, works on surprisingly similar lines. But, as has been indicated, the best proof that the myths of North America have not been sophisticated by those of Europe and Asia is the circumstance that the aboriginal atmosphere they contain is so marked that even the most superficial observer could not fail to observe its presence. In the tales contained in this volume the facts of Indian life, peculiar and unique, enter into every description and are inalienably interwoven with the matter of the story.

In closing, the author desires to make a strong appeal for a reasoned and charitable consideration of the Indian character on the part of his readers. This noble, manly, and dignified race has in the past been grossly maligned, chiefly by persons themselves ignorant and inspired by hereditary dislike. The Red Man is neither a monster of inhumanity nor a marvel of cunning, but a being with like feelings and aspirations to our own. Because his customs and habits of thought differ from ours he has been charged with all manner of crimes and offences with which he has, in general, nothing to do. But that he ever was a demon in human shape must be strenuously denied. In the march of progress Indian men and women are to-day taking places of honour and emolument side by side with their white fellow-citizens, and many gifted and cultured persons of Indian blood have done good work for the race. Let us hope that the ancient virtues of courage and endurance which have stood the Indian people in such good stead of old will assist their descendants in the even more strenuous tasks of civilization to which they are now called.

MAP
TO ILLUSTRATE
LINGUISTIC FAMILIES
OF
NORTH AMERICAN INDIANS

MILES
0 100 200 300 400 500

# BIBLIOGRAPHY

THE annexed bibliography, although full, is far from being exhaustive, but it is hoped that readers who desire to follow up the whole or any separate department of study connected with the Red Race of North America will find in it reference to many useful volumes. It is claimed that the list represents the best of the literature upon the subject.

ADAIR, JAMES: *The History of the American Indians.* London, 1775.

AMERICAN ANTIQUARIAN SOCIETY: *Transactions and Collections (Archæologia Americana)*, vols. i.–vii.; Worcester, 1820–85. *Proceedings*, various numbers.

*American Archæologist* (formerly *The Antiquarian*), vol. ii., *Columbus.* 1898.

AMERICAN ETHNOLOGICAL SOCIETY. *Transactions*, vols. i.–iii.; New York, 1845–53. *Publications*, vols. i.–ii.; Leyden, 1907–9.

AMERICAN PHILOSOPHICAL SOCIETY. *Minutes and Proceedings: Digest*, vol. i.; Philadelphia, 1744–1838. *Proceedings*, vols. i.–xliv.; Philadelphia, 1838–1905. *Transactions*, vols. i.–vi.; Philadelphia, 1759–1809. *Transactions*, New Series, vols. i.–xix.; Philadelphia, 1818–98.

ANTHROPOLOGICAL SOCIETY OF WASHINGTON. *Transactions*, vols. i.–iii. Washington, 1881–85.

ARCHÆOLOGICAL INSTITUTE OF AMERICA. *Papers*, American Series, vol. i., Boston and London, 1881 (reprinted 1883); vol. iii., Cambridge, 1890; vol. iv., Cambridge, 1892; vol. v., Cambridge, 1890. *Annual Report*, first to eleventh; Cambridge, 1880–90. *Bulletin*, vol. i.; Boston, 1883.

ASHE, THOMAS: *Travels in America performed in 1806; for the purpose of exploring the Rivers Alleghany, Monongahela, Ohio, and Mississippi, and ascertaining the Produce and Condition of their Banks and Vicinity.* London, 1808.

ATWATER, CALEB: *Description of the Antiquities discovered in the State of Ohio and other Western States.* (In *Archæologia Americana*, vol. i., 1820.)

BACON, OLMER N.: *A History of Natick, from its First Settlement in 1651 to the Present Time.* Boston, 1856.

# BIBLIOGRAPHY

BAEGERT, JACOB: *An Account of the Aboriginal Inhabitants of the California Peninsula.* Translated by Charles Rau. (Smithsonian Report for 1863 and 1864 ; reprinted 1865 and 1875.)

BAKER, C. ALICE: *True Stories of New England Captives.* Cambridge, 1897.

BANCROFT, GEORGE: *History of the United States.* 9 vols. Boston, 1838–75.

BANCROFT, HUBERT HOWE: Works. 39 vols. San Francisco, 1886–90. (Vols. i.–v., *Native Races* ; vi.–vii., *Central America* ; ix.–xiv., *North Mexican States and Texas* ; xvii., *Arizona and New Mexico* ; xviii.–xxiv., *California* ; xxv., *Nevada, Colorado, Wyoming* ; xxvi., *Utah* ; xxvii.–xxviii., *North-west Coast* ; xxix.–xxx., *Oregon* ; xxxi., *Washington, Idaho, Montana* ; xxxii., *British Columbia* ; xxxiii., *Alaska* ; xxxiv., *California Pastoral* ; xxxv., *California inter Pocula* ; xxxvi.–xxxvii., *Popular Tribunals* ; xxxviii., *Essays and Miscellany* ; xxxix., *Literary Industries.*)

BANDELIER, ADOLF F.: *Historical Introduction to Studies among the Sedentary Indians of New Mexico.* (Papers of the Archæological Institute of America, American Series, vol. i., Boston, 1881.)

—— *Final Report of Investigations among the Indians of the South-western United States, carried on mainly in the Years from* 1880 *to* 1885. (Papers of the Archæological Institute of America, American Series, vol. iii., Cambridge, 1890 ; vol. iv., Cambridge, 1892.)

BARRATT, JOSEPH: *The Indian of New England and the North-eastern Provinces: a Sketch of the Life of an Indian Hunter, Ancient Traditions relating to the Etchemin Tribe, etc.* Middletown, Conn., 1851.

BARTON, BENJAMIN S.: *New Views of the Origin of the Tribes and Nations of America.* Philadelphia, 1797. *Ibid.,* 1798.

BARTRAM, JOHN: *Observations on the Inhabitants, Climate, Soil, Rivers, Productions, Animals, and other Matters worthy of Notice made by Mr. John Bartram, in his Travels from Pensilvania to Onondago, Oswego, and the Lake Ontario in Canada, to which is annexed a Curious Account of the Cataracts of Niagara, by Mr. Peter Kalm.* London, 1751.

BARTRAM, WILLIAM: *Travels through North and South Carolina, Georgia, East and West Florida, the Cherokee Country, the Extensive Territories of the Muscogulges or Creek Confederacy, and the Country of the Chactaws.* Philadelphia, 1791. London, 1792.

# BIBLIOGRAPHY

BATTEY, THOMAS C.: *Life and Adventures of a Quaker among the Indians* Boston and New York, 1875. *Ibid.*, 1876.

BEACH, WILLIAM W.: *The Indian Miscellany: containing Papers on the History, Antiquities, Arts, Languages, Religions, Traditions, and Superstitions of the American Aborigines.* Albany, 1877.

BEAUCHAMP, WILLIAM M.: *The Iroquois Trail; or, Footprints of the Six Nations.* Fayetteville, N.Y., 1892.

BELL, A. W.: *On the Native Races of New Mexico.* (*Journal* of the Ethnological Society of London, New Series, vol. i., Session 1868–69; London, 1869.)

BELL, ROBERT: *The Medicine-man; or, Indian and Eskimo Notions of Medicine.* (*Canada Medical and Surgical Journal*, Montreal, March–April, 1886.)

BLISS, EUGENE F. (Editor): *Diary of David Zeisberger, a Moravian Missionary among the Indians of Ohio.* 2 vols. Cincinnati, 1885.

BOAS, FRANZ: *Songs and Dances of the Kwakiutl.* (*Journal of American Folk-lore*, vol. i.; Boston, 1888.)

—— *Chinook Texts.* (*Bulletin* 20, Bureau of American Ethnology; Washington, 1895.)

—— *The Mythology of the Bella Coola Indians.* (*Memoirs* of the American Museum of Natural History, vol. ii., *Anthropology*, i.; New York, 1898.)

—— *Kathlamet Texts.* (*Bulletin* 26, Bureau of American Ethnology. Washington, 1901.)

—— *Tsimshian Texts.* (*Bulletin* 27, Bureau of American Ethnology. Washington, 1902.)

BOLLAERT, WILLIAM: *Observations on the Indian Tribes in Texas.* (*Journal* of the Ethnological Society of London, vol. ii., 1850.)

BOLLER, HENRY A.: *Among the Indians. Eight Years in the Far West: 1858–1866. Embracing Sketches of Montana and Salt Lake* Philadelphia, 1868.

BONNELL, GEORGE W.: *Topographical Description of Texas; to which is added an Account of the Indian Tribes.* Austin, 1840.

BOSCANA, GERONIMO: *Chinigchinich; a Historical Account of the Origin, Customs, and Traditions of the Indians at the Missionary Establishment*

# BIBLIOGRAPHY

*of St. Juan Capistrano, Alta California, called the Acagchemem Nation.* (In Alfred Robinson's *Life in California*; New York, 1846.)

BOURKE, JOHN G.: *The Snake-Dance of the Moquis of Arizona; being a Narrative of a Journey from Santa Fé, New Mexico, to the Villages of the Moqui Indians of Arizona.* New York, 1884.

BRICKELL, JOHN: *The Natural History of North Carolina; with an Account of the Trade, Manners, and Customs of the Christian and Indian Inhabitants.* Dublin, 1737.

BRINTON, DANIEL G.: *Myths of the New World.* New York, 1868.

—— *National Legend of the Chahta-Muskokee Tribes.* Morrisania, N.Y., 1870.

—— *American Hero-myths: A Study in the Native Religions of the Western Continent.* Philadelphia, 1882.

—— *Essays of an Americanist.* Philadelphia, 1890.

—— *The American Race.* New York, 1891.

BROWNELL, CHARLES DE W.: *The Indian Races of North and South America.* Boston, 1853.

BUCHANAN, JAMES: *Sketches of the History, Manners, and Customs of the North American Indians, with a plan for their Melioration.* Vols. i.–ii. New York, 1824. *Ibid.*, 1825.

BUREAU OF AMERICAN ETHNOLOGY (SMITHSONIAN INSTITUTION): *Annual Reports*, i.–xxvi.; Washington, 1881–1908. *Bulletins*, 1–49; Washington, 1887–1910. *Introductions*, i.–iv.; Washington, 1877–1880. *Miscellaneous Publications*, 1–9; Washington, 1880–1907. *Contributions to North American Ethnology* (q.v.).

BUSHNELL, D. I., Jr.: *The Choctaw of Bayou Lacomb, St. Tammany Parish, Louisiana.* (*Bulletin* 48, Bureau of American Ethnology; Washington, 1909.)

CALLENDER, JOHN: *An Historical Discourse on the Civil and Religious Affairs of the Colony of Rhode-Island aud Providence Plantations in New-England, in America.* Boston, 1739. (*Collections*, Rhode Island Historical Society, vols. i.–iv.; Providence, 1838.)

CAMBRIDGE ANTHROPOLOGICAL EXPEDITION TO TORRES STRAITS: *Reports*, vol. ii., parts i. and ii. Cambridge, 1901–3.

CARR, LUCIEN: *Food of certain American Indians.* (*Proceedings* of the American Antiquarian Society, New Series, vol. x.; Worcester, 1895.)

# BIBLIOGRAPHY

CARR, LUCIEN : *Dress and Ornaments of certain American Indians. (Proceedings* of the American Antiquarian Society, New Series, vol. xi. ; Worcester, 1898.)

CARVER, JONATHAN : *Travels through the Interior Parts of North America, in the Years* 1766, 1767, *and* 1768. London, 1778.

—— *Three Years through the Interior Parts of North America for more than Five Thousand Miles.* Philadelphia, 1796.

—— *Carver's Travels in Wisconsin.* New York, 1838.

CATLIN, GEORGE : *Illustrations of the Manners and Customs and Condition of the North American Indians.* 2 vols. London, 1841. *Ibid.,* London, 1866.

—— *Letters and Notes on the Manners, Customs, and Condition of the North American Indians.* 2 vols. New York and London, 1844.

—— *O-kee-pa : a Religious Ceremony ; and other Customs of the Mandans.* Philadelphia, 1867.

CHAMPLAIN, SAMUEL DE : *Voyages : ou Journal des Découvertes de la Nouvelle France.* 2 vols. Paris, 1830.

CHARLEVOIX, PIERRE F. X. DE. *Histoire et Description générale de la Nouvelle France.* 3 vols. Paris, 1744.

CLARK, W. P. : *The Indian Sign Language.* Philadelphia, 1885.

COLDEN, CADWALLADER : *The History of the Five Indian Nations of Canada, which are dependent on the Province of New York, America.* London, 1747. *Ibid.,* 1755.

CONANT, A. J. : *Footprints of Vanished Races in the Mississippi Valley* St. Louis, 1879.

*Contributions to North American Ethnology.* Department of the Interior, U.S. Geographical and Geological Survey of the Rocky Mountain Region, J. W. Powell in charge. Vols. i.–vii., ix. Washington, 1877–93.

CORTEZ, JOSÉ : *History of the Apache Nations and other Tribes near the Parallel of 35° North Latitude. (Pacific Railroad Reports,* vol. iii., part iii., chap. 7 ; Washington, 1856.)

COUES, ELLIOTT (Editor) : *History of the Expedition of Lewis and Clark to the Sources of the Missouri River and to the Pacific in* 1804–5–6. A new edition, 4 vols. New York, 1893.

CURTIN, JEREMIAH : *Creation Myths of Primitive America in relation to the Religious History and Mental Development of Mankind.* Boston, 1898.

# BIBLIOGRAPHY

CURTIS, EDWARD S. : *The American Indian.* 4 vols. New York, 1907–9.

CUSHING, F. H. : *Zuñi Fetiches.* (*Second Report,* Bureau of American Ethnology ; Washington, 1883.)

—— *Outlines of Zuñi Creation Myths.* (*Thirteenth Report,* Bureau of American Ethnology ; Washington, 1896.)

—— *Zuñi Folk-tales.* New York, 1901.

DALL, WILLIAM H. : *Tribes of the Extreme North-West.* (*Contributions to North American Ethnology,* vol. i. ; Washington, 1877.)

—— *The Native Tribes oj Alaska.* (*Proceedings* of the American Association for the Advancement of Science, 1885, vol. xxxiv. ; Salem, 1886.)

DAWSON, GEORGE M. : *Notes and Observations of the Kwakiootl Peopie oj the Northern Part of Vancouver Island and Adjacent Coasts made during the Summer of* 1885, *with Vocabulary of about* 700 *Words.* (*Proceedings and Transactions* of the Royal Society of Canada, 1887, vol. v. ; Montreal, 1888.)

—— *Notes on the Shuswap People of British Columbia.* (*Proceedings and Transactions* of the Royal Society of Canada, 1891, vol. ix., sect. ii. ; Montreal, 1892.)

DE FOREST, JOHN W. : *History oj the Indians of Connecticut from the Earliest Known Period to* 1850. Hartford, 1851. *Ibid.,* 1852, 1853.

DEANS, JAMES : *Tales jrom the Totems oj the Hidery.* (*Archives* of the International Folk-lore Association, vol. ii. ; Chicago, 1889.)

DELLENBAUGH, F. S. : *North Americans of Yesterday.* New York and London, 1901.

DIXON, R. B. : *Maidu Myths.* (*Bulletins* of the American Museum of Natural History, vol. vii., part ii. ; New York, 1902.)

DODGE, RICHARD I. : *Our Wild Indians.* Hartford, 1882.

DONALDSON, THOMAS : *The Moqui Indians of Arizona and Pueblo Indians oj New Mexico.* (*Extra Census Bulletin,* Eleventh Census, U.S. ; Washington, 1893.)

DORSEY, GEORGE A. : *Arapaho Sun Dance : The Ceremony oj the Offerings Lodge.* (*Publications* of the Field College Museum, Anthropological Series, vol. iv. ; Chicago, 1903.)

—— *Mythology oj the Wichita.* (Carnegie Institution of Washington, Publication No. 21 ; Washington, 1904.)

# BIBLIOGRAPHY

DORSEY, GEORGE A. : *Traditions of the Osage.* (*Publications* of the Field College Museum, Anthropological Series, vol. vii., No. 1 ; Chicago, 1904.)

—— *The Cheyenne.* Part i., *Ceremonial Organization* ; part ii., *The Sun Dance.* (*Publications* of the Field College Museum, Anthropological Series), vol. ix., Nos. 1 and 2 ; Chicago, 1905.)

—— *The Pawnee : Mythology.* Part i. (Carnegie Institution of Washington, *Publication No.* 59 ; Washington, 1906.)

—— AND KROEBER, A. L. : *Traditions of the Arapaho.* (*Publications* of the Field College Museum, Anthropological Series, vol. v. ; Chicago, 1903.)

DORSEY, J. OWEN : *Osage Traditions.* (*Sixth Report,* Bureau of American Ethnology ; Washington, 1888.)

—— *The Cegiha Language.* (*Contributions to North American Ethnology,* vol. vi. ; Washington, 1890.)

—— *A Study of Siouan Cults.* (*Eleventh Report,* Bureau of American Ethnology ; Washington, 1894.)

DRAKE, SAMUEL G. : *Book of the Indians of North America.* Boston, 1833. *Ibid.,* Boston, 1841 ; Boston [1848].

DUNN, JACOB P. : *True Indian Stories.* With Glossary of Indiana Indian names. Indianapolis, 1908. *Ibid.,* 1909.

EMERSON, ELLEN R. : *Indian Myths ; or, Legends, Traditions, and Symbols of the Aborigines of America.* Boston, 1884.

EWBANK, THOMAS : *North American Rock-writing.* Morrisania, N.Y., 1866.

FAIRBANKS, G. R. : *History of Florida,* 1512–1842. Philadelphia, 1871.

FEWKES, J. W. : *Tusayan Katcinas.* (*Fifteenth Report,* Bureau of American Ethnology ; Washington, 1897.)

—— *Tusayan Migration Traditions.* (*Nineteenth Report,* Bureau of American Ethnology, part ii. ; Washington, 1900.)

FISCHER, JOSEPH : *Discoveries o the Norsemen in America.* London, 1903.

FLETCHER, ALICE C. : *Indian Story and Song from North America.* Boston, 1900.

FOSTER, J. W. : *Prehistoric Races of the United States & America.* Chicago, 1878.

# BIBLIOGRAPHY

FOWKE, GERARD : *Stone Art*. (*Thirteenth Report*, Bureau of American Ethnology ; Washington, 1896.)

GASS, PATRICK : *Journal of the Voyages and Travels oj a Corps of Discovery, under Command of Lewis and Clark*. Pittsburg, 1807. *Ibid.*, Philadelphia, 1810 ; Dayton, 1847 ; Welsburg, Va., 1859.

GATSCHET, ALBERT S. : *A Migration Legend of the Creek Indians*. Vol. i., Philadelphia, 1884 (Brinton's Library of Aboriginal American Literature, No. 4) ; vol. ii., St. Louis, 1888 (*Transactions* of the Academy of Sciences, St. Louis, vol. v., Nos. 1 and 2).

GENTLEMAN OF ELVAS : *A Narrative of the Expedition oj Hernando de Soto into Florida*. Published at Evora, 1557. Translated from the Portuguese by Richard Hakluyt. London, 1609. (In French, B.F., Hist. Coll. La., part ii. ; 2nd ed., Philadelphia, 1850.)

GRINNELL, GEORGE BIRD : *Pawnee Hero-stories and Folk-tales*. New York, 1889.

—— *Blackfoot Lodge Tales*. New York, 1892.

HALE, HORATIO : *Iroquois Book of Rites*. Philadelphia, 1883.

HECKEWELDER, JOHN G. E. : *An Account of the History, Manners, and Customs of the Indian Nations who once inhabited Pennsylvania and the Neighbouring States*. Philadelphia, 1819. (Reprinted, *Memoirs* of the Historical Society of Pennsylvania, vol. xii. ; Philadelphia, 1876.)

HEWITT, J. N. B. : *Legend oj the Founding oj the Iroquois League*. (*American Anthropologist*, vol. v. ; Washington, 1892.)

—— *Orenda and a Definition of Religion*. (*American Anthropologist*, New Series, vol. iv. ; Washington, 1891.)

—— *Iroquoian Cosmology*. (*Twenty-first Report*, Bureau of American Ethnology ; Washington, 1903.)

HOFFMAN, WALTER J. : *The Midē'-wiwin, or ' Grand Medicine Society,'* of the Ojibwa. (*Seventh Report*, Bureau of American Ethnology ; Washington, 1891.)

HOLMES, WILLIAM H. : *Aboriginal Pottery oj the Eastern United States*. (*Twentieth Report*, Bureau of American Ethnology ; Washington, 1903.)

HOUGH, WALTER : *Antiquities of the Upper Gila and Salt River Valleys in Arizona and New Mexico*. (*Bulletin* 35, Bureau of American Ethnology ; Washington, 1907.)

370

# BIBLIOGRAPHY

HRDLIČKA, ALEŠ: *Physiological and Medical Observations among the Indians of the South-western United States and Northern Mexico.* (*Bulletin* 34, Bureau of American Ethnology; Washington, 1908.)

HUNTER, JOHN D.: *Memoirs of a Captivity among the Indians of North America.* London, 1823.

JOHNSON, ELIAS: *Legends, Traditions, and Laws of the Iroquois, or Six Nations.* Lockport, N.Y., 1881.

*Journal of American Ethnology and Archæology*, vols. i.–iv. Boston and New York, 1891–94.

*Journal of American Folk-lore*, vols. i.–xxiii. Boston and New York, 1888–1910.

KANE, PAUL: *Wanderings of an Artist among the Indians of North America.* London, 1859.

KELLY, FANNY: *Narrative of my Captivity among the Sioux Indians.* 2nd ed. Chicago, 1880.

KOHL, J. G.: *Kitchi-gami: Wanderings round Lake Superior.* London, 1860.

LAFITAU, JOSEPH FRANÇOIS: *Mœurs des Sauvages amériquains, comparées aux Mœurs des Premiers Temps.* 2 vols. Paris, 1724.

LARIMER, SARAH L.: *Capture and Escape; or, Life among the Sioux.* Philadelphia, 1870.

LE BEAU, C.: *Aventures; ou Voyage curieux et nouveau parmi les Sauvages de l'Amérique Septentrionale.* 2 vols. Amsterdam, 1738.

LEE, NELSON: *Three Years among the Comanches.* Albany, 1859.

LELAND, C. G.: *Algonquin Legends of New England.* Boston and New York, 1885.

LEWIS, MERIWETHER: *The Travels of Captains Lewis and Clark, from St. Louis, by way of the Missouri and Columbia Rivers, to the Pacific Ocean; performed in the Years 1804, 1805, and 1806.* London, 1809. *Ibid.,* Philadelphia, 1809.

—— AND CLARK, WILLIAM: *History of the Expedition of Captains Lewis and Clark to the Sources of the Missouri, across the Rocky Mountains, 1804–6.* 2 vols. Philadelphia, 1814. *Ibid.,* Dublin, 1817; New York, 1817.

—— —— *The Journal of Lewis and Clark to the Mouth of the Columbia River beyond the Rocky Mountains.* Dayton, Ohio, 1840.

371

# BIBLIOGRAPHY

LEWIS, MERIWETHER, AND CLARK, WILLIAM : *Original Journals of the Lewis and Clark Expedition*, 1804–6. Edited by R. G. Thwaites. 8 vols. New York, 1904–5.

LONG, JOHN : *Voyages and Travels oj an Indian Interpreter and Trader, describing the Manners and Customs of the North American Indians.* London, 1791.

LOSKIEL, GEORGE HENRY : *History of the Mission oj the United Brethren among the Indians in North America.* London, 1794.

LUMHOLTZ, CARL : *Tarahumari Dances and Plant-worship.* (*Scribner's Magazine*, vol. xvi., No. 4 ; New York, 1894.)

LUMMIS, CHARLES F.: *The Man who Married the Moon, and other Pueblo Indian Folk-stories.* New York, 1894.

McGEE, W. J. : *The Siouan Indians.* (*Fifteenth Report*, Bureau of American Ethnology ; Washington, 1897.)

MALLERY, GARRICK : *Sign-language among North American Indians.* (*First Report*, Bureau of American Ethnology ; Washington, 1881.)

—— *Picture-writing of the American Indians.* (*Tenth Report*, Bureau of American Ethnology ; Washington, 1893.)

MATTHEWS, WASHINGTON : *Navaho Legends.* Boston and New York, 1897.

MOONEY, JAMES : *The Sacred Formulas of the Cherokees.* (*Seventh Report*, Bureau of American Ethnology ; Washington, 1891.)

—— *The Ghost-dance Religion and the Sioux Outbreak oj 1890.* (*Fourteenth Report*, Bureau of American Ethnology, part ii. ; Washington, 1896.)

—— *Myths of the Cherokee.* (*Nineteenth Report*, Bureau of American Ethnology, part i.; Washington, 1900.)

NADAILLAC, MARQUIS DE : *Prehistoric America.* Translated by N. D'Anvers. New York and London, 1884.

NORDENSKIÖLD, G. : *Cliff-dwellers of the Mesa Verde.* Translated by D. Lloyd Morgan. Stockholm and Chicago, 1893.

NORTH-WESTERN TRIBES OF CANADA : *Reports on the Physical Characters, Languages, Industrial and Social Condition of the North-Western Tribes of the Dominion of Canada.* (In *Reports* of the British Association for the Advancement of Science, 1885–98 ; London, 1886–99.)

PAYNE, EDWARD J. : *History of the New World called America.* 2 vols. Oxford and New York, 1892.

# BIBLIOGRAPHY

PEABODY MUSEUM OF AMERICAN ARCHÆOLOGY AND ETHNOLOGY: *Archæological and Ethnological Papers*, vols. i.–iii., 1888–1904. *Memoirs*, vols. i.–iii., 1896–1904. *Annual Reports*, vols. i.–xxxvii., 1868–1904. Cambridge, Mass.

PENSHALLOW, SAMUEL : *The History of the Wars of New-England with the Eastern Indians.* Boston, 1726. (*Collections* of the New Hampshire Historical Society, vol. i., Concord, 1824 ; reprint, 1871.)

PERROT, NICOLAS : *Mémoire sur les Mœurs, Coutumes, et Religion des Sauvages de l'Amérique Septentrionale, publié pour la première fois par le R. P. J. Tailhan.* Leipzig and Paris, 1864.

PETITOT, EMILE : *Traditions indiennes du Canada Nord-Ouest.* Alençon, 1887.

PIDGEON, WILLIAM : *Traditions of De-coo-dah ; and Antiquarian Researches, comprising extensive Explorations, Surveys, and Excavations of the Wonderful and Mysterious Remains of the Mound-builders in America.* New York, 1858.

POWERS, STEPHEN : *Tribes of California.* (*Contributions to North American Ethnology*, vol. iii. ; Washington, 1877.)

RAFN, K. C. : *Antiquitates Americanæ.* Copenhagen, 1837.

SCHOOLCRAFT, HENRY R. : *Algic Researches.* 2 vols. New York, 1839.

—— *Historical and Statistical Information respecting the Indian Tribes of the United States.* Philadelphia, 1851–57.

SHORT, JOHN T. : *North Americans of Antiquity.* 2nd ed. New York, 1880.

SIMMS, S. C. : *Traditions of the Crows.* (*Publications* of the Field College Museum, Anthropological Series, vol. ii., No. 6 ; Chicago, 1903.)

SMITH, ERMINNIE A. : *Myths of the Iroquois.* (*Second Report*, Bureau of American Ethnology ; Washington, 1883.)

SMITH, JOHN : Works, 1608. Edited by Edward Arber. English Scholar's Library, No. 16. Birmingham, 1884.

SMITHSONIAN INSTITUTION : *Annual Reports*, 1846–1908 ; Washington, 1847–1909. *Contributions to Knowledge*, vols. i.–xxiv. ; Washington, 1848–1907. *Miscellaneous Collections*, vols. i.–iv. ; Washington, 1862–1910.

SNELLING, WILLIAM J. : *Tales of the North-West : Sketches of Indian Life and Character.* Boston, 1830.

# BIBLIOGRAPHY

STEVENSON, MATILDA C.: *The Zuñi Indians; their Mythology, Esoteric Fraternities, and Ceremonies.* (*Twenty-third Report*, Bureau of American Ethnology; Washington, 1904.)

SWANTON, JOHN R.: *Haida Texts and Myths.* (*Bulletin* 29, Bureau of American Ethnology; Washington, 1905.)

—— *Tlingit Myths and Texts.* (*Bulletin* 39, Bureau of American Ethnology; Washington, 1909.)

THOMAS, CYRUS: *Introduction to the Study of North American Archæology.* Cincinnati, 1903.

U.S. GEOLOGICAL AND GEOGRAPHICAL SURVEY OF THE TERRITORIES, F. V. Hayden in charge. *Bulletins*, vols. i.–vi.; Washington, 1874–82. *Annual Reports*, vols. i.–ix.; Washington, 1867–78.

VIRCHOW, RUDOLF: *Crania ethnica americana.* Berlin, 1892.

VOTH, H. R.: *Oraibi Summer Snake Ceremony.* (*Publications* of the Field College Museum, Anthropological Series, vol. iii., No. 4; Chicago, 1903.)

WAITZ, THEODOR: *Anthropologie der Naturvölker.* 4 Bd. Leipzig. 1859–64.

WARREN, WILLIAM W.: *History of the Ojibways, based upon Traditions and Oral Statements.* (*Collections* of the Minnesota Historical Society, vol. v.; St. Paul, 1885.)

WHEELER, OLIN D.: *The Trail of Lewis and Clark, 1804–1904.* 2 vols. New York, 1904.

WILL, G. F., AND SPINDEN, H. J.: *The Mandans: Study of their Culture, Archæology, and Language.* (*Papers* of the Peabody Museum of American Archæology and Ethnology, vol. iii., No. 4; Cambridge, Mass., 1906.)

WINSOR, JUSTIN: *Narrative and Critical History oj America.* 8 vols. Boston and New York, 1884–89.

# GLOSSARY AND INDEX

# NOTE ON PRONUNCIATION

WORKERS in Indian mythology and linguistics have in some instances created a phonology of their own for the several languages in which they wrought. But, generally speaking, the majority of Indian names, both of places and individuals, should be pronounced as spelt, the spelling being that of persons used to transcribing native diction and as a rule representing the veritable Indian pronunciation of the word.

Among the North American Indians we find languages both harsh and soft. Harshness produced by a clustering of consonants is peculiar to the north-west coast of America, while the Mississippi basin and California possess languages rich in sonorous sounds. A slurring of terminal syllables is peculiar to many American tongues.

The vocabularies of American languages are by no means scanty, as is often mistakenly supposed, and their grammatical structure is intricate and systematic. The commonest traits in American languages are the vagueness of demarcation between the noun and verb, the use of the intransitive form of the verb for the adjective, and the compound character of independent pronouns. A large number of ideas are expressed by means of either affixes or stem-modification. On account of the frequent occurrence of such elements American languages have been classed as ' polysynthetic.'

# GLOSSARY AND INDEX

## A

ABNAKI. A tribe of the Algonquian stock, 25

ABORIGINES, AMERICAN. Theories as to the origin of, 5-13, 17-22

ACAGCHEMEM. A Californian people ; myths of, 350-355

ADAM OF BREMEN. And Norse voyages to America, 16

AÉ. The first woman, in an Acagchemem creation-myth, 353

AHSONNUTLI. Principal deity of the Navaho, called the Turquoise Man-woman, 121-122

AKAIYAN. A brave ; in Algonquian legend of the origin of the Beaver Medicine, 184-187

ALEUTIAN INDIANS. Custom of, resembles that of Asiatic tribe, 11

ALGON. A hunter ; in the story of the Star-maiden, 152-156

ALGONQUIAN STOCK. An ethnic division of the American Indians, 24-27

ALGONQUINS. The name applied to members of the Algonquian stock, 24 n. ; tribes and distribution of, 24-25 ; early history, 25 ; an advanced people, 26 ; costume of, 58 ; marriage-customs of, 73 ; creation-myth of, 107-108 ; belief of, respecting birds, 110 ; belief of, respecting lightning, 112 ; and the owl, 111 ; and the serpent of the Great Lakes, 113 ; Michabo the chief deity of, 119-120 ; and the soul's journey after death, 129 ; the festivals of, 133 ; dialect of the priests of, 136 ; myths and legends of, 141-216 ; conflict with the Caniengas, 225, subdued by the Iroquois, 227 ; and the King of Rattlesnakes, 248

ALLOUEZ, FATHER. Incident connected with, related by Brinton, 100-101

AMERICA. Origin of man in, 5-22 ; resemblance between tribes of, and those of Asia, 6, 10-12 ; discoveries of prehistoric remains in, 7-10 ; early communication between Asia and, 6, 12

ANAYICOYONDI. A goddess of the Pericues, wife of Niparaya, 355

ANIMISM, 80

ANNIMIKENS. A brave ; hunting adventure of, 55

APACHES. A tribe of the Athapascan stock, 22 ; of Arizona, houses of, 47 ; costume of, 59 ; fetishes of, 89-90 ; and the points of the compass, 131

APALACHEES. A tribe of the Muskhogean stock, 27

APISIRAHTS (The Morning Star). Son of the Sun-god, in Blackfoot myth ; in the stories of Scar-face, or Poïa, 198-205

ARAPAHO. A tribe of the Algonquian stock, 25 ; dwellings of, 48

ARGALL, CAPTAIN SAMUEL. Mentioned in the story of Pocahontas, 32, 36

ARIKARA. A tribe of the Caddoan stock, 28

ART, INDIAN, 62-63

ASGAYA GIGAGEI (Red Man). A thunder-god of the Cherokees, 126

ASHOCHIMI. A Californian tribe ; Coyote, a deity of, 124

ASIA. Ethnological relationship between America and, 6, 10-13

ASSINIBOINS. A tribe of the Siouan stock, 28 ; their method of cooking flesh, 11

ATHAPASCANS. An ethnic division of the American Indians, 22-23 ; costume of, 58 ; and the soul's journey after death, 129

ATÍUS TIRÁWA. Principal deity of the Pawnees, 122 ; in the story of the Sacred Bundle, 307 ; in the story of the Bearman, 308, 310, 311

ATOTARHO. A legendary hero of the Iroquois, chieftain of the Onondagas, 217, 225–226 ; Hiawatha a warrior under, 225 ; at first opposes Hiawatha's federation scheme, but later joins in it, 226

ATTAJEN (Man, or Rational Being). In Acagchemem myth, a semi-divine being, a benefactor of the human race, 354

AUGHEY, DR. Prehistoric remains discovered by, 8

AUZAR. In Acagchemem myth, reputed mother of Ouiamot, 354

AWONAWILONA (Maker and Container of All). The Zuñi creative deity, 106, 121

AZTECS. An aboriginal American race ; the Shoshoneans related to, 29

# B

BABEENS. A tribe of the Athapascan stock ; carvings of, 63

BANCROFT, H. H. On the mythological beliefs of the Californian tribes, 348–350 ; on the beliefs of the Tinneh, 357–358

BARTRAM, W. On the priesthood of the Creeks, 136

BEAR DANCE. Pawnee ceremonial ; story of the originator of the, 308–311

BEAR, THE GREAT. In Blackfoot legend of the origin of the Bear-spear, 188–190

BEAR-MAN. The story of the, 308–311

BEAR-SPEAR. Blackfoot legend of the origin of, 187–190

BEARSKIN-WOMAN. The story of, 182–184

BEAVER. I. A creative deity of the Sioux, chief of the Beaver family ; Ictinike and, 269–270, 271. II. In Haida myth ; story of the feud between Porcupine and, 318–320

BEAVER, THE GREAT (Quah-beet). Algonquian totem-deity ; in myth of Glooskap and Malsum, 142 ; in legend of origin of the Beaver Medicine, 185–187

BEAVER, LITTLE. In legend of origin of the Beaver Medicine, 185–187

BEAVER MEDICINE. Legend of the origin of, 184–187

BEAVER PEOPLE. The beavers personified, in Haida myth ; in the story of Beaver and Porcupine, 318–320

BIG WATER. The Pacific Ocean ; in the story of Scar-face, 203

BIRD, THE. In Indian mythology, 109–111

BLACK TORTOISE, TOMB OF THE. An earth-mound, 19–20

BLACKFEET. A tribe of the Algonquian stock, 24, 25 ; legends of, 182–184, 187–190, 193–212 ; the Sun Dance of, 204 ; Nápi, the creative deity of, 205

BLUE JAY. A mischievous totem-deity of the Chinooks, 124–125, 323 ; stories of, and his sister Ioi, 323–327 ; and the Supernatural People, 323–324, 327, 329–332, 339–340 ; in the story of Stikūa, 342–348

BOAS, FRANZ. Extract from version of the Coyote myth related by, 124

BOSCANA, FATHER GERÓNIMO. On the beliefs of Californian tribes, 350–354

BOURBEUSE RIVER. Prehistoric remains discovered at, 7

BOURKE, J. G. Description of an Apache fetish by, 89–90 ; on ' phylacteries ' (fetishes), 90

BOY MAGICIAN. The story of the, 238–242

BRÉBEUF, FATHER. Incident connected with, related by Brinton, 100 ; and the after-life of the Indians, 130

BRINTON, D. G. On the Shoshoneans, 29 ; extract from translation of the Wallum-Olum by, 77–78 ; on the religion of the Indians, 97–101 ; on Indian ' good ' and ' bad ' gods, 104–105 ; on Indian veneration of the eagle, 110–111

BRUYAS, FATHER. Mentioned, 104

BUFFALO DANCE. A festival of the Mandans, 134–135

BUFFALO-STEALER. The legend of, 208–212

BUNDLES, SACRED. Collections of articles supposed to possess magical potency, 92, 308

BUREAU OF AMERICAN ETHNO-LOGY. Quotations from *Bulletins* of, 17, 21, 45–49, 55–59

BURIAL CUSTOMS, INDIAN, 128

BUSK. A contraction for Push-kita, name of a Creek festival, 133–134

BWOINAIS. A Chippeway warrior; war-songs of, 71–72

## C

CADDO. I. An ethnic division of the American Indians, 28, 304. II. A tribe forming a part of the stock of the same name, 28

CAHROCS. A Californian tribe; deities of, 349–350

'CALAVERAS' SKULL. Prehistoric relic; discovery of, 8

CALIFORNIA. Prehistoric remains discovered in, 8; the tribes of, diversity among, 348; mythological beliefs of the tribes of, 348–356

CANIENGAS. One of the two political divisions of the Iroquois family, 225

CARVER, CAPTAIN JONATHAN. On Sioux methods of reckoning time, 132

CATLIN, G. On the Pipe-stone Quarry, 116, 117–118

CAYUGAS. A tribe of the Iroquois stock, 224

CHÂCOPEE, or WHITE FEATHER. A Sioux hero; the story of, 296–301

CHAREYA (The Old Man Above). Deity of the Cahrocs, 350

CHARLEVOIX, P. On incident relating to origin of the Indians, 12

CHEROKEES. A tribe of the Iroquois stock, 23; as mound-builders, 21; and the eagle, 111; and the owl, 111; hunter-and thunder-gods of, 125–126; and the points of the compass, 131; and the priesthood, 136; dialect of the priesthood of, 136; subdued by the Iroquois, 227; the Iroquois attacks on, 246; and the King of Rattle-snakes, 248; their legend of the origin of medicine, 249–251

CHEYENNE. A tribe of the Algonquian stock, 25; the great tribal fetish of, 91

CHICKASAWS. A tribe of the Muskhogean stock, 27; and earth-mounds, 21

CHILKAT. A tribe of the Thlingit stock; costume of, 58

CHIMPSEYANS. An ethnic division of the American Indians; carvings of, 63

CHINIGCHINICH (Almighty). Deity of the Acagchemems, called also Ouiamot, 352, 354–355

CHINOOKS. A tribe of the Chinookan stock, 322; Coyote a principal deity of, 123, 124; Blue Jay a deity of, 124; mode of burial of, 128; belief of, regarding the soul, 129; cranial deformation among, 322; myths of, 322–348; story of their contests with the Supernatural People, 329–332

CHIPPEWAYS, or OJIBWAYS. A tribe of the Algonquian stock, 25; dwellings of, 48; carvings of, 63; called 'Pillagers,' 68; war-customs of, 68–69; a legend of, 152–156; Manabozho (or Michabo a demi-god of, 223

CHOCTAWS. A tribe of the Mus-khogean stock, 27; cranial deformation among, 27; dialect of the priesthood of, 136

CHURCH, CAPTAIN BENJAMIN. One of the early settlers; his methods in fighting the Indians, 31

CHUTSAIN. A malevolent spirit of the Tinneh, 358

# GLOSSARY AND INDEX

CITY OF THE MISTS. Home of Po-shai-an-K'ia, the father of the Zuñi 'medicine' societies, 95

CLALLAMS. A tribe of the Salish stock; carvings of, 63

CLARKE, J. On the Pipe-stone Quarry, 116–117

CLIFF- AND ROCK-DWELLINGS, 48–49

CLOUD-CARRIER. The story of, 156–159

COCOPA. A tribe of the Yuman stock; dwellings of, 47; costume of, 59

COLORADO. Prehistoric remains discovered in, 8

COLOURS. The Indians and, 60–62

COLUMBUS. And the Discovery, 1, 2

COMANCHES. A tribe of the Shoshonean stock, 28; dwellings of, 48

COMMUNITY HOUSES, 45–47

COMPASS, POINTS OF THE. Significance to the Indians, 131

CONANT, A. J. On the group of earth-mounds in Minnesota, 20

CONQUEROR, THE. A deity mentioned in the myth of Coyote and Kodoyanpe, 123

COSTUME OF THE INDIANS, 55–59

COUNTRY OF THE GHOSTS. Same as Spirit-land, which see

COYOTE. See Italapas

COYOTE PEOPLE, THE GREAT. A Zuñi clan, 95–96

CRANIAL DEFORMATION. Practised among the Muskhogeans, 27; among the Choctaws, 27; among the Chinooks, 322

CREATION-MYTHS, 106–109, 350–353

CREEKS. A tribe of the Muskhogean stock, 27; and earth-mounds, 21; and the eagle, 110; and the owl, 111; Esaugetuh Emissee, the chief deity of, 122; the Pushkita, a festival of, 133–134; the priests of, 136

CREES. A tribe of the Algonquian stock, 25; legend of origin of their Young Dog Dance, 190–

193; how they caught eagles, 190–191

CROWS. A tribe of the Siouan stock; in a Blackfoot legend, 193–196

## D

DAKOTA. An ethnic division of the American Indians, same as Sioux, which see

DAY OF THE COUNCIL OF THE FETISHES. A Zuñi fetish festival, 96

DAY-AND-NIGHT MYTH. A Blackfoot, 205–208

DEKANEWIDAH. A Mohawk chieftain; assists Hiawatha in his federation scheme, 226

DELAWARES. A tribe of the Algonquian stock, 25; in the story of Frances Slocum, 37–38, 41

DÉNÉ. Same as Tinneh, which see

DEVIL. In Indian mythology, 349

DEVIL DANCES, 135

DEVIL'S CASTLE. Place in Siskiyou, California; regarded by natives as abode of malignant spirits, 349

DEVIL-FISH. Supernatural beings in Haida myth; story of an Indian and the daughter of a, 320–321

DEVOURING HILL. The story of the Rabbit and the, 302–303

DICKSON, DR. Discovery of prehistoric remains by, 7

DIGHTON WRITING ROCK, 16

DJŪ. A river mentioned in Haida myth, 314

DOGRIB INDIANS. A tribe of the Athapascan stock; myth of heaven-climber resembles that of Ugrian tribes of Asia, 11

DROWNED CHILD. The story of the, 285–287

DWELLINGS, INDIAN, 45–49

## E

EAGLE. Indian veneration for, 110–111

EJONI. The first man, in an Acagchemem creation - myth, 353

ELEGANT. An Indian beau ; in the story of Handsome, 160-162

ENO (Thief and Cannibal). A name of Coyote among the Acagchemem tribes, 351

ES-TONEA-PESTA (The Lord of Cold Weather). In the story of the Snow-lodge, 151-152

ESAUGETUH EMISSEE (Master of Breath). Supreme deity of the Muskhogees, 122 ; in creation-myth, 108

EYACQUE (Sub-captain). A name of Coyote among the Acagchemem tribes, 351


F

FACE-PAINTING, 59-62

FAIRY WIVES. The story of the, 170-175

FEATHER-WOMAN. A beautiful maiden ; in the legend of Poïa, 200-203

FEATHER-WORK. Indian skill in, 63

FESTIVALS, INDIAN, 133-135

FETISHISM. Swanton on totemism and, 84-85 ; origin and nature of the fetish, 87-89 ; Apache fetishes, 89-90 ; Iroquoian fetishes, 91 ; Huron fetishes, 91 ; Algonquian fetishes, 91 ; the Cheyenne tribal fetish, 91 ; Hidatsa fetishes, 92 ; Siouan fetishes, 92 ; Hopi fetishes, 92-93 ; Zuñi fetishism, 93-97 ; fetishism associated with totemism, 93

FEWKES, J. W. And fetishes of the Hopi, 92

FINE-WEATHER-WOMAN. Haida storm-deity ; in the myth of the origin of certain demigods, 314 ; origin of, as the mother of Sïñ, 314-316

FIVE NATIONS, THE. A federation of the Iroquois, called also the Grand League, 23, 24 ; the tribes composing, 23, 224-225 ; Hia-watha the founder of the league, 23 ; influence upon European history, 223, 227 ; called also Six Nations and Seven Nations, 224 ; Hiawatha's early efforts toward federation, 225 ; the federation inaugurated, and completed, 226 ; growth of the power of, 227 ; the Peace Queen appointed by, 263 ; the office of Peace Queen abolished, 265

FLATHEADS. Name applied to the Choctaws by the whites, 27

FLETCHER, MISS A. C. On dwellings of the Omaha, 48

FLYING SQUIRREL. A creative deity of the Sioux ; Ictinike and, 271

FOXES. A tribe of the Algonquian stock, 25, 71

FRIENDLY SKELETON. The story of the, 242-246

FUTURE LIFE. The Indian idea of, 127


G

GÉBELIN, COURT DE. And the Dighton Writing Rock, 16

GENETASKA. A Peace Queen ; the legend of, 262-265

GHOST PEOPLE. The souls of the dead, the inhabitants of Spiritland, 129, 130 ; Ioi and Blue Jay among, 324-326, 327

GHOST-LAND. Same as Spiritland, which see

GILA-SONORA. An ethnic division of the American Indians ; costume of, 59

GITSHE IAWBA. A Chippeway brave ; hunting exploit of, 54-55

GLOOSKAP (The Liar). A creative deity of the Algonquins, twin with Malsum, 141 ; his contest with Malsum, 141-142 ; resembles the Scandinavian Balder, 142 ; creates man, 143 ; contest with Win-pe, 143-144 ; his gifts to man, 144-145 ; and Wasis, the baby, 145-146 ;

381

leaves the earth, 146–147; a sun-god, 147; and Summer and Winter, 147–149; his 'wigwam,' 149

GOD. The Indian idea of, 101

GODS, INDIAN. Character of, 103–105; description of the principal, 118–126

GRAND COUNCIL of the Five Nations, 224, 226

GRAND LEAGUE, or KAYANERENH KOWA. A federation of the Iroquois, known also as the Five Nations. *See under* Five Nations

GREAT DOG. A totem-deity, 137

GREAT EAGLE. A totem-deity, 137

GREAT HEAD. A malevolent being, in Iroquois myth; a legend of, 232–235

GREAT MAN. Name for a chief deity among Californian tribes, 348

GREAT SPIRIT, THE, or MANITO. Supreme Indian deity; and the origin of smoking, 116

GREAT WATER. The Pacific; in the story of the Snake-wife, 290, 292

GREATEST FOOL. Supernatural being in Haida myth; in the story of Master-carpenter and South-east, 317

GREENLAND. Early voyages from, to America, 13, 14–16


H

HAIDA. A tribe of the Skittagetan stock; houses of, 46–47; myths and legends of, 312–321

HAMPTON INSTITUTE. And education of the Indians, 79

HANDSOME. A beautiful maiden; the story of, 159–162

HAOKAH. Thunder-god of the Sioux, 125

'HARRYING OF HADES.' American Indian myth provides examples of, 332, 340–341

HEALING WATERS. The legend of the, 257–260

HELLU-LAND (Land of Flat Stones). In legend of Norse voyage to America, 14, 15

HERBERT, SIR THOMAS. His *Travels* quoted, 4–5

HERJULFSON, BIARNE. And the Norse discovery of America, 13–14

HIAWATHA (more properly HAI-EN-WAT-HA; = He who seeks the Wampum-belt). A legendary hero of the Iroquois, 217, 223–228; represented also as of Algonquian race, 223; effect of Longfellow's poem on the history of, 223; Longfellow's confusion in identity of, 223; historical basis for the legends, 223; founder of the League of the Five Nations, 223–224; a warrior under Atotarho, 225; his plans for federation, 225; adopted into the Mohawk tribe, 226; his scheme consummated, 226

HIDATSA. A tribe of the Sioux; fetishes of, 92; have no belief in a devil or hell, 104

HI'NUN. Thunder-god of the Iroquois, 217; myths relating to, 218–222; great veneration for, 222

HOBBAMOCK, or HOBBAMOQUI (Great). Beneficent Indian deity, 105

HOFFMANN, W. J. On Algonquian fetishes, 91

HOGAN. An Indian dwelling, 49

HOPI, or MOQUI. A tribe of the Shoshonean stock; as cotton-weavers, 56, 73; fetishes of, 92–93; festivals of, 135

HUNTING, INDIAN, 50–55

HUPA. A tribe of the Athapascan stock; costume of, 59; method of reckoning age, 133

HURONS. A tribe of the Iroquois stock, 23; marriage among, 73; fetishes of, 91; the dove regarded as sacred by, 111; and the soul's journey after death, 129; originally one people with the Iroquois, 224; in the conflict between the Caniengas and

Algonquins, 225 ; war with the Onondagas, 225; annihilated by the Iroquois, 227 ; a legend of, 248

I

ICE-COUNTRY. In Algonquian myth, 147

ICTINIKE. An evil spirit, in Sioux myth ; adventures of, 266–271

ILLINOIS. A tribe of the Algonquian stock ; in a Seneca legend, 236–238

' INDIAN.' The name wrongly applied to the North American races, 1

INDIANA. Primitive implements found in, 7 ; earth-mounds found in, 17, 18

INDIANS, NORTH AMERICAN. The theory that they came from the East, 1–2 ; early controversy as to origin of, 2–3 ; identified with the lost Ten Tribes, 3 ; other theories of origin of, 4 ; theory of their Welsh origin, 4–5 ; origination of American man in the Old World, 5–6 ; scientific data relating to origin of, 5–13, 17–22 ; affinities with Siberian peoples, 10–12 ; probably migrants from Asia, 12–13 ; ethnic divisions of, 22–29 ; geographical distribution of the tribes of, 22–29 ; industry of, 26 ; early wars between whites and, 29–31 ; early relationship with whites, 29–30 ; deportation of, as slaves, 31 ; confinement of, to ' reservations,' 31 – 32 ; stories of whites and, 32–45 ; and kidnapping of white children, 36–45 ; dwellings of, 45–49 ; tribal law and custom among, 50 ; hunting among, 50–55 ; dress of, 55–59 ; and face-painting, 59–62 ; and colours, 60–62 ; art of, 62–63 ; war-customs of, 63–72 ; position of women among, 72–73 ; marriage among, 73 ; and child-life, 73–74 ; and totemism,

74–76, 80–87 ; picture-writing among, 76–78 ; enlightenment of, 79, 360 ; and fetishism, 87–97 ; and religion, 97–105, 140 ; ideas of God, 101 ; character of gods of, 103–105 ; creation-myths of, 106–109 ; serpent-and bird-worship among, 109–115 ; and the use of tobacco, 115–118 ; the gods of, 118–126 ; and ideas of a future life, 127–128 ; burial customs of, 128 ; and the soul's journey after death, 129 ; and the spirit-world, 129–130, 139–140 ; reverence for the four points of the compass, 131 ; methods of time-reckoning, 131–133 ; festivals of, 132, 133–135 ; the medicine-men of, 135–140 ; original character of the mythologies of, 359 ; worthiness of the race, 359–360

IoI. A deity of the Chinooks, sister of Blue Jay ; stories of, 323–327

IOSKEHA (White One). One of the twin-gods of the Iroquois, 121

IOWA. I. The State ; prehistoric remains discovered in, 8. II. A tribe of the Sioux stock, 266 ; legends of, 266–271

IROQUOIS (Real Adders). An ethnic division of the American Indians, called also Long House People, 23–24, 224 ; the Five Nations of, 23, 24, 223–227 ; community houses of, 45 ; costume of, 58 ; marriage customs of, 73 ; name for fetish, 85 ; and the serpent of the Great Lakes, 113 ; the twin-gods of, 121 ; and the soul's journey after death, 129 ; myths and legends of, 217–265 ; Hi'nun, the chief deity of, 217 ; Hiawatha, a mythical hero of, 217 ; originally one people with the Hurons, 224 ; the two political branches of, 224–225 ; growth of the power of, 227

IROQUOIS CONFEDERACY. See Five Nations

ISLAND OF THE BLESSED. In the story of the Spirit-bride, 163–165

ITALAPAS or ITALAPATE, (Coyote). A principal deity of the Chinooks and Californian tribes, 123–124, 350 ; in the myth of Ouiot, 351

## J

JAPAZAWS. A chief, 32

JEWS. American aborigines identified with, 3–4

## K

KATCINA. A clan of the Hopi tribe ; and the tribal festivals, 135

KAYANERENH KOWA. The Grand League, or Five Nations, a federation of the Iroquois. See under Five Nations

KENTUCKY. Earth-mounds found in, 18

KEWAWKQU'. A race of giants and magicians, in Algonquian myth ; conquered by Glooskap, 145

KICHAI. A tribe of the Caddoan stock, 28

KICKAPOOS. A tribe of the Algonquian stock, 25

KIDNAPPING by Indians, 36 ; a story of, 37–45

KIEHTAN. Beneficent Indian deity, 105

KING OF GRUBS. In the myth of the Thunderers, 222

KING OF RATTLESNAKES. The legend of, 248

KING PHILIP'S WAR, 30–31

KINGFISHER. A creative deity of the Sioux ; Ictinike and, 271

KINGSBOROUGH, LORD. And the identity of the American aborigines, 3

KIOWA. An ethnic division of the American Indians ; dwellings of, 48 ; picture-writing records of, 77 ; the year of, 132

KITTANITOWIT. A manufactured name for the supreme Indian deity, 105

KOCH, DR. Prehistoric remains discovered by, 7

KODOYANPE. Principal deity of the Maidu, 123, 124

KOHL, J. G. On Indian face-painting, 59–62

KOKOMIKIS. The Moon-goddess, wife of the Sun-god ; in the stories of Scar-face, 199–204

KOLUSCHES. An ethnic division of the American Indians ; customs of, resemble those of Asiatic tribes, 10–11

KOOTENAY. An ethnic division of the American Indians ; Coyote the creative deity of, 124

KUM. A semi-subterranean lodge of the Maidu, 47

KUTOYIS (Drop of Blood). A hero in Algonquian myth ; legends of, 212–216

## L

LAKE SUPERIOR. Prehistoric remains discovered in district of, 8

LAND OF THE SUN. Indian abode of bliss, 127

LAND OF THE SUPERNATURAL PEOPLE. Region inhabited by a semi-divine race, 129–130 ; in Chinook myth, 323–324, 327–332, 337–338

LANGUAGE. Resemblance between that of American and Asiatic tribes, 12 ; the basis of ethnic classification of American tribes, 22

LEIF THE LUCKY. Legend of voyage of, to America, 14–15

LELAND, C. G. On Algonquian mythology, 143

LENI-LENÂPÉ. A tribe of the Algonquian stock ; the Wallum-Olum of, 77–78

LIGHTNING. Indian belief regarding, 111–112

LIPANS. A tribe of the Athapascan stock, 22

LITTLE DEER. Chief of the Deer tribe, in Cherokee myth, 249, 250

LITTLE MEN. Twin thunder-gods of the Cherokees, 126

LONE-DOG WINTER-COUNT. A picture-writing chronicle of the Dakota, 77

LONG HOUSE PEOPLE. A name applied to the Iroquois, 224, 227

LONGFELLOW, H. W. And the identity of Hiawatha, 223

LORD OF THE DEAD. Indian deity ; the owl sometimes represented as the attendant of, 112

LOUCHEUX. A division of the Tinneh stock ; the myth of the moon-god of, 357-358

LOX, or LOKI. Algonquian deity, a reincarnation of Malsum, 143 ; reminiscent of the Scandinavian Loki, 143 ; in the story of the Fairy Wives, 174-175

LYELL, SIR CHARLES. On discovery of prehistoric remains, 7

## M

MA-CON-A-QUA. The Indian name of Frances Slocum, 44

MADOC. Legend of, 4

MAIDU. A Californian tribe ; dwellings of, 47 ; creation-myth of, 123 ; Coyote and Kodoyanpe deities of, 123 ; the seasons of, 133

MAIZE. Chippeway story of the origin of, 180-182

MAKER-OF-THE-THICK-SEA-MIST. Haida deity ; in the story of Master-carpenter and Southeast, 318

MALICIOUS MOTHER-IN-LAW. Story of the, 176-180

MALSUM (The Wolf). A malignant creative deity of the Algonquins, twin with Glooskap, 141-143, 149 ; contest with Glooskap, 141-142 ; appears later in Algonquian myth as Lox, or Loki, 143 ; future conflict with Glooskap, 149

MAN. Origin of, in America, 5-22

MANABOZHO. Same as Michabo, II, which see

MANDANS. A tribe of the Siouan stock ; community houses of, 45 ; creation-myth of, 109 ; the dove regarded as sacred by, 112 ; the Buffalo Dance, a festival of, 134-135

MANITO (The Great Spirit). I. Supreme deity of the Algonquins, probably same as Michabo ; and the lightning, 112. II. A general term for a potent spirit or the supernatural among the Algonquins and Sioux, 114. III. Supreme deity of the Iroquois ; in the legend of the Healing Waters, 257-260

MARK-LAND (Wood-land). In legend of the Norse voyage to America, 14, 15

MARRIAGE among the Indians, 73

MARTEN. An idle brave ; in the story of the Fairy Wives, 170-172

MASON, JOHN. One of the early settlers ; and the feud with the Pequots, 30

MASTER OF LIFE. In the story of the Spirit-bride, 164

MASTER-CARPENTER. A supernatural being, in Haida myth ; story of his contest with Southeast, 316-318

MEDA. A 'medicine' society of the Algonquins, 119

MEDA CHANT. An Algonquian religious ceremony, 114

MEDECOLIN. Sorcerers, in Algonquian myth ; conquered by Glooskap, 145

MEDICINE-MEN, or SHAMANS, 135-140 ; as priests, 136 ; as healers, 136-138 ; 'journeys' of, to Spirit-land, 139-140 ; instituted by Attajen, 354

'MEDICINE.' A term signifying magical potency, usually of a healing order ; Seneca legend of the origin of, 230-232 ; Cherokee legend of the origin of curative medicine, 249-251

MEN-SERPENTS. The story of the, 273-275

MENOMINEES. A tribe of the Algonquian stock, 25

MIAMI. A tribe of the Algonquian stock ; in the story of Frances Slocum, 40, 41

MICE. Two supernatural beings in Chinook myth, 339–340

MICHABO (The Great Hare). I. Supreme deity of the Algonquins, probably same as Manito, 119–120 ; in creation-myth, 107–108. II. A demi-god of the Ojibways, called also Manabozho ; confusion of, with Hiawatha, 223

MICMACS. A tribe of the Algonquian stock, 25 ; subdued by the Iroquois, 227

MILKY WAY. Called the Wolf-trail by the Indians, 204

MINAS, LAKE. In Nova Scotia ; Glooskap leaves the earth upon, 146

MINNESOTA. Primitive implements found in, 7 ; earth-mounds found in, 18, 19–20

MINNETAREES. A tribe of the Hidatsa stock ; creation-myth of, 109

'MIOCENE BRIDGE.' And the origin of man in America, 6

MOHAVE. A tribe of the Yuman stock ; costume of, 59

MOHAWKS. A tribe of the Iroquois stock, 24, 224, 225 ; and the twin-gods myth of the Iroquois, 121 ; Hiawatha may have belonged to, 223, 226 ; Hiawatha adopted into, 226

MOHEGANS. Same as Mohicans, which see

MOHICANS, or MOHEGANS. A tribe of the Algonquian stock, 25 ; a community house of, 45 ; subdued by the Iroquois, 227

MON-DA-MIN. The maize-plant ; story of the origin of, 180–182

MONTAGNAIS. A tribe of the Algonquian stock, 25

MOON-GODDESS. See Kokomikis

MOOSE. A brave, a great hunter ; in the story of the Fairy Wives, 170–172

MOOWIS. A counterfeit brave ; in the story of Elegant and Handsome, 161–162

MOQUI. Same as Hopi, which see

MORGAN, L. On Indian community houses, 45–46

MORNING STAR. See Apisirahts

MOUNDS. Prehistoric earthen erections found in America, 17–22 ; in animal form, 17-18 ; purpose of, 18 ; contents of, 18–19, 21 ; description of a group, 19–20 ; the builders of, 20–21 ; age of, 21–22

MUSK-RAT. A creative deity of the Sioux ; Ictinike and, 270–271

MUSKHOGEANS. An ethnic division of the American Indians, 27 ; costume of, 58 ; marriage-customs of, 73 ; creation-myth of, 108

N

NAKOTAT. A Chinook village ; in the myth of Stikŭa, 341, 345

NANTAQUAUS. Son of the chief Powhatan, 33

NANTENA. Spirits or fairies, in Tinneh mythology, 358

NÂPI. The creative deity of the Blackfeet ; in a day-and-night legend, 205, 208 ; in the legend of Buffalo-stealer, 208–212

NARRAGANSETS. A tribe of the Algonquian stock, 25

NARVAEZ, PANFILO DE. And the Muskhogean people, 27

NATCHEZ. I. The city ; discoveries of prehistoric remains at, 7. II. A tribe of the so-called Natchesan stock ; and earth-mounds, 21 ; and the eagle, 112

NAVAHO. A tribe of the Athapascan stock, 22 ; a dwelling of, 49 ; costume of, 59 ; belief of, respecting birds and the winds, 110 ; Ahsonnutli the chief deity of, 121–122 ; belief of, respecting the soul, 129 ; and the points of the compass, 131

NEBRASKA. Prehistoric remains discovered in, 8

NEKUMONTA. An Iroquois brave ; in the legend of the Healing Waters, 257–260

NEMISSA. A Star-maiden; in the story of Cloud-carrier, 156–159

NEW ORLEANS. Prehistoric remains discovered at, 7

NEW YORK. State of; conflict between Indians and the early settlers in, 30

NEZ PERCÉS. A tribe of the Sahaptian stock; dwellings of, 47

NIPARAYA. A supreme deity of the Pericues, 355–356

NIPMUCS. A tribe of the Algonquian stock, 25

NOCUMA. A creative deity of the Acagchemems, 352–353

NOKAY. A noted Chippeway hunter; hunting exploit of, 54

NOOTKAS. A tribe of the Nootka-Columbia stock; dwellings of, 47; Quahootze, a deity of, 100

NOPATSIS. A brave; in the legend of the origin of the Beaver Medicine, 184–187

NORSEMEN. Discovery of America by, 13–14, 16; early voyages of, to America, 14–16; left no traces of their occupation, 16

NOTTOWAYS. A tribe of the Iroquois stock, 23

NUNNE CHAHA. A hill mentioned in the Muskhogean creation-myth, 108


O

OHIO. I. The State; primitive implements found in, 7; earth-mounds found in, 17, 18. II. The river; attempt to maintain as Indian boundary, 25

OJIBWAYS. Same as Chippeways, which see

OKINAI. In the story of Bearskin-woman, 183–184

OKULAM (Noise of Surge). Name given to giant in Chinook myth of the Thunderer, 335

OLCHONES. A Californian tribe; sun identified with supreme deity by, 350

OLD MAN ABOVE. I. Name for supreme deity among Californian tribes, 348. II. The Chareya of the Cahrocs, 350

OLD WHITE BEAR. Chief of the Bear tribe, in Cherokee myth, 249

OMAHAS. A tribe of the Siouan stock; dwellings of, 48; Ictinike a war-god of, 266

ONE ABOVE. Name for supreme deity among Californian tribes, 348

ONEIDAS. A tribe of the Iroquois stock, 24, 224, 225; inaugurate the federation of the Five Nations, 226

ONNIONT. A mythological serpent, 91

ONONDAGAS. A tribe of the Iroquois stock, 224; Hiawatha probably belonged to, 223; war with Caniengas and Hurons, 225; Atotarho a chief of, 225; and Hiawatha's federation scheme, 226

ORENDA. Magical power, 112

OSAGES. A tribe probably of the Algonquian stock; dwellings of, 48

OTTER-HEART. The story of, 165–170

OUIAMOT. Same as Chinigchinich, which see

OUIOT (Dominator). I. A demi-god of the Acagchemems, 351–352. II. A tyrannous ruler, 353–354

OWL, THE. Indian veneration for, 113


P

PAHE-WATHAHUNI (The Devouring Hill). The story of the Rabbit and, 302–303

PAIUTES. A tribe of the Yunian stock; houses of, 47

PALMER, CAPTAIN G. Work by, quoted, 3–4

PAMOLA. An evil spirit, in Algonquian myth; conquered by Glooskap, 145

# GLOSSARY AND INDEX

PAWNEES. A confederacy of tribes of the Caddoan stock, 28, 304; and the tribal fetish of the Cheyenne, 91; and thunder, 112; Atíus Tiráwa, the chief deity of, 122; and the Young Dog Dance, 190; subdued by the Iroquois, 227; strong religious sense of, 304; myths and legends of, 304–311; story of the origin of their Sacred Bundle, 304–308

PAYNE, E. J. On resemblance of customs of American and Asiatic tribes, 10–11

PEACE QUEEN. A maiden appointed by the Five Nations to be arbiter of quarrels; the legend of Genetaska the, 262–265; the office abolished, 265

PEBBLE-RATTLER. Haida wind-deity; in the story of Master-carpenter and South-east, 318

PEQUOTS. A tribe of the Algonquian stock; feud between the whites and, 30

PERICUES. A Californian tribe; the hostile divinities of, 355–356

PETIT ANSE. Place in Louisiana; prehistoric remains discovered at, 7

PHILIP. An Indian chief, called 'King Philip'; war of, with the whites, 30–31

PICTURE-WRITING, INDIAN, 76–78

PIGMIES. Iroquois belief in a race of, 229; a legend of, 246–248; perhaps actually a prehistoric American race, 248

PIMAS. A tribe of the Pueblo stock; costume of, 59; method of keeping records, 133

PIPE-STONE QUARRY. Source of the Indian's pipe; description of, 116–118

PLAGUE DEMON. Iroquois deity, 264

PLAINS INDIANS. Costume of, 58; artistic work of, 62; rank among, indicated by feathers worn, 63; marriage among, 73

POCAHONTAS. Daughter of the chief Powhatan; the story of, 32–36

POÏA (Scar-face). The legends of, 196–205

PORCUPINE. One of the Porcupine People, in Haida myth; story of the conflict between Beaver and, 318–320

PO-SHAI-AN-K'IA. A Zuñi deity, father of the 'medicine' societies, 95; in creation-myth, 107

POWELL, CAPTAIN NATHANIEL. And the story of Pocahontas, 32–36

POWERS, STEPHEN. On evil spirits in Indian mythology, 349–350

POWHATAN. A chief, father of Pocahontas, 32, 33

POWHATANS. A tribe of the Algonquian stock, 25; belief of, respecting birds, 110.

PRATT, CAPTAIN R. H. His school for the education of Indian children, 79

PREHISTORIC REMAINS. Discoveries of, 7–10

PREY BROTHERS. A priesthood of the Zuñi, 96

PREY-GODS. Deities of the Zuñi, 94–97

PRIESTHOOD of the Indian tribes, 135–136

PRINCE OF SERPENTS. A deity who dwelt in the Great Lakes, 112, 113

PUEBLOS. I. An ethnic division of the American Indians; buildings of, 47, 49; costume of, 57, 59; artistic work of, 63; festivals of, 135. II. Indian community houses, 46, 48

PUSHKITA. A festival of the Creeks, 134

## Q

QUAAYAYP. A son of the Pericue deity Niparaya, 355

QUAH-BEET (Great Beaver). Algonquian totem-deity; in myth of Glooskap and Malsum, 142

QUAHOOTZE. Deity of the Nootkas, 100

QUAPAWS. A tribe of the Caddoan stock; and earth-mounds, 21

## R

RABBIT. Personified animal in Sioux myth ; Ictinike and, 266–268 ; and the Sun, 301–302 ; and Pahe-Wathahuni, the Devouring Hill, 302–303

RAFN, K. C. Cited, 14 ; and the Dighton Writing Rock, 16

RATTLESNAKE. Indian regard for the, 113–115

RAVEN. Personification in Chinook myth ; in the story of Stikŭa, 342–348

RED PIPE-STONE ROCK. The first pipe made at, 116

RED-STORM-CLOUD. A Haida wind-deity ; in the story of Master-carpenter and Southeast, 317

RESERVATIONS, INDIAN, 31–32

RESURRECTION. Indian belief in, 128

ROBIN. A deity of the Chinooks, brother of Blue Jay, 125, 330, 332

ROGEL, FATHER. Incident connected with his missionary work, 105

ROLFE, JOHN. Husband of Pocahontas, 32

ROOT-DIGGERS. A tribe of the Shoshonean stock, 28

## S

SACRED BUNDLE. The story of the, 304–308

SACRED OTTER. A hunter ; in the story of the Snow-lodge, 150–152

SALISH INDIANS. A tribe probably of the Algonquian stock ; houses of, 47 ; costume of, 58

SALMON. The story of, 282–285

SANTEES. A tribe of the Siouan stock, 28

SASSACUS. Pequot chief ; his village destroyed, 30

SAUKS. A tribe of the Siouan stock, 71

SAYADIO. A young Wyandot brave ; the legend of, 260–262

SCALPING. Nature of the act, 66 ; preservation of scalps, 67

SCAR-FACE. See Poïa

SCHOOLCRAFT, H. R. On Indian hunting, 52–55 ; on Indian warfare, 66–72 ; on the Indian's use of tobacco, and his pipe, 115–118 ; and the identity of Hiawatha, 223

SECOTAN. An Indian village in North Carolina, 48

SEMINOLES. A tribe of the Muskhogean stock, 27 ; costume of, 58

SENECAS. A tribe of the Iroquois stock, 225, 226 ; the so-called, in Oklahoma, 24 ; join the Grand League, 226 ; story of the origin of the 'medicine' of, 230–232 ; legend of, 236–238

SERPENT, THE. In Indian mythology, 109–111, 114 ; worship of, 112–114 ; reverence paid to, 135

SHADOW-LAND. Same as Spirit-land, which see

SHANEWIS. Wife of Nekumonta ; in the legend of the Healing Waters, 257–260

SHAWNEES. A tribe of the Algonquian stock, 25 ; as mound-builders, 21 ; and the King of Rattlesnakes, 248

SHOSHONEANS (Snakes). An ethnic division of the American Indians, 28–29 ; costume of, 59

SHUSHWAP INDIANS. A Srlish tribe ; Coyote the creative deity of, 124

SILVER CHAIN. Name applied to the Grand Council of the league of the Five Nations, 226

SÎÑ. Sky-god and principal deity of the Haida ; myth of the incarnation of, 314–316

SINNEKES. One of the two political divisions of the Iroquois, 224, 225

SIOUX, or DAKOTA. An ethnic division of the American Indians, 28, 266 ; superstition of, resembles that of the Itelmians of Kamchatka, 11 ; dwellings of, 48 ; face-painting among,

61–62; war-customs of, 68; fetishes of, 92; belief of, respecting the winds, 110; and the eagle, 111; and the rattle-snake, 114; Haokah, the chief thunder-god of, 125; Waukheon, a thunder-god of, 126; Unktahe, the water-god of, 126; and the soul's journey after death, 129; the year of, 132; methods of time-reckoning of, 132–133; myths and legends of, 266–303

SIROUT (Handful of Tobacco). One of the first men, in an Acagchemem creation-myth, 353

SITS-BY-THE-DOOR. The story of, 193–196

SKRÆLINGR. Name given by Norsemen to American natives, 13; attack the early Norse voyagers, 15

SKULL, DEFORMATION OF THE. Practised by the Muskhogean peoples, chiefly by Choctaws, 27; among the Chinooks, 322

SKY-COUNTRY. In a version of the story of Poïa, 201–205

SKY-GOD. Of the Haida—see Siñ

SLOCUM, FRANCES. The story of, 37–45

SMOKE-EATER. A being with magical powers, in Chinook myth, 330

SMOKING among the Indians, 115–118; legend of the origin of, 116; importance of, in Indian life, 131

SNAKE-OGRE. The story of the, 278–282

SNAKE-WIFE. The story of the, 287–292

SNOW-BODGE. The story of the, 149–152

SOKUMAPI. A young brave; in Blackfoot story of the origin of the Bear-spear, 187–190

SOTO, HERNANDO DE. And the Muskhogean people, 27

SOUL. The journey of the, after death, in Indian belief, 129

SOULS, THE LAND OF. In the legend of Sayadio, 260–261

SOUTH-EAST. A Haida deity representing the south-east wind; contest of, with Master-carpenter, 316–318

SPIDER MAN. In the legend of Poïa, 201, 202

SPIRIT-BRIDE. The story of the, 162–165

SPIRIT-LAND. Abode of mortals after death, 129–130; the lesser soul of sick persons taken to, 129, 139–140; 'visits' of medicine-men to, 139–140; in the story of the Spirit-bride, 162–165; in the story of Sayadio, 260–261; Ioi and Blue Jay in, 324–326

SQA-I. A town in the Queen Charlotte Islands; the contest of Master-carpenter and South-east at, 316–318

SQUIER, E. G. And the earth-mounds, 18

STAR-BOY. First name of Poïa, or Scar-face, 201, 203

STAR-COUNTRY, THE. In the story of Algon, 155–156; in the story of Cloud-carrier, 156–159; in the story of the Fairy Wives, 173

STAR-MAIDEN. The story of the, 152–156

STIKŭA. Wife of Blue Jay; the story of, 341–348

STONE GIANTESS. The story of the, 254–257

STONE GIANTS. A malignant race, in Iroquois myth, 217, 228–229, 255–257

STYLES, DR. And the Dighton Writing Rock, 16

SUMMER. Queen of the Elves of Light, in Algonquian myth; Glooskap and, 148–149

SUN, THE. In Indian creation-myth, 106; worship of, 113, 350; in Sioux myth, the Rabbit and, 301–302

SUN DANCE. Blackfoot ceremony for the restoration of the sick; Poïa brings the secrets of, to the Blackfeet, 204

SUN-CHILDREN. Extract from the story of the two, 93–94

SUN-COUNTRY. In the story of Scar-face, 198–200

SUN-GOD. In the stories of Scar-face, 197–205 ; in a Blackfoot day-and-night myth, 208 ; the Sioux deity, Ictinike the son of, 266

SUPERNATURAL PEOPLE, THE. A semi-divine race, 129–130 ; Blue Jay and, 124–125, 323–324, 327, 329–332 ; Haida myth of the origin of certain, 312–314 ; in Chinook myth, 323–324, 327–332, 337–338

SUSQUEHANNOCKS. A tribe of the Iroquois stock, 23

SWAMP FIGHT. A battle between Indians and whites, 31

SWANTON, J. R. On totemism, 84–87

SWEET GRASS HILLS. In the legend of Buffalo-stealer, 209

## T

TA-UL-TZU-JE. An Indian ; the fetish of, 90

TACU. In Californian myth, reputed father of Ouiamot, 354

TACULLIES. A tribe of the Tinneh stock ; a superstition of, 358

TAKAHLI. A South American tribe ; moral sense of, 98

TAKER-OFF-OF-THE-TREE-TOPS. Haida wind-deity ; in the story of Master-carpenter and South-east, 318

TARENYAWAGO. Master of ceremonies in the Land of Souls ; in the legend of Sayadio, 261

TAWISCARA (Dark One). One of the twin-gods of the Iroquois, 121

TECUMSEH. An Algonquin chief ; war of, with the whites, 25

TETONS. A tribe of the Siouan stock, 28

TEXAS. Indians of ; and earth-mounds, 21

THORWALD. Brother of Leif the Lucky ; voyage of, to America, 15

THREE TESTS. The story of the, 275–278

THUNDER-BOYS. Twin thunder-gods of the Cherokees, 126

THUNDER-GODS, INDIAN, 125–126 ; analogous to thunder-gods of the aboriginal Mexican peoples, 126

THUNDER-MEN. Man-eating beings in Sioux myth ; in the story of the Snake-wife, 290–292 ; transformed into the thunder-clouds, 292

THUNDERER. A supernatural being, in Chinook myth, 334–338

THUNDERER'S SON-IN-LAW. The story of the, 332–341

THUNDERERS. The people of Hi'-nun, the Iroquois thunder-god ; a myth relating to, 219–222

TIDAL-WAVE. Haida storm-deity ; in the story of Master-carpenter and South-east, 318

TIHUGUN (My Old Friend). A beneficent deity of the Tinneh, 358

TIME. Indian methods of reckoning, 131–133

TINNEH, or DÉNÉ. A division of the Athapascan stock, 22, 356 ; poverty of, in mythological conceptions, 356–357 ; beliefs of, 357–358

TIPI. An Indian tent-dwelling, 48, 49

TIPPECANOE. Battle of the, 25

TLINGIT. A tribe of the Koluschan stock ; houses of, 46–47

TO-MORROW. Haida deity, mother of South-east ; in the story of Master-carpenter, 318

TOBACCO. Use of, among the Indians, 115–116 ; legend of the origin of smoking, 115

TOBET. I. A ceremonial dancer of the Acagchemems, 355. II. The costume worn by the tobet, 355

TOSAUT. A rock mentioned in creation-myth of the Acagchemem tribes, 352, 353

TOTEMISM. Influence of, upon marriage, 73 ; story of an adventure with a totem, 74–75 ; story of a totem-vigil, 75–76 ; origin of, among the Indians,

# GLOSSARY AND INDEX

80–81 ; wide extension of, 81, 82–83 ; development of the totem into a deity, 82 ; rules of, 83 ; severity of totemic rule, 83 ; Swanton on, 84–87 ; associated with fetishism, 93 ; influence upon the growth of 'morality,' 102

TSUL 'KALU (Slanting Eyes). A hunter-god of the Cherokees, 125–126

TUPARAN. Same as Wac, which see

TUSCARORAS. A tribe of the Iroquois stock, 23 ; and the twin-gods myth of the Iroquois, 121

TWIN-GODS of the Iroquois, 121

TYRKER, or TYDSKER. In legend of Norse voyage to America, 14, 15

TZI-DALTAI. Fetishes of the Apaches, 89–90


## U

UNDERWORLD. Sioux story of an adventure in, 292–296

UNITED STATES GOVERNMENT. And the Indians, 32, 79

UNKTAHE. Water-god of the Dakota, 126

UTONAGAN. A totem-spirit ; an Indian's adventure with, 74–75


## V

VANCOUVER, G. And Indian dwellings, 47

VIRGINIA. Earth-mounds found in, 18 ; wars between whites and early settlers in, 29–30


## W

WABASKAHA. An Omaha brave ; the story of, 271–273

WABOJEEG. An Indian chief ; hunting exploit of, 54 ; a war-song of, 70–71

WABOSE, CATHERINE. The adventure of, 75–76

WAC. A supreme deity of the Pericues, called also Tuparan, 356

WAKANDA. A deity of the Omaha ; in the story of Wabaskaha, 272 ; in the story of the Snake-wife, 288

WAKINYJAN (The Flyers). Sioux wind-deities who send storms, 110

WALES. Legend that North American Indians came from, 4–5

"WALLUM-OLUM." Picture-writing records of the Leni-Lenâpé, 77–78

WAR-DANCE, INDIAN, 65, 69–70

WARFARE AND WAR-CUSTOMS, INDIAN, 63–72

WASIS. A baby, in Algonquian myth ; Glooskap and, 145–146

WATER MANITOU. In a Chippeway legend, 179

WATER-GOD. Of the Dakota, 126 ; in an Iroquois legend, 286–287

WAUKHEON (Thunder-bird). A thunder-god of the Dakota, 126

WAYNE, GENERAL A., 26

WEASEL. Name of the Fairy Wives, 172

WEST WIND, THE. I. Algonquian deity, father of Michabo, 120. II. Deity of the Iroquois, brother of Hi'nun, 217 ; destroys the Stone Giants, 228–229

WHALE-MEAT-CUTTER. A being with magical powers, in Chinook myth, 330

WHITE FEATHER. See Chácopee

WHITES. Familiar name for European settlers in America ; early wars with Indians, 29–31 ; early relationship with Indians, 29–30, 32 ; Blackfoot idea of the originator of, 208

WHITNEY, PROFESSOR J. D. Discovery of 'Calaveras' skull by, 8

WICHITA. A tribe of the Caddoan stock, 28 ; grass hut of, 48

WICKIUP. An Indian dwelling, 49

WIGWAM. An Indian dwelling, 49

# GLOSSARY AND INDEX

WILSON, PROFESSOR D. On the Chinooks, 322

WIN-PE. A giant sorcerer, in Algonquian myth; Glooskap and, 143–144

WINE-LAND. In legend of Norse voyage to America, 15

WINNEBAGO. A tribe of the Siouan stock; as mound-builders, 21

WINSLOW, E. On the gods of the Indians, 105

WINTER. A giant, in Algonquian myth; Glooskap and, 147–148

WISCONSIN. Earth-mounds found in, 17

WITCHCRAFT. Iroquois belief in, 229

WOLF-TRAIL. Indian name for the Milky Way, 204

WOMEN, INDIAN. Position of, 72–73; skill of, in weaving, 73

WONDERFUL KETTLE. The story of the, 251–254

WYANDOTS. A tribe of the Iroquois stock; allied with Algonquian tribes, 25; a legend of, 260–262

WYOMING. Prehistoric remains discovered in, 8

## Y

YANKTONS. A tribe of the Siouan stock, 28

YCAIUT (Above). One of the first women, in an Acagchemem creation-myth, 353

YOUNG DOG DANCE. Legend of the origin of the, 190–193

YUCHI. A tribe of the Uchean stock; and earth-mounds, 21

## Z

ZINZENDORF, THE COUNT OF. Story of the rattlesnake and, 114–115

ZUÑI. A tribe of the Zuñian stock; fetishism among, 93–97; creation-myth of, 106–107; Awonawilona, the chief deity of, 106, 121; and the eagle, 111; and the serpent, 113; the year of, 132; dialect of the priesthood of, 136